Fighting Against the Odds

New Perspectives on the History of the South

Florida A&M University, Tallahassee
Florida Atlantic University, Boca Raton
Florida Gulf Coast University, Ft. Myers
Florida International University, Miami
Florida State University, Tallahassee
University of Central Florida, Orlando
University of Florida, Gainesville
University of North Florida, Jacksonville
University of South Florida, Tampa
University of West Florida, Pensacola

Fighting Against the Odds

A History of Southern Labor Since World War II

Timothy J. Minchin

Foreword by John David Smith, Series Editor

University Press of Florida
Gainesville · Tallahassee · Tampa · Boca Raton
Pensacola · Orlando · Miami · Jacksonville · Ft. Myers

10 09 08 07 06 05   6 5 4 3 2 1

Library of Congress Cataloging-in-Publication Data
Minchin, Timothy J.
Fighting against the odds: a history of southern labor since World
War II / Timothy J. Minchin; foreword by John David Smith.
p. cm. — (New perspectives on the history of the South)
Includes bibliographical references and index.
ISBN 0-8130-2790-X
    1. Labor—Southern States—History. 2. Labor unions—
Southern States—History. 3. Labor movement—Southern
States—History. I. Title. II. Series.
HD8083.S9M56 2004
331.88'0975'09045—dc22   2004054194

The University Press of Florida is the scholarly publishing
agency for the State University System of Florida, comprising
Florida A&M University, Florida Atlantic University, Florida Gulf
Coast University, Florida International University, Florida State
University, University of Central Florida, University of Florida,
University of North Florida, University of South Florida,
and University of West Florida.

University Press of Florida
15 Northwest 15th Street
Gainesville, FL 32611-2079
http://www.upf.com

To my son Alexander

Contents

Foreword

La Trobe University historian Timothy J. Minchin's compact, fast-paced, and well-written study of southern labor since World War II is a landmark synthesis of the last two decades' scholarship on the history of working southerners. Focusing on both workplace struggles and on the workers' broader lives, Minchin charts the complex changes that southern workers experienced as the region's crucial and once dominant textile industry declined and new groups of laborers, especially Latino migrants, entered the southern workplace. Despite the South's postwar economic transformations, its antipathy to unions has remained virtually constant. "The weakness of organized labor," Minchin explains, "has remained a distinctive southern trait throughout the post-1945 period, just as the region as a whole has retained elements of a separate identity even as it has increasingly 'Americanized.'"

Indeed, in the post–World War II years the South, a region that always possessed a lower proportion of unionized workers than the rest of the country, remained, according to one union leader, "organized labor's number one regional problem." In the early 1950s, nearly 40 percent of America's manufacturing workers held union cards. In the South, however, fewer than 17 percent of laborers belonged to unions. Southern managers in textiles and furniture manufacturing routinely paid their workers 30–50 percent lower wages than workers in other parts of the United States. Boosters of southern economic development marketed their region as "pro-business"—the land of low wages and few unions. Not surprisingly, unions repeatedly tried to make deep inroads into the southern labor force. But they failed. "There is," Minchin notes wryly, "something different about the South when it comes to unions."

Like the best recent scholarship in southern working-class history, Minchin draws heavily on oral history interviews (many of which he conducted himself) and focuses clearly on race, gender, and ethnicity in his analyses. Rejecting earlier arguments that characterized southern textile and other workers as exceptional—inherently apathetic and incapable of group organization, militancy, and protest—he underscores instead the workers' agency and solidarity. For example, southerners participated actively in the 1934 general textile strike that ultimately mobilized over 170,000 workers. In the 1960s African American labor activists led the way in forcing both companies and unions to provide equal opportunities for black southerners. In 1976 southern unionists sparked the national boycott of the J. P. Stevens textile company. This was part of the first "corporate campaign" initiated by an American union.

Following the lead of other labor historians, Minchin identifies the various causes that have worked to inhibit the development of unions in the South. In the 1934 walkout, for instance, weak union leadership, not worker apathy, contributed to the strike's collapse. "In particular," Minchin adds, workers "repeatedly confronted hostile and determined opposition from management." Southern businessmen went to great lengths to resist unionization. "Many were willing to harass or dismiss union supporters, aware that even if these workers were reinstated, it would take years before this remedy was secured." Managers also were prone to shut down plants that favored union representation. In other cases they forced unionists to withstand lengthy and costly walkouts. Continuing their longstanding anti-labor discriminatory practices, after World War II southern state governments continually resisted the organization of their employees by prohibiting collective bargaining by state and local employees. Supported by local clergy, factory owners went to great lengths to convince their employees that union organizers were Communists—agents of the Red menace. When other anti-labor tactics failed, southern managers employed violent means to suppress union organization.

Minchin describes additional difficulties that the South's labor force, notably textile operatives, confronted in organizing. The textile industry relied on easily replaceable unskilled or semi-skilled workers, it tended to stockpile production, and its many small factories were dispersed in remote towns across a large geographic area. Mill owners wielded seemingly insurmountable control and influence over their workers, especially as they were the dominant employer in the area. These characteristics overwhelmingly favored management and impeded collective action by unions.

The South's dual system of de facto and de jure segregation also posed serious problems for labor organizers determined to unite workers irregardless of skin color. "In the postwar period," Minchin writes, "building interracial unions proved a constant headache for organized labor, especially as white workers repeatedly voted with their feet if they felt that blacks were becoming too active in the union." Minchin doubts that "a stronger civil rights stance would have allowed unions to make more progress in the South as a whole." Focusing on capturing the support of black workers, Minchin explains, "was problematic because it risked alienating whites, who made up the majority of the workforce in most industries. In cases where unions did give strong support to civil rights, in fact, they invariably lost support among whites."

Well into the 1980s, Minchin writes, southern workers—male and female, black, white, and Hispanic—continued to fight for such basic rights as better pay and the recognition of grievance procedures. The uphill battle yielded few victories, however, as wages in the region remained lower there than in other sections of the country and unions continued to be marginalized and weak. "While southern workers were used to fighting against the odds," Minchin adds, "in the last two decades of the twentieth century they faced a particularly hostile climate, as a determined management offensive undermined existing unions and stifled organizing efforts."

Today, Minchin observes, labor organization in the South remains an uphill struggle. Unions are weak in the region and, aside from some success in organizing workers in the public sector, the proportion of unionized private sector southerners continues to decline. For ideological and economic reasons, during their history southern elites have consistently opposed unions as dangerous, radical, and "un-American." Ironically, its persistent antipathy to unions in the postwar decades identifies the South as distinctive in the American experience. Minchin tells this intriguing story well in his engaging and compelling book.

John David Smith
Series Editor

Acknowledgments

As I researched and wrote this book, I was helped by many people in the South. I would particularly like to thank my friend Richard Zieger, who provided me a place to stay while I worked in Chapel Hill, North Carolina. In addition, I am grateful to Chuck and Vonnie Spence, who welcomed me into their family when I was working in Alabama. Like many scholars, my efforts were greatly assisted by helpful and skilled archivists and librarians. The librarians at the Wilson Library at the University of North Carolina at Chapel Hill were particularly helpful in guiding me through the holdings of the North Carolina Collection and the Southern Historical Collection. The archivists at the Southern Labor Archives at Georgia State University also ensured that my trawls through their collections were productive. I would also like to thank the staff at the Southern Regional Council in Atlanta. They provided me with many valuable materials on southern workers, especially reports put together by their Southern Labor Institute.

In retrieving secondary works, I was helped greatly by the efficiency of the Interlibrary Loans department at the University of St. Andrews. The research and writing of this book was supported by grants from the Carnegie Trust for the Universities of Scotland and the Leverhulme Trust, and I would like to thank them for this funding. I am also grateful to my colleagues at La Trobe University for all their support. I particularly wish to thank Tim Murray, Alan Frost, and Jim Hammerton, while John Salmond has been a fine source of friendship and valuable advice for many years. I would also like to thank the editors at the University Press of Florida for dealing with the manuscript in an efficient way and helping me throughout the publication process. I am especially grateful to Meredith Morris-Babb, who was a great source of encouragement throughout. The comments provided by the two readers of the initial manuscript were both generous and helpful. In particular, they allowed me to add material on some topics that I had overlooked. I am especially grateful to Bob Zieger, who provided many valuable suggestions. Throughout the researching and writing process, I have also been encouraged by John David Smith, who graciously agreed for this book to be included in his series on the South. Finally, I would like to thank my family for all their love and support, especially my wife Olga and my parents. I am proud to dedicate this book to my son Alexander, who was born as it was being prepared.

Introduction

In the fall of 1966, University of Texas academic F. Ray Marshall put the finishing touches to a general study of southern workers that he had been working on for over a decade. In *Labor in the South*, published by Harvard University Press the following summer, the respected scholar and subsequent secretary of labor summarized union efforts to make progress in the southern states over the previous fifty years. Written at a time when few scholars explored the history of southern workers, Marshall's work was truly pathbreaking. Although labor history was rapidly emerging as an important discipline in American universities, most early practitioners concentrated on writing the history of organized workers in the northern states rather than looking at the South, where unions had consistently struggled to establish themselves.

Since *Labor in the South* was published, much has changed. "Far from remaining an intellectual backwash," noted historian Douglas Flamming in 1992, "southern labor history has emerged as one of the most vibrant fields in American historiography." In the 1980s and 1990s, southern labor historians produced a rich variety of studies exploring the history of southern workers, some of which secured major scholarly prizes. Several volumes of essays have also explored the history of southern workers, building on the pioneering collections edited by Gary M. Fink and Merl E. Reed in the 1970s. New work has drawn on archival collections set up since the 1960s, particularly manuscripts held by the Southern Labor Archives at Georgia State University and the transcripts of interviews making up the Southern Oral History Program at the University of North Carolina. Despite the growth of the subject, however, there has been no general, synthetic book written on southern workers since Marshall completed his study, which was based on material gathered in the 1950s. As Robert H. Zieger noted in 1997, such a work is "long overdue."

This book aims to go some way toward updating Marshall's account by providing a concise history of southern labor since World War II. Concentrating on the postwar period, it does not pretend to be a comprehensive account, but it is hoped that it brings together some of the recent writing on southern workers, while complementing more general surveys of southern history since World War II. It gives particular emphasis to events that have occurred since the publication of Marshall's book, such as the rise in public employee unionism. From the mid 1960s on, the demands of increasingly assertive government workers generated major strikes across the South, symbolized by the high-profile struggles in Memphis (1968) and Charleston (1969). In other sectors, too, there have been high-profile organizing campaigns in recent years, including the lengthy battle with textile-maker J. P. Stevens. The economic decline of the textile industry, the South's major employer for most of the twentieth century, and the influx of Latino migrants into the southern workplace, are important recent developments that are also explored here.

Marshall's work, while still valuable, was written from the labor economist tradition that was dominant before the emergence of the "new" labor history. As a result, it concentrated on economic context and institutional union history rather than the broader aspects of workers' lives. This study aims to balance the two approaches by exploring workplace struggles as well as being informed by new scholarship. Recent scholarship, for example, has relied heavily on oral history, often an indispensable source in writing the history of working southerners. *Labor in the South* contained few workers' voices, but this account tries to give some idea of how employees themselves felt about their jobs and the important protests that they participated in. In recent studies, southern labor historians have also explored the experience of African Americans in much greater detail and have established their agency much more effectively. A considerable degree of attention is given here to the importance of race in southern labor history, especially in the post–World War II period, when the struggle for civil rights dominated workers' lives.

Since World War II, organized labor has made repeated efforts to organize the South, where the proportion of unionized workers has consistently been lower than in the rest of the country. From the "Operation Dixie" of the 1940s through to the "Operation Sunbelt" of the 1970s, labor leaders launched major drives to try and recruit southerners to their cause. All of these efforts ended in failure, and historians have spent a great deal of time exploring why the South remained stubbornly nonunion. As Bryant Simon noted in a 1997 examination of the issue, the big question of why there are so few unions in the South "stalks every examination of the history of working people and industrialization in the South."

Ultimately, unions' failure to organize the South had important implications for the entire United States. Between 1950 and 1975, the South's economy grew at an average annual rate of 4.4 percent, compared to 3.4 percent nationally, with every industry except mining performing better in Dixie than in the country as a whole. The steady economic growth of the southern states, much of it based on "runaway shops" from the North, undermined unions at the national level. The South came to represent, in the words of one union leader, "organized labor's number one regional problem." Operating from a declining membership base, however, unions' need to make progress in the South increased as their capacity to do so fell.

Much historical attention has focused on the textile industry, which was the South's largest employer and the focus of repeated organizing efforts. If they could get textile workers to join with them, union leaders argued, then others would inevitably follow. In explaining why these hopes never materialized, early accounts described southern textile workers as culturally resistant to unions, a deviation from American norms. Most observers agreed with Progressive reformer Sinclair Lewis, who depicted the southern textile workforce as "cheap and contented." Some accounts even asserted that southern textile employees were a social or physical "type" afflicted with physical or mental deformities. In his influential *Mind of the South* (1941), for instance, Wilbur Cash pictured southern textile men with "chinless faces, microcephalic foreheads, rabbit teeth, [and] goggling dead-fish eyes," while women were "characteristically stringy-haired and limp of breast at twenty, and shrunken hags at thirty or forty."

In the 1980s and 1990s, work by a growing body of southern historians challenged many of the conclusions of these earlier studies. Anxious to dispel negative stereotypes, a new generation of historians argued forcefully that southern workers were capable of militancy and protest. In short, they were little different from their counterparts in other regions of the United States. This approach was led by the pioneering *Like a Family: The Making of a Cotton Mill World*, which for the first time established the agency of southern textile workers. Rather than being viewed simply as the obedient tool of industrialists, a group of authors led by Jacquelyn D. Hall showed how workers themselves helped to shape the culture of the evolving mill villages in the early twentieth century. *Like a Family* also helped to highlight the activism of southerners in launching the 1934 general textile strike, a major protest that involved more than 170,000 people. More recent work by Janet Irons and John A. Salmond has further detailed the participation of southerners in the walkout and has argued that weak union leadership, and not a lack of militancy among participants, was the major cause of the strike's collapse.

In all of their recent work, historians have strongly challenged the idea that southern workers were inherently culturally resistant to unions. Southerners, after all, initiated the largest strike in American history and were at the forefront of many other struggles. Emphasizing the similarities between the South and the rest of the country is undoubtedly very important, for it has corrected earlier interpretations that viewed southern employees as peculiarly exceptional, culturally unable to protest.

In fact, unions in the South faced a particularly severe range of obstacles, which hindered their progress much more effectively than worker apathy or resistance to unions. In particular, they repeatedly confronted hostile and determined opposition from management. Southern executives, of course, were not unique in being antiunion, but they were peculiarly effective at resisting organized labor. Many were willing to harass or dismiss union supporters, aware that even if these workers were reinstated, it would take years before this remedy was secured. Management also showed a particular willingness to close plants that voted for union representation, or they forced their employees to endure costly strikes. These tactics were especially pronounced in the post–World War II period, as a strong union movement repeatedly tried to organize the region in which they were weakest. In vigorously resisting these efforts, southern executives also often received an unusual level of support from public authorities. During the postwar period, southern governments themselves vehemently opposed the unionization of public employees. Departing from national trends, most southern states kept laws on their books that prohibited collective bargaining among public employees, just as they also had earlier passed a disproportionate number of "right-to-work" laws in the 1940s and 1950s.

Some southern employers were also willing to employ violence in order to fight off unions. As Stephen H. Norwood's recent study of strikebreaking has argued, after World War II *violent* resistance to organized labor faded away in other parts of the United States but persisted in the South. During Operation Dixie, many union activists were threatened, intimidated, and beaten. In subsequent years, organizers repeatedly found southern hospitality wanting when they ventured into the region. In the late 1970s, for instance, five bullets were fired into the car of a United Steelworkers organizer in Florida, while company security men or police beat other organizers. In the 1970s and 1980s, in fact, employers increasingly relied on professional security firms who often harassed and injured union supporters. During the J. P. Stevens campaign of the 1970s, police shadowed union organizers and conducted illegal surveillance of their meetings. "Violence," concluded *The Economist* on November 17, 1979, "is never far from the surface of labor organizing drives in the South."

Executives, particularly in the textile industry, had powerful economic reasons for fighting against organized labor. In low-wage industries such as textiles and furniture, southern companies had established their dominance by paying wages that were 30 to 50 percent lower than in other regions. As a result, unions, which openly sought to raise southern wages in order to protect the jobs of their better-paid members in the North, were seen as a direct threat. Business groups such as the Southern States Industrial Council (SSIC), organized in the 1930s, argued repeatedly in favor of a regional wage differential. In the South, they asserted, the cost of living was lower and industrial workers were still paid more than their counterparts in agriculture. In the postwar period, outside firms were also increasingly drawn to the region by this wage differential, which southern political and economic leaders used to market their region.

Unions in the South also faced other particular obstacles. The region's largest industry, textiles, was notoriously difficult to organize. Most jobs were unskilled or semiskilled, ensuring that employees could be easily replaced. The industry was often prone to overproduction, ensuring that employers were frequently willing to stockpile goods and endure labor disputes. The logistics of organizing such a vast industry were themselves daunting; hundreds of small plants were scattered across a broad area stretching from southern Virginia through to northern Alabama, requiring overstretched organizers to travel vast distances. In the North, textile plants were usually located in large urban centers; but in the South, mills were typically built in small towns where they were invariably the largest employer. Marshall's work itself highlighted that union membership was more likely among workers living in large urban centers, especially as employers and local elites were able to cooperate more effectively in small communities. Acutely aware that the mill had given them the best-paying job available in the area, southern textile operatives were especially vulnerable to economic pressure from their employers.

The race issue was also a particular problem in a region with such a large African American population. Throughout the post–World War II period, the southern states contained the highest proportion of African Americans in the country, ensuring that unions often had to unite blacks and whites together in order to organize successfully. They had to do so, moreover, in a region where legal racial segregation, or Jim Crow, existed until the 1960s. Right through to the present day, managers have consistently used the "race card" against organized labor. As veteran textile union leader Bruce Raynor commented in 1998, "Southern employers, traditionally in a work force that's mixed, make race an issue. They tell the workers that the union is for the black workers and try to separate the white workers. I've never seen a hard-fought campaign in the South where employers didn't use that issue to divide workers." In the postwar period, building interracial unions proved a constant headache for organized labor, especially as white workers repeatedly voted with their feet if they felt that blacks were becoming too active in the union. In the South, this white exodus from black-led unions was also encouraged by the legal negation of union security laws, which ensured that union membership was purely voluntary.

Certainly, the failure of organized labor in the South was partly a reflection of broader problems. Since the early 1950s, organized labor has declined across the country. From coast to coast, unions have been hurt by the decline of manufacturing industries in which most of their members toiled. Union leaders everywhere complained that labor laws failed to protect the right to organize, especially in the face of determined opposition. It is still the case, however, that levels of union organization in the South have consistently lagged well behind other American regions. In the early 1950s, for instance, the percentage of American workers who belonged to unions was more than twice what it was in the South. Despite the growth in public employee unionism, southern government workers were also less likely to hold union cards than their counterparts in other regions. In 1987, in fact, only 21.2 percent of southern public workers were organized compared to over 45 percent nationwide.

Home to many southern manufacturing plants, the Carolinas have consistently been the least unionized states in the country. In 1974, 6.8 percent of North Carolina's nonfarm workers belonged to unions, compared to a national average of 26.2 percent. In 2001, the proportion of U.S. workers represented by unions had fallen to 13.5 percent, but North and South Carolina continued to have the lowest rates in the country—just 3.6 and 4 percent respectively.

There is, in short, something different about the South when it comes to unions. The weakness of organized labor has remained a distinctive southern trait throughout the post-1945 period, just as the region as a whole has retained elements of a separate identity even as it has increasingly "Americanized." Since World War II, this general southern distinctiveness has undeniably diminished. Increasing prosperity reduced the region's poverty, while civil rights legislation led to the dismantling of the Jim Crow system of legal racial segregation. At the same time, many observers have emphasized the region's continuing distinctiveness, noting that southerners clung to a regional identity that stressed morality and a different pace of life. Rates of churchgoing remained higher in the region than elsewhere, and southerners held more conservative views than the rest of the country on moral issues such as abortion, the death penalty, and school prayer. An important additional element of this persistent southern identity that needs to be recognized is antiunionism, because even as the region has Americanized, it has never embraced organized labor to the extent that the rest of the country has.

A Double-Edged Sword

World War II and Southern Workers

On the eve of World War II, the South was the poorest region in America, but by the end of the conflict it had been transformed by four years of unprecedented economic growth. The war, which did so much to end the Great Depression and regenerate the American economy as a whole, had a particularly striking impact on the southern states. Between 1941 and 1945, many southern workers enjoyed rising wages and an improving standard of living, and an unprecedented number experienced the benefits of union membership. An acute labor shortage also created new opportunities for women and African Americans, who gained access to a much greater range of industrial jobs than they had ever held before.

The war was not simply a positive experience for southern workers, however, especially as the rapid economic growth it generated also had a downside. Despite receiving better wages, workers also had to cope with heavy workloads and long hours. In many southern communities, dramatic economic expansion created housing shortages that were felt most acutely by working people. Although they saw temporary improvements, both women and African Americans struggled to make lasting gains in the southern work place during the war. Despite an acute labor shortage, many southern companies remained reluctant to hire African Americans, and when they did they were anxious to retain traditional segregated hiring patterns.

In other ways, too, southern executives resisted fundamental change. Although there was some wartime growth in southern union membership, resistance to organized labor remained strong in Dixie, and there were signs even before the conflict was over that few southern executives had decided to reconcile themselves to a union presence. The war indeed generated a conservative backlash against unionism, as managers waited anxiously to roll back the tenuous gains that organized labor had made in the region. Throughout the war, in fact, southern employers resisted all "outside" interference in their business decisions, whether it be from unions or the federal government. Hiring and firing, they insisted, was strictly their business.

In strictly economic terms, the war certainly benefited the South. Just three years before Pearl Harbor, the Roosevelt administration had been so concerned about southern poverty that it had labeled the underperforming region "the Nation's Number One economic problem." With lucrative defense contracts to distribute, the federal government set about tackling southern poverty; during the war, it awarded 17.6 percent of all military contracts to the region, spending over $5 billion in all. The Roosevelt administration hoped that wartime investment would deter future depression and aid economic growth, hopes that proved to be partially justified. The war completely reshaped the southern economy, as 3.2 million people left rural areas to pursue new opportunities. The flight from the land alleviated rural overpopulation, which had plagued the region for generations. Most rural migrants found work in the booming defense plants. Between 1939 and 1943, the number of southerners employed in industry increased from 1.6 million to a high of 2.8 million. While communities across the region prospered, this growth was especially noticeable in cities that became important defense centers, such as Mobile, Alabama, Norfolk, Virginia, and Beaumont, Texas.

Southerners who had struggled to make ends meet now found that they had steady work at much higher wages than they had ever received before. The economic turnaround was especially noticeable in communities dependent on heavy manufacturing industries, which had been hardest hit by the depression. In the early 1930s, Birmingham had been the country's most depressed city. Around 25 percent of the city's workforce was unemployed, as steel plants, the mainstay of the local economy, were operating at only 20 percent of capacity. "It was rough," recalled local steelworker Hosea Hudson. "You talking about a rough time, that was a rough time. Birmingham is a cold place when it does get real cold. It got cold in those days. It got to where you could not find a stick on the ground as large as a baby's wrist to make a fire out of in your house. The ground was clean of any kind of anything to make a fire." By the early 1940s, however, Birmingham's steel mills, like other heavy industries across the region, were booming. Such was the demand for steel, in fact, that even retired plants were pressed into service.

The South's leading industry boomed during the war. By the end of the 1930s, textiles, which had played a key role in building the New South after the Civil War, had clearly established itself as the region's dominant employer. In 1937, the South had 72 percent of the industry's value, its textile mills employing ten times as many workers as tobacco, the only other industry that came close to it in terms of value of product. The southern textile industry had grown significantly in the period immediately after the Civil War, when merchants who had made money out of the tenant and sharecropping systems set up the first mills. Ignoring the impoverished African American community, the new industrialists recruited their employees from among landless white farmers. The industry was promoted as the salvation of poor whites and this, together with cultural taboos against employing black men close to large numbers of white women, ensured that no more than 2 percent of southern textile employees were black at the time of World War II.

Lower wages and longer hours were crucial in allowing southern textile mills to gradually expand while those in New England, the industry's birthplace, slowly contracted. Until the New Deal, southern textile workers regularly worked fifty-five to sixty hours a week. In Massachusetts, in contrast, a forth-eight-hour week had been mandated in 1919, pushing neighboring Rhode Island and New Hampshire to follow suit. Southern states also gained an advantage by permitting night-work for women. Above all, however, the lack of competing industries and the absence of unions allowed southern textile executives to pay much lower wages than their counterparts in the North. In 1907, for example, female ring spinners in the South were paid just $5.71 a week compared to the $7.36 a week they received in New England. The South offered manufacturers other cost advantages; utility rates were cheaper, and prior to the 1930s child labor was also far more prevalent than in New England, where protective labor laws kept the young out of the mills. Between 1923 and 1933, the South's competitive advantage proved compelling, as 40 percent of New England's textile factories closed, taking almost 100,000 jobs with them. Over the same period, the percentage of textile workers based in Dixie rose from 46 to 68 percent.

In the 1930s, southern textile mills had struggled to earn a profit, and many workers suffered reduced hours. Based on full capacity of two forty-hour shifts, the industry never exceeded 90 percent production between 1933 and 1939, while in some years output dropped to 57 percent. This all changed with the outbreak of the war. During the conflict, capacity utilization based on this same measure averaged 133.2 percent. Across the region, textile mills ran at full capacity, turning out uniforms, tents, and other vital supplies for the military. In the spring of 1943 alone, the army ordered eighteen million undershirts, ten million blankets, seventy-eight million pairs of socks, sixty million yards of mosquito netting, and eighteen million sleeping bags. During the war as a whole, over 80 percent of cotton textile production was for military orders. Across the region, textile mills took on more and more workers in order to fulfill these orders. Between 1940 and 1943, employment in the textile industry of Floyd County, Georgia, increased by over a third. Over the same period, Dan River Mills in Danville, Virginia took on over 4,000 extra staff. In all, over 14,000 employees toiled in Dan River's sprawling complex of mills located just above the North Carolina state line. By the end of the war, over 400,000 people worked in the hundreds of mills located across the southern textile belt, which stretched from Danville through the Carolinas and into northern Georgia and Alabama.

During the war, personal income in the South more than doubled. Both whites and blacks left low-paying jobs and secured more lucrative work in war industries. Facing pressure to hold onto their precious staff, low-paying employers were pushed to increase their wages. Textile workers' pay rose steadily as a result, more than doubling over the course of the conflict from 42 to 86 cents an hour. Between January 1, 1941 and August 1, 1946, southern textile executives gave eight industry-wide pay increases and, even allowing for rising consumer prices, real wages in the industry increased by more than 50 percent between 1941 and 1945. Although many of the industries that grew during the war were not suitable for peacetime production, even after reconversion the region retained about half the wartime addition to its factory force. Pent-up civilian demand fuelled further growth, keeping southern textile mills operating on a full-time basis for more than four years after the cessation of hostilities.

Such rapid economic growth also had a downside for many ordinary southerners. In many respects, in fact, the war was a double-edged sword for southern workers. The wage gains came at a price, as many staff became exhausted by the long hours and relentless pace of work. In southern textile mills, machines ran twenty-four hours a day at record speeds and were often tended to by worn out operatives. Between 1942 and 1944, accident rates in Georgia's mills rose by 48 percent. The war also had a disruptive effect on established communities, especially as many people left their home areas and relocated to towns where they had found defense work. With car ownership reaching a greater proportion of the population, more and more people also commuted to work from farther afield. George Waldrep's study of textile towns in Spartanburg County, South Carolina notes that these developments, while breaking down mill workers' isolation from broader society, also undermined the strong sense of community previously present in the close-knit mill villages. The protection for the rights of organized labor provided by the National War Labor Board (NWLB) also came at a price as, in return, national unions agreed to a broad no-strike clause that robbed them of the ability to protest against harsh working conditions. When workers did violate the agreement, they often threatened the legitimacy of their unions.

Dramatic economic expansion also produced problems outside the work place. The movement of thousands of migrants into defense work frequently led to overcrowding. When Du Pont built an explosives plant in the small town of Childersburg, Alabama, its population rose sharply from 500 to over 14,000, producing severe housing shortages. In Pascagoula, Mississippi, the rapid expansion of shipbuilding during the war increased the population from 4,000 in 1940 to 30,000 in 1944. In 1942, the burgeoning Gulf Coast community was described as full of "trailer parks, rusty boarding houses, old homes with charm but limited sanitary facilities, and even tents." In many other towns, housing problems were created by rapid population increases, while public facilities such as schools, hospitals, and transport were also stretched to the limit. "The war has brought unprecedented conditions," reported Birmingham's police commissioner. "Stations, depots, carriers, buses, streetcars . . . are crowded to capacity; sidewalks . . . are congested; stores and elevators are filled with people." Southern blacks, who even before Pearl Harbor were confined to living in overcrowded segregated areas, were disproportionately hurt by the housing crisis. "There is not a single available house for colored," noted one wartime report in Memphis. Overcrowding sometimes sparked racial tension, especially on public transport, where many protests were led by young African Americans frustrated with the persistence of discrimination at a time when their country was supposed to be fighting to uphold democratic values.

As the economy expanded and more and more men departed to serve in the military, southern companies found it difficult to fill jobs. As shortages became acute, southern employers, like their counterparts across the country, gradually turned to women to staff positions. A dramatic break with precedent, some historians have seen this move as highly significant.

Women workers, they argue, gained access to an unprecedented range of jobs and proved that they could carry them out successfully. World War II was, in the words of William H. Chafe, "a milestone for women in America."

The evidence from the South does provide some support for these claims. The war did lead to women gaining access to a range of new jobs and they proved to men and to themselves that they could perform them well. At the same time, however, women were only hired as a last resort, and it was always clear that this was a temporary expedient. Female war workers also often had to endure unequal pay, long hours, and inadequate childcare facilities.

On the plus side, many southern women did make breakthroughs into new jobs. In defense centers such as Mobile and New Orleans, women secured a range of nontraditional positions, including managing parking lots, driving taxis and trucks, welding and repairing aircraft and ships, and working in machine shops. Some of the better-paid defense jobs provided starting wages of $35 a week, more than double the amount paid to southern textile employees at the time. Even in the cotton mills, women's opportunities improved markedly. Executives in the lily-white industry were reluctant to hire blacks, so white women were the obvious labor source to tap when men left. In Floyd County, Georgia, located in the heart of the state's textile belt, women's share of textile jobs increased from 38 to 43 percent between 1940 and 1943. In many industries, some single women left the home to enter the workforce for the first time, but more common was the reentry of married women who had previously quit work in order to raise their families.

Some women did report a sense of liberation when they received their first paychecks. The experience of becoming economically independent and proving that they could operate "male" jobs was important, and some who had performed nontraditional tasks passed onto their children a belief that females should not be confined to domestic roles. Peggy Terry, a Kentucky war worker interviewed by Studs Terkel after the conflict, felt that the availability of well-paying industrial jobs was "a big break" for women workers who had not worked in plants before. Her work, she explained to the veteran interviewer, caused her to travel more widely and mix with a much more diverse group of friends than she had known growing up in a small Kentucky town. "I believe the war was the beginning of my seeing things," she explained.

The war also challenged the views of some male executives and union leaders about women's inability to perform "male" jobs. In Mobile, the competence of female welders openly challenged male prejudice. "Frankly, they surprised me," admitted one welding supervisor. "But it's the finest surprise I know, and certainly a welcome one." "Management on the shipyards during the war were absolutely surprised at the ability of the women workers to learn jobs and work," remembered former shipyard manager John VanDillon: ". . . I'm sure that patriotism had a lot to do with it. . . . It was a joy to see really."

While often acquiring a grudging respect for their female employees, managers only hired them out of necessity. At the Bell Aircraft Corporation plant in Atlanta, where the B-29 bomber was assembled, women were only employed after the male labor supply had been exhausted. It was the same story elsewhere. In September 1942, the director of vocational education in Mobile's public school system noted candidly that, "We have scraped the bottom of the barrel as far as men are concerned, and women are going to have to take over the war industry program." Women were being trained for shipyard jobs, explained the *Mobile Register*, because there was no alternative. "There isn't a mentally and physically fit unemployed man left in Mobile, unless he doesn't have to work," it commented candidly.

Once employers had made their decision to recruit women, they were mobilized with stridently patriotic appeals. In Mobile, a full-page advertisement in the local paper declared: "To the Women of Mobile: Uncle Sam Says: I Need You! . . . You are needed in the war jobs and in other essential civilian jobs directly aiding the war effort in Mobile NOW." Not surprisingly, many responded dutifully to such appeals. Michelina LaCerva, Rosemary Jones, and Ruth Arcenaux, the first women hired at the Rheem Manufacturing Plant in New Orleans, explained that, "We hope to turn out our work fast, so that the ones we love can blast the Japs." While patriotism was an important motive, other women took defense jobs for economic reasons and to gain new skills. For some, war work also helped alleviate the loneliness they felt while their loved ones were at war. As Louisiana war worker Merle Weigel wrote to her husband: "I'm so glad I have a job for it keeps me busy all day and when I get home at night I'm tired and can sleep."

The strident appeals concealed the reality that conditions for the women defense employees were often poor. The emphasis on maintaining production meant that the pace of work was often relentless. Peggy Terry, employed at a shell-loading plant in Viola, Kentucky, related that it was very difficult for staff to take any breaks from the production line. "You could only get a drink of water if you went to the cafeteria," she recalled, "which was about two city blocks away. Of course you couldn't leave your machine long enough to go get a drink. I drank Coke and Dr. Pepper and I hated 'em. I hate 'em today. We had to buy it, of course. We couldn't leave to go to the bathroom, 'cause it was way the heck over there." Many women were also called into the workforce without adequate provisions for childcare, meaning that single females or those whose children had already left home were best placed to take advantage of new opportunities. Although defense jobs often paid well, women were not rewarded as well as men, and they still had to cope with the heavy workloads and long hours that were the lot of most war workers. While women's performance led to some male managers and government officials changing their views, others—especially those more removed from the shop floor—continued to view females as less reliable and more prone to absenteeism, reflecting the cultural belief that they were casual workers who only worked for "pin money." Male coworkers and many unions were also hostile to women's entry into male-dominated workplaces.

As many studies have highlighted, women's wartime employment failed to fundamentally alter traditional ideas about gender roles. Employers still viewed women as a temporary expedient to help the war effort, and it was always clear that these were men's jobs. Companies continually stressed that their female employees were keeping jobs "warm" for men. Many even sought to hire women from the community who had relations working in the same plant, ensuring that they would not oppose layoffs at the end of the war. A 1943 pamphlet published by southern lumber employers was typically keen to insist that the presence of women would not overturn traditional employment patterns: "Nearly all the women workers interviewed at the mills, both white and colored, said they are working in the lumber plants to help win the war—back up their men-folks in the armed forces and to make additional money to increase the family budget."

At the end of the war, many women workers faced strong social pressure to return to their traditional domestic roles. The returning serviceman, a 1945 article in *Home Beautiful* told its readers, "was head man again. . . . Your part in the remaking of this man is to fit his home to him, understanding why he wants it this way, forgetting your own preferences." Across the country, women were laid off to make way for men, even though surveys indicated that many wanted to hold onto their jobs.

In durable goods industries, for example, women's share of the workforce fell by 50 percent. Overall, women comprised 60 percent of all workers let go by employers in the early months after the war and were laid off at a rate 75 percent higher than men. In some industries, however, it took longer for women to be pushed aside than others. The southern textile industry, in particular, continued to boom until 1949, ensuring that many women held onto their jobs for several years after the conflict had ended.

Like women, African Americans struggled to make lasting employment gains in the South during the war. On the whole, the conflict failed to alter the fundamental problems facing black southerners. Black men continued to be overwhelmingly confined to menial, laboring jobs, finding that companies and government agencies were extremely reluctant to upgrade them into skilled or even semiskilled positions. Black women, in contrast, still found it very difficult to get hired in southern industry at all, with many companies willing to recruit white women from far away in order to avoid hiring them. Despite the fact that the war was promoted as a fight for democracy, segregated facilities also continued to exist in southern plants, reflecting the inferior status of African Americans in southern society. Many companies also provided their white employees with more facilities than blacks. In a range of defense plants, for example, companies provided cafeterias that only whites were allowed to use, forcing blacks to eat on the job or in an inferior, segregated area near the kitchen.

On the eve of World War II, African Americans remained underrepresented in southern industries. This was especially true for black women. In the South's leading industries, African American females only worked as cleaners and never made up more than 2 percent of the workforce. Many white workers employed black women as domestic helpers for very low wages, and they often opposed them being employed in industry as a result. Only the tobacco industry had a history of black female employment, yet even here they were confined to the dirtiest, least desirable jobs. In contrast, black men were hired in a broad range of manufacturing industries, but they were confined to heavy, labor-based jobs for which they were seen as particularly suitable. Even during the war, when labor shortages were acute, African American men faced determined resistance from both employers and white workers if they tried to move into more skilled positions.

In the two years prior to U.S. entry into World War II, the economy took off as defense plants supplied the allies with materials. African

Americans, however, did not secure a fair share of these new opportunities. Along the Gulf Coast, none of the booming shipyards employed black welders. The Delta Shipyard in New Orleans employed over 6,000 staff but only sixty of them were black, and they were confined to working as office porters or "common laborers." The situation was little better in the North, with aircraft factories in northern cities such as Detroit hiring blacks only for a small number of "mop-and-broom" jobs. Responding to a government questionnaire, over half of companies said they would not hire blacks. After civil rights leader A. Philip Randolph threatened a mass march on Washington in order to demand an end to discrimination in defense industries, President Roosevelt intervened. In June 1941, Executive Order 8802 obliged employers and unions to provide for "full and equitable participation of all workers in the defense industries without discrimination." The order's mandate was to be enforced by a Fair Employment Practices Committee (FEPC) responsible for investigating complaints of discrimination and for recommending action.

Despite the existence of the FEPC, traditional segregated hiring practices remained resistant to change. Determined to limit the upgrading of black workers, both employers and workers fought to maintain the racial status quo. At one Mobile shipyard, the company refused to upgrade blacks, calling the suggestion "impractical and utopian," while at others white workers pressed to keep blacks out of skilled jobs. Many southern whites hated the FEPC, which Alabama Governor Frank Dixon termed a "crackpot reform" and a "kangaroo court obviously dedicated to the abolition of segregation." Southerners repeatedly attacked the federal commission, claiming that it had, in the words of the Shreveport Chamber of Commerce, "created ill will between races." Resistance came not just from employers and workers but also from regionally based federal agencies, which, mainly staffed by local people, played a crucial role in determining job assignments.

Despite this broad-based resistance, southern employers, who were ultimately responsible for selecting new staff, played the central role in maintaining traditional segregated job assignments. Part of their dislike for the FEPC stemmed from their opposition to any outside interference in their business; hiring and firing, they insisted, were management prerogatives and not the business of any outside groups, whether government officials or union leaders. At the same time, southern executives also deflected blame by repeatedly insisting that their white employees would not stand for blacks being placed in nontraditional jobs. "We cannot put

Negroes in our office," explained one employer. "Everybody would quit, beginning with the manager." Managers at the AVCO-Vultee plant in Nashville similarly claimed that they could not hire more blacks because this would create racial tensions that could threaten war production. In September 1943, following lengthy hearings, the FEPC criticized the discriminatory hiring practices of the major railroads, but southern employers led opposition to the committee's findings. "It is wholly impractical, and indeed impossible, for these railroads to put into effect your Committee's Directives," declared one group of employers. "Any attempt on their part to comply . . . for instance, to promote Negroes to locomotive engineers or train conductors, would inevitably disrupt their peaceful and cooperative relations with their employees . . . and would most gravely and irreparably impair the whole war effort." Across the region, employers clearly viewed black workers as a last resort, and they were often willing to tolerate labor shortages or import whites from remote areas rather than integrate nontraditional jobs. In many areas, employers also faced pressure from property owners who complained bitterly that black agricultural laborers were leaving the land and taking industrial jobs.

At the Bell Aircraft plant in Atlanta, one of the largest defense plants in the region, blacks were restricted to a small range of unskilled jobs. Between 1942 and 1945, only 2,500 were hired out of a total workforce of nearly 30,000, helping to explain why Atlanta's African American population never secured their full share of defense opportunities. Most of those taken on were restricted to traditional menial tasks. The company, which had "reassured" local leaders about its racial policies when it located in Atlanta, gave whites positions as draftsmen, radio installers and supervisors, yet blacks were only offered openings as laborers, porters, janitors, and metal cleaners. FEPC investigations revealed that even black college graduates were being offered jobs as laborers. African American workers at the plant complained to the FEPC about a broad range of problems, including wage differentials, discriminatory job classifications, newspaper advertisements specifying race, as well as refusal to train and hire. Like many other employers, Bell managers defended the company's record by claiming that it was afraid of work stoppages by whites. Plant manager James Carmichael blamed racism at the plant on "lower type" whites, "undeveloped hill-billies of Georgia with deeply entrenched prejudice."

The FEPC itself lacked the power to force real change in racial hiring practices. Across the South, African American workers enthusiastically appealed to the federal agency, yet it had no enforcement capability. Commission leaders also lacked the political will to tackle segregation. Its first chair, Mark Etheridge, was reluctant to confront southern racial practices; when the agency held hearings in Birmingham to investigate discrimination in southern defense industries, he told his audience: "No power in the world—not even . . . Allied and Axis [armies together] could now force the Southern white people to the abandonment of the principle of social segregation." Following Etheridge's resignation, Roosevelt downgraded the commission by placing it under the War Manpower Commission (WMC). Throughout the war, Roosevelt was reluctant to address racial issues, insisting that the nation's priority was to pull together in order to secure victory against fascism. The time, he insisted, was not right to confront contentious issues such as segregation. Lacking political support, the FEPC could do little more than expose and catalogue racist employment practices at major defense plants, unable to provide black complainants with a satisfactory settlement.

Local officials who ran the United States Employment Service (USES) in the South also helped to maintain a segregated labor market. As well as providing industrial training, local USES offices were responsible for gathering information on labor supply and demand and referring job applicants to employers. In 1944, a federal investigator reported that most of the USES offices in the South exhibited "open disregard" for fair employment principles. Exclusionary practices, while not unique to the South, proved more difficult to break down in a region where, unlike the North, legal racial segregation existed right across society. Federal investigator John Beecher went as far as to call black training programs provided by the USES a "pathetic farce." These programs either excluded blacks altogether or prepared them only for a much more limited range of jobs than whites. In May 1942, the USES's training programs in Memphis had enrolled 1,084 whites but just ninety-eight blacks. USES offices frequently had a direct influence over hiring. Across the textile belt, for example, USES officials with clear notions of "black" and "white" jobs helped to maintain traditional job assignments in the region's mills. "[T]here are no Negroes used in manufacturing, except as common labor," noted one report from Floyd County, Georgia. Officials repeatedly justified the exclusion of blacks from production jobs by claiming that they were "unskilled," yet they did not apply the same criteria to white applicants.

On the few occasions when blacks did carry out more skilled jobs, they were, like women workers, frequently not paid equally because they were classified differently. Throughout the war, many complained to the FEPC about discriminatory pay rates. At the Buckeye Cottonseed Oil Company in Memphis, African American millwrights were paid 44 cents an hour, while their white counterparts received between 88 and 98 cents. Black bricklayers at another plant made just 47 cents an hour, while whites received up to $1.62 for the same job. At the Gibbs Gas Engine Shipyard in Jacksonville, Florida, African Americans were paid only 60 cents an hour, "the lowest common labor price," for performing skilled grinding work on ships' hulls while whites made $1.20 an hour. "I grit my teeth and go on," wrote black grinder William Kitchen to the FEPC, "but it doesn't get any better, and I know it is because I am colored. I would be getting more if I was white, but white or colored this work must be done."

When blacks were upgraded into nontraditional jobs, there was, as executives had warned, resistance from whites. Whites remained especially keen to limit any shop floor contact with blacks. "There is serious racial prejudice within the Bell plant," reported FEPC regional director A. Bruce Hunt in 1944, "so serious that rivets and other dangerous articles have been thrown by whites at Negroes while at work because the whites objected to Negroes coming into certain departments." The employment of white women could also make it more difficult to hire or upgrade black men owing to the cultural taboo about close contact between the two. At the large Firestone rubber plant in Memphis, black men remembered that during wartime they had to walk through the plant with their eyes down because of the racial tension. Even after V-J Day, a riot almost erupted in the plant after a white woman accused a black man of urinating in front of her.

Similar problems occurred in some textile plants where acute labor shortages pushed companies to experiment with upgrading a few black pioneers into nontraditional jobs. In 1944, whites at Dan River Mills, the largest single textile plant in the South, walked out after the company hired black spinners for the first time. At Muscogee Mill in Columbus, Georgia, whites also struck when blacks were placed in nontraditional jobs. When a textile mill in Alabama increased its hiring of blacks, the Southern Regional Council reported, "the whites became indignant to the point of grouping up in the mill gates and threatening the Negroes as they came to work one morning."

These racial disturbances help to explain why many executives claimed that they could not upgrade blacks because their white employees would not tolerate it. At the same time, however, both companies and unions could have taken a stronger stance. Bell Aircraft managers refused to reprimand white employees who threatened blacks. At Dan River Mills, the company responded to the white workers' walkout not by holding firm in their decision to hire black spinners but by removing them instead, a move that local union officials also supported. When faced with white protest, other companies similarly backed down, scaling back or totally abandoning efforts to upgrade their black staff.

Nevertheless, the threat of organized and violent white resistance was real. In May 1943, white workers at the Alabama Dry Dock and Ship-building Company (ADDSCO) in Mobile rioted after blacks were placed on nontraditional welding jobs following pressure from the FEPC, which was concerned that whites monopolized skilled positions at the giant yard. Reporting on the disturbance, the *Mobile Register* described how "stones, sticks, and pipes" were used by the rioters in a "head-battering melee." Whites rioted not just because they feared that blacks would be given skilled jobs at their expense, but also because they worried that black male workers would be placed close to white women, highlighting the importance of sexual fears in maintaining industrial segregation in the South. As the *Register* explained, the violence had been triggered by "indiscreet mingling of white and Negro workers." The paper called for "Absolute Segregation" of the races as "an unalterable policy" in order to prevent further costly interruptions to war production.

Following the riot, Mobile remained tense for several days, with sales of alcohol banned throughout the surrounding county and U.S. Army Troops from nearby Brookley Field called in to restore order. Two days later, however, when some black employees returned to the yard, whites walked off the job and troops were again required to prevent more violence. As a result of the disturbances, ADDSCO lost 160,000 man-hours of work. Following talks, company and union representatives, together with civil rights leaders and FEPC staff, agreed to offer four segregated gangways to blacks, although in reality they only ever received two complete gangways and two half gangways. The compromise disappointed local civil rights activist John Le Flore, who denounced it as an "emasculation" of the commission's purpose and called for "equitable integration." FEPC leaders themselves expressed some disappointment with the agreement, but noted that it had ensured that some blacks did receive nontraditional jobs, even though they remained segregated.

The Mobile riot reflected broader white anxieties that the war was leading to a breakdown in the racial status quo. Across the South, whites circulated rumors that blacks were becoming increasingly assertive and duplicitous. Many gossiped that black domestics were forming secret "Eleanor Clubs," inspired by the first lady's commitment to organized labor and racial equality. As one North Carolinian angrily wrote, "I hear the cooks have been organizing Eleanor Clubs, and their motto is 'A white woman in every kitchen by Christmas.'" Although investigations by the FBI concluded that these clubs did not exist, many southern whites still clung to the belief that black women were covertly organizing, highlighting their fears that they would no longer be able to afford domestic help. These rumors also reflected some southern whites' dislike of unionization and their belief that organized labor was an outside force that could whip up discontent among southern blacks. "The Negroes have formed unions demanding higher wages and working conditions and it is almost impossible to find any help at all," complained one woman. "I don't know about the Eleanor Clubs, but I think they had a hand in trying to organize the Negroes."

Throughout the war, African American women found it particularly difficult to secure good-paying industrial jobs, yet their need for such work was acute. The low wages paid to their menfolk ensured that black women had always participated in the labor force in large numbers. Across the South, most were restricted to working as domestics or as launderers, either privately or for dry cleaning companies. In southern textile communities, the labor of black domestics was crucial in allowing large numbers of white women to work in the mills. On the eve of World War II, for example, women held close to 40 percent of southern textile jobs. Lucy Taylor, who grew up in the textile town of Roanoke Rapids, North Carolina, recalled that, "my mother had a colored woman who helped her. She'd be at our house when Mama was working in the mill. This colored woman's name was Pat Simmons. . . . Pat's family and a lot of the other colored used to live down by the cemetery. They had a right hard time. People didn't pay them much. If Pat didn't get to work some, they just didn't have food." On the eve of World War II, in fact, black domestics in the Piedmont textile belt were paid as little as $1 to $3 a week.

This reliance on black domestics ensured that many white workers particularly opposed the hiring of black women into industry. Across the region, whites were anxious not to lose their domestic "help," and managers, for their part, were often reluctant to risk alienating their white employees. Executives were also unwilling to hire black women because they lacked a tradition of manufacturing employment. As a result, black women were only hired in industrial jobs during the war as a last resort, and they were mainly confined to janitorial or menial positions.

Many of the black women who did secure defense work were assigned to heavy, physical jobs that had previously been given to black men. Across the South, black women were in fact classified with black men as common labor, rather than as "female." At a box-making factory in Brewton, Alabama, for example, African American women fired boilers and handled lumber while white women operated stitching machines. In Memphis, black women at the Firestone tire plant were hired as tire stackers, a heavy job previously carried out by black men. "I didn't like it," recalled Evelyn Bates, who worked as a wartime stacker. Like many of her counterparts, however, Bates was acutely aware that she had few options. "I didn't have any other choice because I wanted to work," she explained. "If you quit that job you didn't get another factory job probably. Not a black woman. You might go to a little cafe, do housework or something like that, but factory jobs were hard for black women to get." Like their male counterparts, many black women also complained that they were pushed hard by unsympathetic white supervisors. "You had a white woman always over you," recalled Irene Branch, another Firestone employee. "She gonna see that you work . . . you couldn't go to the bathroom and stay no time. If you did, she'd come in there and get you."

When the war ended, southern whites were anxious to reverse the tenuous gains that both African American men and women had been able to make in the southern work place. The FEPC, which southern Democrats helped to terminate in 1946, noted in an overview of its work that blacks had only entered war work "very late." "They were unable," it continued, "because of racial barriers, to transfer to other employment. And their low seniority, in those industries in which they are still employed, subjects them to the risk of further displacement by returning veterans." Across the country, indeed, African Americans found that companies and unions were keen to reimpose prewar hiring patterns. "It is now clear," reported the FEPC in June 1946, "that Negro workers have lost large parts of their wartime employment gains and are finding that peacetime industry offers only the traditional openings of the years before 1940."

The experience of many individual southern workers confirms this observation. In Mobile, Horace Crenshaw, who had been one of the small number of African Americans able to work as a wartime welder in the local shipyards, tried to secure a similar position after the conflict, but was told by company supervisors that "they only had labor jobs for blacks at that time." In Savannah, John Bonner similarly remembered that though some blacks had secured work as truck drivers at the large Union-Camp paper mill during the war, when the conflict ended, management "took them off." Even though they had been performing the job for some time, black truck drivers were told by the company that they were not qualified and were replaced with whites. Many other African Americans had similar experiences. At International Paper Company in Georgetown, South Carolina, Emmanuel Johnson remembered that a handful of blacks had been given a nontraditional production job during the war, but they were sent back to "common labor" positions as soon as the company had enough returning white veterans: "Those men started returning back and being discharged from the army and navy, out of the service, and Boom!, they took us off. . . . That Sunday morning when they got enough of those guys, they didn't even tell us nothing. That Sunday morning we went up to my job upstairs, they says, 'Don't need you, you can go back downstairs.' Just that quick, without any explanation, without any thank-you or what. . . . They got enough men back, 'don't need you,' but we went back on the same bottom line."

The war was not, however, an entirely negative experience for southern blacks. For men like Johnson, Crenshaw, and Bonner, war jobs brought improved wages, even if only for a short period. For black women, too, industrial jobs, while invariably heavy and menial, were usually the first "public" work that they had been able to secure, and they offered many benefits over domestic work. Apart from shorter hours and higher wages, industrial work allowed African American women to break free of the control of white women who had previously employed them. By performing nontraditional jobs, African Americans also highlighted to themselves and to companies that they were capable of more than laboring work. War jobs brought blacks greater autonomy and visibility, and the complaints that many filed with the FEPC are themselves an indication of this. The FEPC itself helped black communities and organizations to mobilize around employment issues, paving the way for black activism to enforce fair employment laws in the 1960s. Rather than having few avenues to bring their complaints to, African American workers now had a federal body to appeal to, as for the first time the federal government had made fair employment a national policy. During the war, the FEPC processed more than 5,000 complaints, with typical grievances being that supervisors were unfairly barring blacks from skilled work or were unfairly demoting them to menial jobs. The commission's Birmingham hearings also breached racial mores, as black FEPC committee members Earl Dickerson and Milton Webster occupied positions of authority and questioned white witnesses. At the hearings, black professionals also gave evidence, while African American workers testified and voiced their charges of discrimination against both employers and unions.

While African Americans may have struggled to make lasting progress, the war raised their expectations considerably, encouraging an increase in civil rights activism that was to have permanent consequences. The war's rhetoric as a struggle for democracy focused black attention on the paradox that they were being asked to support this fight abroad while segregation still existed at home. In addition, many African Americans realized from military service or industrial work that they had skills that they were previously unaware of. From Virginia to Mississippi, black veterans returned home with a new determination to challenge segregation that eventually culminated in the high-profile civil rights protests of the 1950s and 1960s. Some participated in a broader upsurge in NAACP membership and black voter registration; between 1940 and 1945, for example, the NAACP's membership increased from 50,000 to 450,000, with most growth taking place in the South. Many also brought a new assertiveness into the workplace. In Natchez, Mississippi, for example, Sidney Gibson came back from the war and began efforts to fight discrimination at local plants, confronting unions that were infiltrated by the Ku Klux Klan. In Savannah, meanwhile, black veterans led by George Sawyer pioneered efforts to protest against discrimination at the Union-Camp paper mill, the Georgia city's largest employer. Across the region, African Americans pointed out that they no longer "thought it right" that they should be confined to unskilled work.

As well as giving African American veterans higher expectations and a greater awareness of discrimination, the war also gave them courage and a knowledge of how to defend themselves that was often based on weapons training. Such fortitude was often necessary, as blacks who challenged the status quo were often threatened or attacked. In Baton Rouge, Louisiana, veteran Amos Favorite, who confronted the Ku Klux Klan in his efforts to integrate the Ormet Aluminum plant, claimed that he was no longer afraid after the war. "The army taught me that," he recalled. "I wasn't afraid of nobody. Another thing is I had some good guns here and I wasn't afraid to use them either." In the 1960s, many of these workers initiated legal efforts to try and secure equal employment rights, often citing their war experience as a central part of their activism; Gibson, Sawyer, and Favorite, for example, were all participants in litigation brought under Title VII of the 1964 Civil Rights Act, which prohibited discrimination in employment.

As the war came to a close, many black workers also looked to their unions to fight discrimination. "We know that we are here in the South," complained one group of Birmingham steelworkers to the union's president, "but can't something be done to help this black race to let us feel like we are free in our hall or on our daily occupation[?] We feel like the [local Steelworkers leadership] is not doing its part for the black men." Organized labor, in fact, had a racial record that was mixed at best. At least thirty-one of the American Federation of Labor (AFL) affiliates, mainly craft unions, barred blacks from even joining. On the eve of World War II, the bulk of the federation's southern membership was in these unions, small groups of skilled white craftsmen who had organized in the late nineteenth and early twentieth century. They included the International Association of Machinists (IAM), which had been founded in Atlanta's railroad shops in the late nineteenth century and initially limited membership to whites by a constitutional provision. Later, a secret ritual pledged members to accept only competent white mechanics. In the late 1940s, the union abolished this ritual, but even after this the IAM had very few black members.

During the war, the IAM epitomized the way that unions often colluded with companies to maintain segregation. At a range of defense plants, the union and managers were both anxious to deter the rival Congress of Industrial Organizations (CIO), and they cooperated closely to uphold traditional racial practices. At the AVCO-Vultee aircraft plant in Nashville, where the IAM had bargaining rights, only 0.5 percent of workers were black, and they were confined to a small number of menial jobs such as sweepers and latrine workers. At FEPC hearings in Birmingham, IAM leaders sprang to Vultee's defense. "Management does hire negroes as janitors and in like occupations," they argued. "Obviously negroes are adapted for that kind of work. Most anyone familiar with factory work, especially where aircraft are being built, can understand why management believes that white workers are the most qualified and competent."

Many other AFL unions did accept black members but they usually segregated them into auxiliaries that lacked equal power and rights. This separation occurred because AFL chiefs, while declaring their organization open to "all workers," also maintained a policy of "local autonomy" that delegated decision-making capacity to rank-and-file leaders who were usually reluctant to challenge the racial status quo. Not surprisingly, the AFL publicly denied that it discriminated, citing the large numbers of blacks among its ranks. Rather than advancing racial justice, however, the union federation supported the organization of blacks primarily in order to stop them from depressing the wages of their white colleagues. Avoiding what it called the "wild promises" of the CIO, the AFL portrayed itself as a pragmatic alternative, arguing that blacks should be organized so that they were less likely to act as strikebreakers.

Forged in the 1930s out of a broad-based commitment to organize all industrial workers, the CIO has often been pictured as more racially egalitarian than the AFL. It was true that CIO unions did not prohibit blacks from membership, and the federation had proven willing to organize northern black workers in the 1930s. The IAM's CIO counterpart, the United Automobile Workers (UAW), certainly came into the war with a better racial record, but it still left much to be desired. In several UAW-represented plants, for example, FEPC representatives reported that union officers were helpful to black workers, and UAW-represented plants generally had a higher proportion of African American workers than their IAM counterparts. At the same time, however, UAW locals in the South sanctioned segregated meetings and acceded in traditional job assignments for blacks.

The CIO was a broad church, and the racial record of its member unions varied enormously. Left-led internationals had the strongest ideological commitment to racial equality, while other affiliates felt that blacks needed to be organized in order to stop them undermining the union. During World War II, the leftist Packinghouse Workers Organizing Committee organized blacks and whites together at the large Armour and Swift plants in Fort Worth and conducted union business on an integrated basis. This progressive position was initiated by the union's Chicago-based leadership and was helped by the fact that many blacks worked on the strategically important killing floor. As was the case in earlier interracial organizing efforts—such as longshore workers' struggle to join together at the start of the twentieth century—whites would join with blacks to secure common economic rights, but the alliance proved more fragile if racial questions were addressed, especially by outspoken black activists. At both Armour and Swift, interracial unionism was always a challenge, and the companies' efforts to scare whites away from the union by telling them that it was "a nigro organization" did have some success.

While many union leaders could have acted more forcefully on the race issue, they often faced difficult and genuine dilemmas. As Bruce Nelson has noted in his influential study of ship workers in Mobile, the leaders of the Industrial Union of Marine and Shipbuilding Workers of America (IUMSWA) were trapped between a white majority uninterested in civil rights and increasingly impatient black workers. Activists wanted to use their union as a forum to advance civil rights, but the need to pacify the white majority led IUMSWA chiefs to acquiesce in efforts to limit job opportunities for blacks.

It was when black workers made up the majority of the membership of CIO unions that they were able to most effectively push civil rights issues. In wartime Winston-Salem, North Carolina, a majority-black local of the Food, Tobacco, Agricultural and Allied Workers' Union (FTA) represented workers at the Reynolds tobacco factories and became involved in a broad range of civil rights activities. In the course of the war, members joined the NAACP, participated in voter registration campaigns, and helped elect a black minister to the city's Board of Aldermen. A heavily black Amalgamated Clothing Workers of America (ACWA) local at the Reliance Manufacturing Company in Montgomery also combined union meetings with successful voter registration classes. "We used to have clinics on our lunch hours and at union meetings," recalled former ACWA activist Fannie Allen O'Neal. "People had been down to register and they still hadn't heard if they were registered and they were mad. So it was motivating. We could get people to register." The local's work eventually helped prepare the ground for the 1955–56 Montgomery Bus Boycott, which Reliance workers supported. O'Neal, who went on to work for the state AFL-CIO, credited the labor movement as having "started the process of setting me free."

Other CIO unions were not as progressive. When whites made up the majority of the rank and file, union leaders usually refused to challenge their racial preferences. In the paper industry, one of the few solidly organized southern industries, both the AFL's International Brotherhood of Pulp, Sulphite, and Paper Mill Workers (IBPSPMW) and the CIO's United Paperworkers of America (UPA) organized black workers into segregated local unions. These unions were much more common in IBPSPMW plants, although this partly reflected the fact that the AFL union was much bigger than its CIO counterpart. Seeking to explain the practice, organizers and union leaders repeatedly argued that whites would never have accepted integrated local unions. "If you was going to organize when the industry moved South, the international didn't have no choice," recalled Russell Hall, a former representative of the AFL's paper workers' union. "It wasn't that they believed in it. If you said that you was going to have black and whites in the same union, then the whites wouldn't have joined. So the international didn't have no choice. In order to organize they had to agree to separate locals." To gain a foothold in a region hostile to organized labor, IBPSPMW chiefs were willing to defer to southern whites. As longstanding IBPSPMW president John P. Burke wrote a southern colleague in 1940, "Of course, I fully understand that you boys down South understand this colored problem much better than I do."

Within segregated unions, blacks did gain automatic representation and some experience of leadership, but they found that when they tried to press for greater civil rights they were pushed aside by the more numerous and powerful whites. White local unions and companies negotiated contracts that only offered blacks a limited number of segregated jobs in separate "lines of progression." Although black leaders tried to merge the black and white lines of progression in order to increase their job opportunities, they were simply outnumbered by whites, who were often grouped into three or four separate unions organized according to job classifications. "Our line of progression was like a short ladder up the side of a tall building," asserted Alphonse Williams, the long-serving leader of a black local union at International Paper Company in Mobile, Alabama. "If you stayed on that ladder, it would never get you to the top jobs because you see the top jobs was represented, ranked into the jurisdictions of the other locals, and of course they never consented to merge the lines of progression." "We tried to merge the line of progression," added Williams, who started working at the plant during World War II, "We tried to merge it but we couldn't. They wouldn't agree . . . and basically the other locals sometimes wouldn't agree, see they had all of the biggest and the best jobs."

Nationally, organized labor began the wartime period in a strong position, having made unprecedented membership gains over the previous decade. Encouraged by New Deal legislation, especially the 1935 Wagner Act, which gave federal recognition of workers' right to organize, trade union membership trebled over the course of the 1930s. Following steady growth, 23 percent of the nonagricultural workforce was organized by 1940. The major U.S. industries—steel, automobiles, and coal—had all been brought under the union banner. In the past, organized labor had experienced similar rapid surges in growth, particularly during the World War I era, but now for the first time union leaders had established permanent mass organizations capable of fighting for workers' rights in the nation's largest industries.

Such gains had been limited in the South. Southern workers in fact had a long history of sporadic activism dating back to the 1880s, but employers had consistently refused to recognize unions. At the end of World War I and again in 1929–30, southern workers had enthusiastically flocked into unions but employers had crushed their efforts, leaving few lasting gains. The 1934 general textile strike epitomized this recurring pattern. In the wake of the mass walkout, mill owners blacklisted more than 75,000 strike supporters, helping to kill union sentiment at a time when workers in other areas were swelling the ranks of organized labor. Many of those blacklisted would never work in the mills again. Their fate was well publicized, especially as many of those affected by the harsh tactic traveled widely across the region looking for work. The crushing of the 1934 strike hurt unions in the South for years to come. "I think," commented one southern textile worker in the late 1970s, "what happened in 1934 has a whole lot to do with people not being so union now." The same kind of retribution was not exacted on northern strikers. In New England and the Mid-Atlantic states, employers rehired most union supporters, and these activists played a key role in organizing northern mills later in the decade.

In the South, by contrast, when the CIO's Textile Workers' Organizing Committee (TWOC) tried to sign up recruits in 1937–38, they found that many of their supporters were no longer working in the mills or were fearful of getting involved again. "[T]he solid anti-union hostility of the corporations," recalled TWOC organizer Don McKee, "had brought about a widespread worker fright that paralyzed creative activity to improve the conditions of life and work." The TWOC campaign floundered, faced by determined employer opposition and an economic downturn that further increased workers' fears of economic retribution. The drive left the North solidly organized and the South overwhelmingly nonunion, ensuring that making greater progress in Dixie would remain a high priority of the CIO in the future. At the end of the 1930s, only 10.7 percent of southern workers belonged to unions, compared to 21.5 percent elsewhere. In North Carolina, the leading textile state, only 4.2 percent of nonagricultural workers were organized in 1939. By the time of the outbreak of World War II, the CIO, which had established such a strong presence in the large northern centers, had only 5 percent of its membership in the South.

The low rates of southern union membership were certainly not the result of a lack of organizing effort, as the TWOC drive highlighted. Labor leaders, however, consistently claimed that they faced greater employer opposition in the South than in other parts of the country. During the TWOC campaign, in particular, the force of mill owners' antiunionism surprised experienced labor chiefs, who had felt that the burgeoning labor movement was becoming increasingly mainstream and respectable. Even CIO publicist Lucy Mason, herself a southerner, was surprised at "the misunderstanding and hostility to the CIO . . . in this section." Southern executives resolutely fought the union federation, with many refusing to sign contracts even when they lost elections. "You people in New York don't know what it means to have the politicians, the local state administrators, the press and the public lined up with the employers and against the workers," reported Mason to the CIO's New York office.

Union leaders perhaps exaggerated the differences between the South and the rest of the country. Antiunionism was certainly not unique to Dixie; in northern states unions were vigorously and often violently resisted as well. During the 1937 Little Steel strike in Chicago, for example, eighteen people died, ten of them shot by police who had been housed and partially armed by the Republic Steel Company. There were, however, particularly strong barriers to successful labor organizing in the South. In conquering the South, labor leaders hoped not merely to spread unionism to the region but also to raise southern wages and thereby reduce the region's competitive advantage, thus protecting the jobs of their northern membership. At the same time, the CIO's leaders also aimed to undermine conservative southern Democrats by strengthening the profile of organized labor in the region. As such, unionism was a direct attack on executives, threatening both their pocketbooks and their close ties to the region's dominant conservative politicians. Southern business and political leaders also shared a desire to remain nonunion because they attracted plants to the region by promising that organized labor was weak. In the 1920s and 1930s, for example, southern states had become a haven for New England cotton mills fleeing higher-wage, union labor. For both sides, therefore, the stakes were high.

In the late 1930s, the strength of southern opposition to unionism was revealed vividly in the town of Fitzgerald, Georgia, where workers responded enthusiastically to the CIO but ultimately were defeated by an employer willing to use both legal and illegal methods. After workers at Fitzgerald Cotton Mills voted overwhelmingly for the TWOC, management bluntly refused to recognize the union, closing the mill and circulating forms asking their employees to revoke their union membership. Organizer David Witherspoon Dodge was also abducted and beaten by a group of company supporters who subsequently dumped him on the roadside and told him to get out of town. "We don't want no union and we ain't goner have none," they asserted. Dodge received little help from local law enforcement officials, who absented themselves when he was attacked and subsequently refused to investigate the case. "Fitzgerald law enforcement agencies did nothing," complained the union activist. A federal inquiry into Dodge's abduction led to the arrests and indictments of fifteen men, four mill managers, and eleven employees, but a local jury cleared them all of guilt. The verdict highlighted clearly to union supporters that even the federal government could not protect labor organizers in the South. Like many cases where the TWOC won elections, they never secured a contract in Fitzgerald.

Over the course of the 1930s, the more moderate AFL had fared slightly better in the region than the CIO, which was particularly detested by many southerners. At the Tennessee Valley Authority, where directors encouraged unionism, the older union federation made particular headway. The AFL also signed up new members in the tobacco, paper, and longshore industries, where conservative leaders chartered separate local union branches for black and whites. The bulk of the AFL's southern membership, however, continued to come from craft unions, most of which had been established in the late nineteenth and early twentieth centuries. In 1939, of 388,700 AFL members in the South, over 100,000 were in the building trades and more than 146,000 were in the railroad and related unions.

During World War II, the American union movement as a whole more than doubled in size, with real progress being made in organizing heavy industries. The growth that had started in the 1930s continued, as membership increased from 7.2 million in 1940 to over 14 million by 1945. Some of these gains were made in the South, reflecting the crucial protection provided by federal agencies. Although its declared purpose was to be neutral in labor relations, the NWLB's policies clearly assisted organized labor. During the war, "maintenance of membership" became a common

feature of NWLB directive orders, meaning that management had to require union membership as a condition of employment for all workers
who belonged to the union at the end of an initial fifteen-day escape period. The policy helped organized labor across the South; the Atlanta
Regional Board, for example, granted the provision in sixty-seven of seventy cases it handled in its first year. The board could also require both
sides to adopt specific contract terms, meaning that election results could
be directly translated into labor agreements. As a result, unions no longer
faced the problem, which had dogged them in the South, of winning elections but being unable to secure a contract. The board also had the power
to recommend that government contracts be cancelled or even to seize
plants if firms failed to comply with its rulings. During the war, for the
first time, strong federal protection for workers' rights meant that southern employers' resistance was quelled to some extent.

Federal protection was the driving force behind many of the CIO's
wartime gains in the South. In 1942, the Textile Workers Union of America (TWUA) managed to organize Dan River Mills, the largest textile
company in the region, and, more crucially, to secure a contract that
contained the automatic checkoff of union dues. According to the company's history, managers "vigorously objected" to the clause, "contending
that it was the union's responsibility to collect its dues." Under "intense
pressure" from the NWLB, however, managers were "forced to yield on
this point." The Virginia company's executives never liked the checkoff,
and after the war they succeeded in forcing the union to collect its own
dues.

Across the region, the wartime climate helped unions to make substantial strides. In Memphis, powerful mayor E. H. Crump had been a strident opponent of industrial unionism in the 1930s. The maverick politician promised the open shop to firms that located in his city, claiming that
unlike New York or Chicago, Memphis would not tolerate the CIO's
"nigger unionism." In 1940, when the CIO attempted to organize the
Firestone Rubber plant, the city's largest factory, company toughs bat-
tered labor activists while Crump sat back and verbally attacked the union
federation. During the war, in contrast, with the national climate stressing
the need for unity and federal agencies demanding that firms deal with
unions, Crump was pushed to soften his stance. Organized labor made
major strides as a result, and by 1943 about half of Memphis's 40,000 industrial workers belonged to the CIO, including the Firestone group.
The United Rubber Workers, which organized the Firestone plant, was

also able to establish a strong local at the Goodyear plant in Gadsden, Alabama, where, as in Memphis, prewar organizing efforts had been beaten back by violent resistance, with organizers assaulted and chased out of town by company supporters.

During World War II, unions made organizing gains in a wide variety of other industries. The ACWA was able to sign up several apparel plants, including Reliance Manufacturing Company in Montgomery and the Haggar Company's southern facilities. The AFL also made real progress, claiming a 100 percent increase in membership over the course of the war. The Oil Workers' Union made steady gains in organizing the new refineries that had sprung up in Louisiana and Texas following the discovery of deep oil reserves in the region in 1930. The federation also made strong gains in the shipyards, securing a major breakthrough when it organized over 9,000 workers at the Ingalls shipyard in Pascagoula, Mississippi. These strides helped increase labor's political clout in the region, aiding the emergence of politicians who welcomed labor support, including Governors Ellis Arnall in Georgia and Jim Folsom in Alabama and senators such as Florida's Claude Pepper, Alabama's Lister Hill, and North Carolina's Frank Graham. The CIO tried to mobilize its members to support prolabor candidates, setting up its Political Action Committee (PAC) in July 1943. While nominally nonpartisan, the PAC functioned closely with Roosevelt and liberal elements of the Democratic Party. In the spring primaries of 1944, the PAC claimed that it had helped to defeat several antiunion politicians, including Texas Representative Martin Dies. Despite these successes, however, many workers felt that unions should stay out of politics, and the PAC did not succeed in reshaping the political landscape as comprehensively as its leaders had hoped.

One of the CIO's biggest wartime coups was the successful organizing of the large R. J. Reynolds plant in Winston-Salem, North Carolina, which employed more than 10,000 people. The local union at Reynolds, which became one of the largest in the South, was strongly supported by black activists who looked to it to improve their poor working conditions. Unlike most other southern manufacturers, tobacco companies employed large numbers of African Americans, partly because industrial slavery in the antebellum years had provided a pool of trained employees. In addition, the processing of tobacco lent itself well to a two-tier production process, with blacks performing the nonmechanized processing tasks and whites the cleaner, mechanized work of making the final products. Textile work, in contrast, was much more interconnected, and blacks were excluded from the production process. In 1940, African Americans made up 45.5 percent of tobacco workers in Kentucky, the Carolinas, and Virginia, with roughly equal numbers of men and women toiling in the plants. The South was the home of the tobacco industry, producing around 90 percent of American-made cigarettes. The industry was particularly important to the economy of North Carolina; by 1930, for example, almost two-thirds of all American cigarettes were produced in the Tarheel State.

In Reynolds' factories, as in other southern tobacco plants, blacks were given the heavier, dirtier jobs and had to perform them under the watchful eye of abusive white supervisors. Grassroots activists pioneered efforts to improve these conditions. "We was catching so much hell in Reynolds that we had to do something," recalled Geneva McLendon. "In the first place they gave you a great big work load, more than you could do. . . . And then they stood over you and cussed you out about doing it. 'If you can't get this work out, get your clothes and get out.' Oh, it was rough, it was rough. Everybody would almost cry every day the way they would work you and talk to you. You weren't allowed to open the windows. The heat was almost unbearable. And you wan't allowed to talk to each other. It got so we wasn't going to take it anymore; we had had it." In June 1943, McLendon took part in a work stoppage initiated by over 200 stemmers who were tired of excessive workloads, overbearing supervisors, and hot, dirty working conditions. The strike quickly spread to other departments, paving the way for the establishment of a local union. Recalled rank-and-file leader Robert Black: "The people realized something they had never thought of before; we hold the strength in our hands to stop this company."

After being organized, FTA Local 22 became well known for employing African American officials and organizers, with rank-and-file activist Moranda Smith earning national prominence as the first black woman to sit on the executive board of an international union. Several organizers from the Communist Party proved particularly effective at mobilizing black activists. African American workers claimed that the union had given them a new confidence and respect. "When the union came, it was just like being reconstructed," explained Local 22's Ruby D. Jones. Black activism contributed to white reluctance to join Local 22, however, highlighting again the difficulties of building interracial unions, especially when black activists pushed a strong civil rights agenda. No more than 150 whites ever joined the local, alienated by its strong civil rights record. Racial divisions were encouraged by Reynolds, which looked for an opportunity to break the union. This chance came in 1947, when many white workers sided with the company and crossed a union picket line. Although the local was also undermined by anticommunism, with the press and local radio stations attacking it as communist-dominated during the strike, the failure to recruit white members was a central cause of its demise.

The wartime climate also helped to give migrant agricultural laborers more bargaining power. In the 1930s, a glutted labor market had ensured that migrant laborers, who were overwhelmingly black, toiled in the fields for as little as 30 or 40 cents a day. During the war, however, a tighter labor market and greater federal intervention encouraged laborers to fight back. In particular, the Farm Security Administration's Migratory Camp Program helped laborers to organize, especially as workers could stay in the camps and refuse to work unless their pay demands were met. In Florida, migrant workers repeatedly showed their willingness to protest during the war, causing complaints from owners that labor had the farmer "across the barrel." Toward the end of the conflict, however, employers regained control. In Florida, farm owners cooperated with federal agencies and hired immigrant workers who were deported if they tried to improve their conditions. In 1945, for example, the Farm Labor Supply Program supplied east coast growers with 56,000 foreign workers and 122,000 POWs. In the Arkansas and Mississippi Delta, farmers used their traditional tools of violence and disfranchisement to maintain the upper hand over African American agricultural laborers who had often joined labor or civil rights organizations in the course of the war. Although the wartime activism of Delta agricultural laborers was ultimately repressed, however, it again set the stage for subsequent civil rights protests.

Despite the gains that unions had made in the region, at the end of World War II organized labor was still much weaker in the South than in other parts of the United States. This was especially the case in the key textile industry. At the end of the conflict, the TWUA only represented around 19,000 of North Carolina's 200,000 textile workers. Similarly meager gains occurred in the other southern textile states; in Alabama, Georgia, and South Carolina, which together contained over 350,000 textile employees, the TWUA was able to add only 12,000 new members during the war. In textiles, even the strong protection provided by federal wartime agencies was usually not enough to push recalcitrant employers to accept organized labor. The management of the large Burlington Mills shut down its mills during the war rather than follow a NWLB ruling to bargain with the TWUA, while two other companies had their mills taken over by the U.S. Army because they refused to recognize the board's authority. Even before the war had ended, conservative forces in the South were seeking to restrict labor's rights, as the 1944 passage of "right-to-work" laws in Florida and Arkansas indicated.

In many ways, wartime developments were of crucial importance in postwar southern labor history. The war stored up a considerable degree of antiunion sentiment among employers, who resented being forced to deal with organized labor. Even executives who cooperated with federal agencies disliked government intrusion into their business and looked forward to the end of the conflict, when they hoped to reduce union influence and restore the prewar status quo.

Unions, on the other hand, were dissatisfied with the progress that they had made in the South during the war and looked forward to extending their limited organizing gains. Ultimately, therefore, wartime developments set union leaders and managers on a collision course, as one wanted to extend union influence while the other aimed to reduce it. This was especially the case in the textile industry, where organized labor had made major strides in the northern states during the 1930s and World War II. Throughout the postwar years, in fact, the TWUA and its successors launched repeated efforts to organize the big chain companies, such as Burlington, J. P. Stevens, and Cannon, that had refused to recognize organized labor during World War II. These companies continued to expand their southern operations, driving textile unions to try to organize the burgeoning sector of the industry. These unions used their northern strength to finance their southern forays, but as mill closings gradually weakened this base, their efforts were slowly curtailed.

The Number One Task

Operation Dixie and the Failure of Postwar Organizing

As World War II came to a close, American union leaders were optimistic, and they had good reason to be. They had by now experienced more than a decade of unprecedented growth, as union membership had increased dramatically from under 3 million in 1932 to 14.5 million thirteen years later. Over the course of the war, in particular, organized labor had gained unprecedented power and influence, and labor leaders felt that they were on the move. In 1945, unions won an impressive 82.9 percent of the 5,000 National Labor Relations Board (NLRB) elections held, and during the 1945–46 strike wave corporations were less willing to use violence against organized labor, indicating that they reluctantly accepted a lasting union presence in their plants. The one region of the country that was not solidly unionized, however, was the South. In Dixie, organized labor had not made the same progress, facing determined resistance even during the war. The South's economy was dominated by textiles, the only major manufacturing industry that was not organized. More than 800 mills dotted a wide area from Virginia to Alabama, presenting a huge organizing challenge. Drawing strength from the gains they had made in other regions, however, union strategists believed that the time was right for a major onslaught on the South that would concentrate heavily on the textile plants.

Shortly after the end of World War II, both the AFL and the CIO announced that they would make intensive efforts to organize Dixie's workers. Both staked a lot on their southern forays. In early 1946, CIO president Philip Murray told the federation's executive board that the southern organizing effort was "the most important drive of its kind ever undertaken by any labor union in the history of this country." Similar sentiments were repeatedly echoed by others; organizers had to battle away in Dixie, claimed one strategist, until they had conquered "everything in sight." The AFL also saw its southern drive as very important, describing it as "the most intensive Southern organizing drive ever undertaken by the trade union movement."

Labor leaders put such emphasis on their southern drives because they understood that the region was crucial to the future of the entire union movement. The labor movement, despite its strengths outside the region, could not be secure as long as the South was largely nonunion. Southern wages remained the lowest in the nation, and a much lower percentage of southern workers belonged to unions. Underlining the threat that the region posed to organized northern workers, many companies were increasingly setting up branch plants in Dixie. The CIO had realized for some time that it had to push South. "As long as the south remains unorganized," declared a federation prospectus in 1939, "it constitutes the nation's Number One economic problem and is also a menace to our organized movement in the north and likewise to northern industries." "The organization of the workers in the South," confirmed a resolution passed unanimously at the CIO's 1941 convention, "is the no. 1 task before the CIO."

CIO leaders also used these arguments as a way of securing support and funding from their northern members. Citing low wages in the South, CIO president Murray told a gathering of New Jersey autoworkers, "Lend all the support you can to this Southern drive, because the South, as you doubtless know, constitutes a type of economic millstone thrust around the necks of the people who are working in the North." The South was also home to antiunion, anti-New Deal congressional Democrats who, in alliance with conservative Republicans, had made Congress a citadel of reaction. Labor leaders hoped that if they could increase the number of union members in the South, they would provide a stronger political base for Democratic politicians who would be more supportive of organized labor.

No group of southerners threatened the living standards of northern union members more than the vast number of textile millhands. At the end of World War II, the TWUA had more than 400,000 members, yet only a tiny fraction of them were in the South. Textile workers comprised nearly a third of all southerners employed in basic industries, and around 75 percent of all textile workers lived in Dixie. Drive leaders clearly understood that the fate of their campaign rested on its primary industry. "When you organize the textile industry of the South," declared Van A.

Bittner, the veteran mineworkers' leader selected to head the campaign, "you have not only the textile industry of America organized, but you have practically all industries in the South under the banner of the CIO. So, our main drive . . . has been in the textile industry."

From the start, CIO leaders assigned more organizers to this key industry than to all others combined. As a whole, the union federation's commitment to the drive was impressive; it sent 250 organizers into the region, and affiliated unions contributed more than $1 million. The campaign was officially launched in May 1946, and staff made their most intensive efforts over the first six months. Organizing continued for another six years, however, and Operation Dixie was not officially wound up until April 1953, spotlighting the CIO's intensive commitment to try and unionize the South.

Ultimately, however, both the AFL and CIO's efforts fell flat. The two federations netted only minuscule gains, and most of these were limited to small plants. Both drives ran into determined corporate opposition that reflected a broader conservative backlash against trade unions and liberalism in general. Many southern employers had only recognized unions when the war was on because they had to. Once the conflict was over they were determined to restore the prewar status quo. This backlash affected existing southern union members as well, as companies increasingly forced strikes in order to weaken or eliminate unions altogether. In some respects, the gap between the experience of southern workers and those elsewhere in the United States in these years is striking. Nationally, the immediate postwar years are often viewed as a period when unions became an established part of American life. Radical critics even charged that they had lost the militancy that had helped create them in the 1930s; instead, they have asserted, unions were now excessively bureaucratic, stable, and conservative. In the South, however, very few unions could ever take their existence for granted, and even established locals often came under attack from management and their allies in the immediate postwar years.

Employers were able to draw on many powerful local allies in their fight against organized labor. Most southerners viewed the CIO as much more radical than the AFL, and they concentrated particular energy on opposing it. In many communities, especially small towns in the textile belt, employers had strong influence over the local police, churches, and other community institutions, and these bodies were often mobilized in the company's favor. As Operation Dixie organizer Lloyd Gossett complained: "The Mayor, the police chief, the deputy, the businessmen, the President of the Chamber of Commerce—everybody was against us."

In a region with high rates of church attendance, employers proved particularly adept at using the power of religion. Across the South, organized antilabor propaganda was subsidized by businessmen and appeared from religious sources whenever the CIO appeared. The close ties between companies and local churches surprised organizers. "The company," recalled one, "would not only make radio announcements, they'd get a preacher on Sunday: 'We have a labor organizer in town who is nothing but an agitator and will tell nothing but lies to get you to join and sign a union card and have an election!' The company would put it out in leaflets! And then the preacher would take that leaflet and read it in the pulpit!" In some textile communities, organizers complained that their arrival led to the spontaneous appearance of preachers who set up tents and were soon proclaiming that "the union is the 'mark of the beast.'"

Many of the CIO's problems actually stemmed from the fact that it was trying to organize the South in order to protect its northern membership base, as this allowed its opponents to portray organizers as outsiders who cared little for the real interests of ordinary southerners. Company supporters frequently revived memories of the Civil War. In Floyd County, Georgia, William Howard Lewis, a prominent county commissioner, led opposition to the CIO as they tried to organize several local textile plants as part of their postwar drive. Lewis used the press, a frequent opponent of unions during Operation Dixie, to attack organized labor through a series of lengthy editorials. "The South stands again at Vicksburg," he warned, and was threatened by a new "Northern invasion." CIO staff claimed that Lewis' attacks were making their job more difficult, and their efforts to organize the key Pepperell mill in Lindale faltered. Following a lengthy campaign, the union eventually lost this key election by a four-to-one margin. Across the South, in fact, union leaders and organizers were consistently portrayed as outside aliens. In communications with workers, employers and their allies repeatedly emphasized the "foreign" names of CIO leaders, such as the TWUA's George Baldanzi and the ACWA's Jacob Potofsky. In one clothing plant, managers posted Potofsky's picture on the bulletin board and asked their workers: "Does this man look like he's interested in your welfare?" These kinds of attacks, complained organizers, were used "to the hilt."

The CIO often unwittingly encouraged this opposition. At the start of their campaign, union leaders such as steelworkers' official David

McDonald spoke of the South being "attacked," while the *CIO News* termed the drive a "Holy Crusade." It may have been unofficial, but the term "Operation Dixie" also encouraged the CIO's opponents to use the invasion metaphor. In later years, drive veterans agreed that the name was a strategic mistake, as it had advertised too much and "immediately put people on the defensive." "Here comes Sherman's army again! Be ready!" they noted ironically. In North Carolina, even the liberal Raleigh *News and Observer* wrote that unions had "invaded a war-industrialized South-land with hundreds of organizers and the determination to sign up at least a million new members."

While antiunionism was certainly not unique to the South, it was more intense and lasting in the region than in other parts of the country. In combination with community allies, southern executives proved willing to use violence to fight organizing efforts at a time when it was becoming much more unusual in other regions. During the massive strike wave that had swept across the North in 1945–46, management and police directed less violence at labor than had been the case in the 1930s. Unions effectively discouraged these tactics by comparing companies' use of armed spies with the "storm troop armies of the Fascist nations." In the South, however, violent tactics persisted longer, reflecting the close ties between executives and law enforcement officials. During the first five months of the CIO's campaign, seventeen union organizers and members were severely assaulted. Lucy Randolph Mason, assigned to investigate violations of civil rights for the CIO, was soon overwhelmed by the task. Union leaders' hopes that Mason, a genteel Virginia native, could educate southerners to accept unions proved to be misplaced, as wherever she went she reported detailed violent community opposition to the CIO. In Tifton, Georgia, for example, where she investigated beatings of striking workers by the city police, she wrote of an "exceedingly anti-union" chief of police and a deputy sheriff who told her to stop meddling in what was not her business. In another incident, a county sheriff in Port Gibson, Mississippi, assaulted union supporters and threatened to "shoot their damn heads off."

Mason was simply unable to visit every location where violations of civil rights took place. In Gadsden, Alabama, procompany vigilantes ransacked the CIO's office and threw its furniture out on the street, while in Florence, South Carolina, a mob informed a CIO worker that he would be tarred and feathered if he did not leave immediately. Following a severe beating by a hostile mob, an organizer in Avondale, Alabama was visited in hospital by a procompany police chief who told him that he would be killed if he ever returned to the town. Antiunion workers also participated in such attacks. In Tallapoosa, Georgia, a group of armed men and women abducted a female CIO organizer and, claimed the union, dumped her "like a sack of meal onto a dirt road a long way from anywhere."

Managers used other techniques to fight off the CIO. The firing or harassment of union activists was particularly effective. Managers frequently claimed that union supporters had been fired for leaving their machines or not making production, but workers received the message that supporting the union was risky. Indeed, selective firings often killed organizing drives. At the Morrison Turning Plant, a Tennessee furniture maker, state director Paul Christopher reported that the CIO was "getting along fine" until the company fired "our best man" and "all eight of our remaining volunteer organizers who were signing up people." In a 1950 effort to organize Aladdin Industries, a glass-making factory, the CIO's campaign was derailed by the dismissal of "three key men." Firings made workers fearful, and fear among workers was a problem that organizers referred to again and again. As Christopher wrote of one textile mill where the union's leaders had been fired, "The Borden Mill workers are simply scared." Union leaders also complained that the increasingly understaffed NLRB offered little protection, as the average time between the filing of charges and the issuing of NLRB decisions was twenty-seven months. Consequently, even if the board eventually reinstated those who had been dismissed, the organizing drive would lose momentum as apprehensive workers waited anxiously for the decision. The function of the postwar NLRB, complained TWUA president Emil Rieve, was not to "give decisions" but to "perform autopsies."

Employers were able to generate fear through other methods. Many fought off the CIO by launching intensive campaigns on the eve of elections, where they were able to scare their employees into voting against the union. In the work place, companies frequently assembled workers for "captive audience" meetings where they showed them antiunion propaganda. Executives also mailed letters to workers' homes, telling them that unions were only after their dues, that they would push them to strike, and that their economic demands would cause the plant to close. "Unions cost money," noted a typical letter. "The money to operate them can come but from one source. Money out of your pocket." In a 1951 campaign to organize Davis Cabinet Company, a Nashville-based furniture maker, the company hit back with captive audience speeches and letters to workers from company executives. With a vote of 288 to 137, the firm won the subsequent election handsomely. "Out of 260 membership cards which we had signed we were only able to hold 137," reported organizer J. S. Temple. "This in all probability was due to the anti-Union campaign the Company put on in the last few days before the election."

Top executives often made personal appeals to defeat the union and to maintain the "personal" relationship between the company and its employees. Letters placed workers under a great deal of personal pressure. At Gluck Brothers, a furniture-maker based in Morristown, Tennessee, company owner Harry J. Gluck told staff that unions were an unwanted "outside" presence. "Today is my birthday," he wrote at the close of his letter. "I trust that it will be a happy birthday for me to remember." Union leaders repeatedly complained that the effectiveness of these tactics was helped by the tardiness of the postwar NLRB, as delays between the date when they filed for election and the actual holding of the vote gave companies time to launch their onslaughts. Even if corporate opposition was not particularly virulent, it was often difficult to sustain a campaign's momentum over a long period. "Waiting for the election order in this case presents the usual problems of keeping alive worker interest," noted one typical report.

Even if workers did hold firm and vote the CIO in, unions often faced an uphill struggle to secure a contract. Managers refused to even meet for negotiations or stalled when they did, leaving workers to fear that the union lacked the power to bring the company to heel. In the lumber industry, the CIO won elections at nineteen mills during Operation Dixie but by the end of 1948 had only secured contracts at six of them, largely because of management intransigence. As a result, as the drive wore on lumber workers increasingly voted against the CIO, because they felt that it would be unable to deliver on its promises.

Employers' preelection campaigns were clearly encouraged by the 1947 Taft-Hartley Act. Passed over President Truman's veto, the act aimed to reform federal labor policy by curbing union rights, which Taft-Hartley's proponents felt had been protected too much by the 1935 Wagner Act. The 1935 act, which had created the NLRB in order to protect the right to organize, had helped fuel an unprecedented period of union growth. In the interests of balance, supporters of Taft-Hartley argued that management rights now needed to be strengthened. The new law therefore expanded employers' rights to communicate with their employees. Taft-Hartley's proponents argued that workers had the right to hear "both sides," but unions claimed that the law gave a green light to union busting, especially as it allowed employers to initiate decertification procedures through the NLRB, whereas previously only workers had been allowed to do this. The act also banned both secondary boycotts and strikes arising from jurisdictional disputes among unions. In a reflection of the anticommunist mood of the time, Taft-Hartley also required union officials to sign affidavits stipulating that they were not Communist Party members.

The new legislation was strongly supported by southern congressmen and senators, most of whom were anxious to keep organized labor confined to its northern strongholds. Their backing of Taft-Hartley highlighted why labor leaders hoped to increase the labor vote in the South and undermine conservative southern Democrats. Some of the provisions of the law did particularly hurt unions in the South. Apart from southern employers taking notable advantage of their expanded preelection rights, the ban on secondary boycotts also prevented northern unions from using their power to try and help striking southerners. Although most had been successful at resisting unionization even before the law was passed, Taft-Hartley undoubtedly made it easier for southern employers to fight off organized labor. In November 1947, a few months after the passage of the act, North Carolina director William Smith claimed privately that several textile campaigns had been "stymied due to the enactment of the Taft-Hartley Bill."

Taft-Hartley also allowed states to set right-to-work requirements, outlawing the "closed shop," which made union membership a condition of employment. Southern legislatures led the way in taking advantage of this new opportunity; by the end of 1947, seven of the thirteen southern states had already passed right-to-work laws. These laws further weakened organized labor in the region, giving companies the opportunity to discriminate against union members. With right-to-work laws, complained textile organizer Lawrence Rogin, "any mill that wanted to could beat the union." As federal law required unions to bargain and process grievances for all members of the bargaining unit, they were now faced with having to represent workers who did not pay dues. In succeeding years, this proved to be a major problem, as strategically minded "free-riders" enjoyed the benefits of union contracts but refused to pay dues. Some even filed occasional grievances but were unwilling to sign a membership card, while others joined the union for a specific reason but took advantage of the right-to-work laws to withdraw when they wanted to.

Such behavior exacerbated divisions among workers, whose attention was often turned inward rather than focusing on fighting their employer.

Throughout Operation Dixie, managers also frequently responded to organizing efforts by reassuring their employees that they had their interests at heart, encouraging them to feel positively about their jobs. In some communities, particularly in the textile industry, workers identified closely with the mill owners and hesitated to go against their wishes. This problem was particularly acute in the company town of Kannapolis, North Carolina, home of the family-owned Cannon Mills. Employing over 25,000 people in seven different mills, Cannon Mills was a major organizing target. CIO leaders assigned ten organizers to the Cannon campaign, two-thirds of their total complement in the Tarheel State. Despite this, strategists eventually abandoned the drive without an election due to a lack of support.

From its foundation, the Cannon family had been intimately associated with the cluster of textile mills they constructed just north of Charlotte. In 1886, James W. Cannon had built his first cotton mill in Kannapolis, and after he died his son Charles ran the company for over fifty years, providing a wide range of both housing and recreational facilities. Many workers felt a strong sense of identification with the Cannon family, passing down stories of how Charles Cannon would walk through the mills and help operators out when he saw something wrong with the machinery they were operating. "They loved Mr. Cannon," recalled organizer Robert Freeman, who was born and raised in the North Carolina mill town. "Everybody loved him. He was their daddy. The father, the grandfather, the great-grandfather, all lived here. And everybody looked to Uncle Charlie Cannon. He was a Santa Claus. 'He was good to my daddy. He was good to my granddaddy. He was good to my great-granddaddy. He give us a job, give us a place to live.' They'd say, 'I gotta be faithful to him. Long as he likes me, he'll take care of me.'"

The Cannon family's power stretched into every area of life in the small textile community. To union supporters, Cannon workers lacked freedom, an independent voice in the workplace. Charles Cannon was, in the words of one, "the Godfather of Kannapolis. . . . He controlled this town completely." Other Cannon employees, however, failed to see their plight in this way, instead viewing the company's closeness as protective. Noting the family's influence over the town, one commented, "That's the thing I liked about working for Cannon Mills, is it was more family oriented." Others, like mill worker Julia Hicks, fondly recalled growing up in the company town. "I was like no little rich kid on the block, living in a mill village, but the houses were nice," she asserted. "If something happened all you had to do was make a phone call, someone was here to fix it. Plumbing, lighting, anything that you needed, Mr. Cannon saw that the people were looked after." Throughout the postwar years, this identification with the company continually frustrated efforts to organize the plants. The company also undercut the union's appeal by keeping its wages and benefits on a par with those in other textile centers, meaning that many argued that there was little need to sign union cards. By 1948, North Carolina director William Smith admitted in a report on the Cannon campaign that the CIO had "not been able to generate any real activity there." The failure to organize Cannon Mills, one of the largest companies in the key textile industry, represented a crushing defeat for the CIO.

Operation Dixie also took place during the height of the Cold War, and executives and their supporters did not hesitate in using anticommunist propaganda against organized labor. The CIO's efforts to portray itself as moderate and "American" failed to stop its opponents viewing it as little more than a willing agent of the Soviet Union. One organizer recalled that across the South, employers told their employees that "CIO" stood for "Christ is Out, Communism is On." In Rome, Georgia, the local press greeted the arrival of organizers with the headline, "Operation Dixie: The Iron Curtain Descends." Only a small number of CIO unions did have communist members, largely a hangover from the 1930s, when party activists had helped to organize mass production workers in the large northern cities. In 1949, in an attempt to head off anticommunist propaganda, the CIO purged these left-led unions, leading to a messy and protracted battle that frequently diverted staff attention from organizing. On the ground in the South, CIO staff wasted, in the words of one, "a good deal of time" battling the renegade unions rather than trying to sign up new members.

Throughout 1948 and 1949, in fact, the communist issue swallowed up a great deal of the CIO's time and resources. The 1948 presidential election divided the federation, as left-led unions supported Progressive Party candidate Henry A. Wallace. Ignoring a January 1948 executive board resolution that criticized third-party politics, they asserted that the Democratic Party was no longer sufficiently responsive to labor's needs. Many congressional Democrats, they pointed out, had voted for Taft-Hartley. This defiance encouraged CIO leader Philip Murray, a Catholic anticommunist who had previously been eager to avoid open conflict, to take a harsher stance. At the 1948 and 1949 CIO conventions, Murray launched a broadside on the pro-Soviet unionists, terming them "sulking cowards" and "apostles of hate" who were, he claimed, internally corrupting the labor movement.

In the two years following the 1948 presidential election, much of the CIO's attention was consumed with expelling the eleven unions with the most consistent pro-Soviet records. Some of the battles became particularly savage, and the South was not spared. In Alabama, there was bitter conflict between the United Steel Workers (USW) and the left-led Mine and Mill Workers, whose leader Maurice Travis lost an eye after a savage beating by his opponents. In Memphis, conservative CIO activist William A. Copeland led raiding campaigns against a predominantly black local of the Furniture Workers' Union that he accused of being communist-dominated. The communist issue turned labor in on itself, especially as AFL unions were also willing to use the weapon against the CIO. In Nashville, for example, the AFL's IAM succeeded in having a 1947 USW organizing victory set aside because the steelworkers' leaders had not signed the noncommunist affidavit required by the Taft-Hartley Act for access to union services. The move triggered a bitter strike that saw the IAM and USW viciously attacking each other.

Since their original split in the 1930s, relations between the AFL and the new federation had been fractious, and during Operation Dixie the two organizations spent a great deal of time and resources fighting against each other rather than trying to organize new plants. Ultimately, neither benefited from such internecine warfare. In a 1951 campaign to organize the Lannon Tannery in Tullahoma, Tennessee, organizers reported that the infighting between the AFL and CIO had helped convince workers that they did not need a union. When CIO staff tried to hand out leaflets at the plant gates, they reported that they were "treated to cursings, jeers, catcalls and other hostile treatment." The fight between the two federations was particularly futile because even when the CIO did make gains at plants that had previously been organized by the AFL, total union representation in the region did not increase.

A range of other problems afflicted the CIO's organizing campaign. In the spring and summer of 1949, Operation Dixie was hurt by the prolonged illness of director Van A. Bittner. In July 1949, after a long period of poor health, the elderly Bittner slipped into a coma and died. His successor, textile union leader George Baldanzi, argued that the answer to the drive's problems lay in a greater concentration of resources. As a result, he implemented "drastic economies," curtailing both funding and the number of active organizers. These cuts, however, took effect as many employers, partly encouraged by the Taft-Hartley Act, were launching increasingly virulent preelection attacks on the CIO.

The relationship between the central Southern Organizing Committee (SOC) and the various international unions was not always smooth, especially as some unions insisted on implementing their own procedures even when they violated those of the SOC. Drive leaders argued that all workers who signed cards should pay a $1 initiation fee, but the money was never collected by many organizers because their own unions did not require it. The failure to collect the fee compounded the drive's financial problems, especially as strategists had counted on this funding. The TWUA led the way in consistently refusing to collect the initiation charge, while UAW organizers collected the fee but held onto it. These inconsistencies caused headaches for state directors and sent out a mixed message to workers. When CIO staff did insist on the fee, equivalent to an hour's wages for many southerners, they also sometimes deterred cash-strapped workers from signing up.

In some campaigns, there were other differences between staff. Bittner and Baldanzi both responded to failures by arguing that organizers needed to be more efficient. Field staff, they asserted, had to concentrate more on "specific targets," yet organizers frequently replied that their superiors were not giving them the resources they needed to secure results. In December 1947, shortly before a key North Carolina textile election, Bittner refused a request from state director William Smith for $2,000 to fund extra publicity and radio time, which Smith felt was important in order to counteract company propaganda. After the funding was denied, the union lost the subsequent election. In many cases, SOC staff also found themselves sidetracked by servicing work, meaning that they did not devote all of their time to reaching potential new members.

The key textile industry presented particular organizing difficulties. For a start, its disparate structure caused real problems. In the 1930s, the CIO's breakthroughs in the northern automobile and steel plants had been helped by the fact that these industries were dominated by a small number of large companies. When one firm was organized, there was genuine pressure on the others to follow. In contrast, textile plants were much smaller and were scattered right across the Piedmont, ensuring that even breakthroughs at the larger facilities left a huge task ahead. In 1947, there were more than 400,000 southern textile workers, but the average plant only employed around 300 people. Most southern textile companies, however, owned more than one plant, which meant that they could easily transfer production away from organized facilities if they needed to. Organizers frequently complained that employers deliberately dispersed their plants in order to frustrate union efforts, and employers certainly were confident that they could switch work to other mills even if one facility was idled because of a strike.

Most southern textile mills were also located in small towns where they were the dominant employer. A small-town location tended to increase corporate control and make community opposition to organized labor more effective. In short, unions were much more likely to succeed when plants were located in large metropolitan areas. Company threats to close factories were particularly compelling in the textile industry precisely because most mills were usually located in small towns where they were the major employer.

During the war, rulings by the NWLB had granted southern textile workers a series of wage increases, and in the immediate postwar era these wages continued to rise because of the national economic boom. Most southern textile workers remembered the 1930s, when they had struggled to earn more than $12 a week, yet just over a decade later they were taking home between three and four times this amount. In addition, many southern textile companies matched any wage increases awarded by local unionized firms, causing unorganized workers to reason that they did not need to join a union in order to experience an improving standard of living. As well as implementing an industry-wide pay raise, for example, management at American Thread Company in Tallapoosa, Georgia, responded to a union campaign by announcing increased insurance benefits and giving their staff more hours. Until 1949, pent-up civilian demand meant that southern textile mills boomed, making it easier for managers to grant their employees steady wage increases. Some savvy workers even used the presence of CIO organizers to exact wage and benefit improvements. Reporting on the failure to organize Du Pont workers, who were represented by company unions, Virginia state director Ernest B. Pugh wrote, "it is apparently just another case of duPont workers using the threat of the CIO to get benefits otherwise withheld from them." Although the CIO's presence helped to raise southern wages, the regional wage gap also persisted, worrying union leaders.

An improving standard of living tended to undercut organized labor's appeal and reinforce the tendency that many textile workers felt toward embracing the status quo. After all, joining the union was risky, as company harassment of activists indicated. Other southern workers were also enjoying a better standard of living in these years; between 1940 and 1950, in fact, steady economic growth produced a dramatic increase in incomes across the region. Between 1940 and 1950, the bank deposits of southerners nearly doubled, and individual income rose by 227 percent. Rural southerners, who had left behind low incomes in the declining farming sector in order to take industrial jobs, particularly felt the improvement, and it was these workers who were often seen as the hardest to organize.

In the 1930s and 1940s, the CIO had spoken in favor of stronger civil rights legislation and had shown a willingness to organize blacks and whites together. In the South, however, the federation had frequently refused to challenge segregation, afraid that this would prevent it from recruiting whites. During Operation Dixie, CIO leaders were acutely aware that many southerners viewed their organization as a force for racial integration. They did reach out to blacks, but they avoided linking union membership to broader social purposes. Van Bittner set the tone, trying to downplay overt references to race and insisting that the CIO was trying to organize both black and white workers "because they are all God's human beings." Bittner and North Carolina director William Smith were what the *Saturday Evening Post* called "practical" men, not "theorists who want a freshly laundered world next Monday morning." Throughout Operation Dixie, the two activists repeatedly emphasized the economic benefits of unionism rather than directly addressing the race issue. As the drive was centered on the lilywhite textile industry, many textile organizers were keen to prevent the race issue from being mentioned. In industries that did employ larger numbers of blacks, organizers proceeded carefully, working separately between the two groups before tentatively trying to bring them together. As organizer Woody Biggs recalled: "You met with whites, okay; you met with blacks, okay; but the day came when you had to meet together. And that first meeting was touchy. I've had it all fall apart right there. Whites just wouldn't do it." Organizers had to be especially careful not to sign up blacks too quickly, as this could encourage whites to abandon their efforts. "If it looked to the whites like you had a black union," recalled Alabama-based organizer Barney Weeks, "and you wanted them to join it, you'd be dead. They wouldn't do it."

This caution, of course, did not stop employers from frequently raising the racial issue against the CIO, telling textile workers, in particular, that the union federation would encourage a breakdown of segregation across the South. The CIO, thundered influential *Textile Bulletin* editor David Clark, was "an organization for Negroes." In other industries, too, employers did not hesitate to use the race issue against the CIO. "Companies race-baited constantly, and the workers would fall for that," charged one former organizer.

Several scholars have criticized the CIO's racial caution, asserting that it could have made more progress by taking a stronger racial stand. Robert Korstad and Nelson Lichtenstein have argued that the civil rights upsurge that occurred during the war made possible "a very different sort of civil rights movement," based around black workers and with strong bonds to the black community. Organized labor, they assert, missed this opportunity. As well as calling for a stronger racial stance, some scholars have also argued that the federation's anticommunism was an important secondary cause of the failed drive, because it robbed organized labor of some of its most progressive and able activists. Writing about the failure of Operation Dixie, Kim Moody asserts that, "This organizing drive collapsed largely because of the CIO's inability to confront racism in the South and, to a lesser extent, the obsession of the CIO leadership with its fight against its former Communist allies."

During Operation Dixie, as had been the case during the war years, African American workers did respond well to organizing efforts, and some of the CIO's few gains occurred in heavily black industries such as lumber and tobacco. Many of these workers looked to unions as a way of fighting segregation. For them, as one recalled, the CIO was always "a question of freedom." The expulsion of the left-led unions also undoubtedly weakened the CIO, depriving it of committed and experienced organizers and distracting the attention of many staff from the key task of signing up new recruits.

At the same time, however, political realities dictated that the CIO would never follow a more radical course. Operation Dixie was primarily funded by the TWUA and the ACWA, ensuring that textiles, rather than industries that employed large numbers of African Americans, would be the primary focus. Strategists also realized that in order to make real progress in the South, they had to organize the textile industry, the region's largest employer. While undoubtedly damaging, the expulsion of the left-led unions also occurred at a time when Operation Dixie had already run out of steam, unable to overcome the plethora of problems that affected it, particularly determined employer opposition.

It is also doubtful that a stronger civil rights stance would have allowed unions to make more progress in the South as a whole. Basing campaigns around African Americans was problematic because it risked alienating whites, who made up the majority of the workforce in most industries. In cases where unions did give strong support to civil rights, in fact, they invariably lost support among whites. In the late 1940s and early 1950s, white workers withdrew from locals of the United Packinghouse Workers' union in Fort Worth when black and Hispanic members started to push nondiscrimination policies. The racial liberalism of Local 22 of the Food and Tobacco Workers in Winston-Salem, North Carolina also led to white workers refusing to join the union and eventually helping to break it. Although anticommunist attacks on Local 22 were clearly a cause of its demise, the union was also weakened by the refusal of many whites to support it; during a strike in 1943, for example, over 3,000 white Reynolds' employees reported to work. When whites broke the picket lines en masse again four years later, Local 22 was permanently destroyed.

Similar dynamics were at work elsewhere. During a bitter 1949 strike at Memphis Furniture Company, a conflict that represented a turning point in the CIO's fortunes in the Tennessee city, white workers refused to join with blacks and instead acted as strikebreakers. At the Greene Brothers Lumber Company in Elizabethtown, North Carolina, most black workers similarly joined the union while their white counterparts stayed away. During a 1948 strike at the large lumber mill, white workers actually cooperated with employers, the police, and community leaders in fighting the CIO. Although the black unionists prevailed in the strike, the failure of whites to join the union ultimately left it vulnerable, and it crumbled in the 1950s. In 1951, the black president complained that he had tried "everything" to get whites to join, but added "it will take a white man to get them into the union."

Even in cases where black and white workers did organize successfully together, they were careful to avoid broader issues of social equality and to concentrate on workplace rights, just as the CIO's leaders tried to do. In the coal industry and in some lumber towns, workers agreed to allow whites to dominate leadership positions because they reasoned that black leadership would destroy their efforts. As such, interracial unionism did not lead to social equality. Instead, it often required a narrow focus on shared economic issues, rather than on broader problems of social equality, in order to be successful. In addition, interracial unionism worked best in all-male industries like coal mining because it was able to avoid the explosive issue of contact between black men and white women. Again, the textile industry, which employed large numbers of women, presented a much more difficult challenge to labor leaders. The CIO's "choices" with regard to the race issue were actually very limited, especially as the federation had to maintain the loyalty of the rank and file in order to survive. Union leaders thus sought compromises between principles and pragmatism, balancing their national stand for racial equality against the need to recruit and hold onto both black and white members in the South.

Confronting a wide variety of problems, the leaders of Operation Dixie tried hard to remain upbeat. If they just stuck to the task, they reasoned, their diligence would eventually be rewarded. While he headed the campaign, Bittner repeatedly chivvied downbeat staff that they could overcome the difficult organizing climate through hard work. Reacting to the 1946 congressional elections in which the Republicans made big gains, the veteran activist wrote, "We can overcome the election results by putting every ounce of energy and all the intelligence that God has given us in our organizational work." Field staff tried hard to follow Bittner's philosophy and stick to their job. "Moving a little slow, but we are still signing up a few each week," noted one organizer. Even in textile campaigns, where defeat followed defeat, field staff worked hard to convince themselves (and their bosses) that the all-important breakthrough was just around the corner. In March 1948, William Smith reported to Bittner that, "While the picture in Textile has been gloomy and does not appear too optimistic at the present time, I can see definite trends toward organization and have a real feeling that the thing is breaking." These reports were undoubtedly designed to maintain morale and perhaps to guard against staff reductions. Striving to remain optimistic, some field representatives even claimed that they would make real progress once the weather improved, yet such hopes rarely proved to be justified.

Despite all their efforts to remain upbeat, on some occasions the frustration of CIO leaders was evident. In early 1948, staff in North Carolina mounted an intensive campaign to organize Proximity Mill in Greensboro. A key part of a local textile chain, the plant was a major facility employing around 2,200 people. On January 16, Smith reported that "no effort is being spared to win this important election." But despite this, the CIO was still soundly beaten, unable, as was so often the case, to counteract intensive company opposition on the eve of the election. Clearly exasperated, Bittner reacted to news of the loss by writing Smith almost immediately. "There is no accounting," he claimed, "for the lack of intel-

ligence on the part of some workers and we will all just have to keep plug-
ging away to do the best we can." The Proximity debacle was, as Smith
admitted, "a bad defeat" because it represented the most important textile
election that the SOC had contested in the Tarheel State. Along with the
Cannon failure, it represented the low point of the CIO's doomed efforts
in textiles. The tide of setbacks also gradually took their toll even on experienced union leaders such as Tennessee director Paul Christopher, a native southerner who had taken part in some of the bitter battles of the
1934 general strike. "I guess we are going to the dogs in Tennessee," he
admitted privately following a string of heavy losses.

Operation Dixie did produce some gains, but most of them occurred
outside of the crucial textile industry. Within the first year, the CIO won
bargaining rights at the largest chemical plant in Oak Ridge, Tennessee,
and secured victories at a variety of tobacco and fertilizer producers.
Drawing on strong support from African American workers, organizers
were also able to bring some lumber mills into the union fold. There were
scattered gains in the furniture industry; in Virginia, for example, five furniture plants were organized over the course of the campaign. In the paper industry, which had expanded rapidly across the region in the 1930s
and 1940s, the CIO also made progress, drawing on employers' fears of
costly work stoppages in capital-intensive operations. Over the South as a
whole, the amount of progress made by the CIO remains unclear, although Marshall estimated that total membership rose from 143,600 in
1939 to 362,200 in 1953. These figures, however, were based on contemporary "union materials" and are probably overstated, especially as the
CIO was unable to secure contracts after many election victories.

On balance, the drive's scattered successes did not justify the large ex-
penditure of resources that the CIO had invested in it. In the first five
months alone, Operation Dixie cost the CIO over $800,000. In the textile
industry, membership had only increased from 70,200 to 81,095, a minuscule gain given the vast effort that had been concentrated on the sector. By
the end of 1946, the cost of the campaign had already pushed CIO leaders
to lay off organizers and slash the drive's budget. In November 1946,
Bittner confidentially informed all district directors that "our appropria-
tions have been cut almost in half." This meant that in subsequent drives,
state directors continually complained that they did not have sufficient
resources to organize the number of plants that their superiors demanded.
"Every state is crying for men," admitted Bittner in September 1947. In
an effort to keep themselves motivated, union leaders often argued that

their election losses had built the foundations for future victory, but in most cases this optimism was misplaced, as the vast majority of plants where the CIO was beaten back were never subsequently organized. Rather than representing the first step in a gradual effort, most campaigns in fact represented the CIO's best effort. Following defeats, union supporters tended to drift away, becoming afraid or disillusioned. After winning elections, employers were also encouraged to believe that their workers genuinely did not want unions, ensuring that they would fight any subsequent organizing efforts with even more intensity and self-belief. In addition, of course, executives could cite the union's record of defeat against it in any subsequent campaign.

The AFL's postwar organizing drive was not as lengthy or high-profile as the CIO's effort, and it failed to generate the same paper trail. Launched in June 1946, the effort was administered by a policy board of over forty functionaries, with funding of $200,000 provided from the AFL's defense fund. The drive drew on the federation's traditional approach of working constructively with southern employers; leaders indeed described one of their central goals as "promoting union-management cooperation in Southern industry." Throughout their effort, AFL leaders lashed out at the CIO, which they viewed as communist-dominated, and they urged employers to cooperate with them as an insurance against "Communist forces." On the race issue, the older union federation claimed that it did not discriminate, asserting that employers were primarily responsible for black workers' job assignments. The AFL also publicized the CIO's frequent reluctance to challenge segregation, asserting that the breakaway federation's reputation for racial progressivism was largely unfounded.

The AFL was able to make some gains. Around 80 percent of organizing victories were secured through the cooperation policy, which encouraged employers to avoid costly labor struggles. The Southern Conference of Teamsters, for example, organized over seventy new companies without going through NLRB elections. The federation clearly fell well short, however, of its declared goal of signing up one million new members within a year. In many cases, the cooperation policy did not prevent the AFL from running into fierce opposition from southerners who viewed all unions as anathema. In the textile and apparel industries, procompany workers and their allies often formed citizens' committees or other anti-union groups to spearhead opposition to the AFL. Carmen Lucia, who supervised the southern organizing drive of the United Hatters, Cap and

Millinery Workers (UHCMW), recalled that the difficult organizing climate in the region deterred all but the most determined: "nobody else from the union organizers wanted to go South. I was the only damn fool that wanted to go." Lucia vividly remembered fierce opposition to unions, especially in small towns where employers exerted strong community control and threatened their employees with dismissal if they supported organized labor.

Across the South, resistance from employers and their community allies stymied the AFL's organizing efforts. By April 1947, drive leader George Googe reported confidentially that due to antilabor opposition, his organizers were "not making any progress insofar as securing new members is concerned." The AFL did not battle against such opposition for as long as its counterpart; by October 1947, seeing the writing on the wall, it abandoned its struggling southern drive. Highlighting the poor relations between the two federations, AFL leaders, who had wanted to operate without "fuss or fanfare," partly blamed the CIO's high-profile drive with stirring up opposition to unions. "[P]ropaganda begets propaganda," charged Googe. Ultimately, the AFL fared no better than its bitter rival, especially in its efforts to organize the textile industry, where the United Textile Workers (UTW) had only managed to secure 5,000 new members. "[T]he results of the Southern Drive did not meet our expectations," acknowledged the president of the UTW after the campaign.

In the immediate postwar years, rising opposition to organized labor also affected southern workers who had already secured a union contract. Across the country, the ending of the wartime restrictions on collective bargaining led to a renewal of strike activity. Unlike the strikes that took place in large northern centers, where strong, established unions demanded higher wages and improved benefits, the southern struggles were usually defensive battles, as fledgling unions struggled to fight off concessionary management demands.

Highlighting southern manufacturers' determination to restore prewar conditions, many strikes occurred in locations where unions had made wartime gains. In early 1946, the AVCO-Vultee aircraft company in Nashville gutted the union contract by unilaterally suspending maintenance of membership, the checkoff of union dues, vacation pay, and seniority rights, all of which they had reluctantly agreed to during the war. Shortly after the war, employers at two Memphis concerns—the Memphis Furniture Company and the American Snuff Company—also forced unions into unwanted strikes by demanding major concessions. In what became a familiar pattern in the postwar South, they then broke the walk-outs by importing large numbers of strikebreakers, a move that was strongly supported by the local police. The city government openly took the side of the companies, as police allowed strikebreakers to carry guns but vigorously enforced a strict injunction against the strikers. United Furniture Workers organizer Carl Curtis claimed that unions were being subject to a determined offensive, as a "clique of manufacturers . . . [had] made up their mind to break the union in their shops." The failed walk-outs gravely weakened organized labor in the industrial city, where the CIO had made some important ground during the war. Following the strikes, explained Curtis, workers were "scared to death" to even come to union meetings.

Southern textile executives were particularly determined to drive back the small gains that organized labor had made in their plants during war-time. Textile executives, union staffers recalled, wanted to restore the pre-war status quo. Between 1946 and 1948, the TWUA was involved in no fewer than thirty-six southern strikes, many of them precipitated by man-agement demands to take away the checkoff of union dues, which they had been forced to accept during the war. As dues payments generally fell away when the checkoff was removed, both sides understood that auto-matic deduction was central to unions' ability to survive as an effective force. As such, union security was at the heart of the postwar textile strikes. In addition, management often sought other concessions, fre-quently attacking seniority provisions that were particularly valued by workers because they felt that they made the workplace fairer.

Workers who had become familiar with the benefits of unionization fought back against concessionary bargaining, which led to some bitter and protracted disputes. Across the region, southern textile workers fought for their rights as fiercely as they had done in earlier walkouts, but their militancy was again not enough to overcome the determined and powerful opposition of employers and their allies, many of whom simply refused to recognize unions' right to exist. Beginning in September 1945, a strike at Gaffney Manufacturing Company lasted for nearly two years, as both sides repeatedly refused to give ground. "It is remarkable to see a group of workers remain on strike for so long a period, with so few break-ing rank and returning to work," wrote union representative Charlie Puckett. A walkout in Athens, Georgia lasted for twenty months, while another at Amazon Cotton Mills in Thomasville, North Carolina went on for close to a year and a half. Very few disputes were resolved in less than six months, as union members refused to cross the picket lines and employers would not back down. Most of these walkouts still ended with the union losing bargaining rights, as managers followed a predictable pattern of securing injunctions and gradually recruiting outside strikebreakers. As new union locals were gradually broken and eliminated, employers succeeded in wiping out even the small gains that labor activists had fought so hard to secure over the previous decade.

Even when unions were able to survive these strikes, they were often gravely weakened. Apart from gutted contracts, some of the damage left by disputes was less obvious. During a six-month-long walkout in 1949–50, a small group of TWUA members at Clifton Manufacturing Company in Clifton, South Carolina, crossed the picket line. Although the union was still able to secure a new contract in this case, the dispute left deep and lingering divisions in the community. More than a half a century later, these scars were still evident. "I don't think most of them's ever got over it," noted former striker Elbert Stapleton in a 1993 interview. Most southern textile communities, like Clifton, were small towns, and in such settings divisions left by labor disputes were keenly felt. Workers who had taken different sides in disputes could not melt into a large community but instead confronted one another constantly, at work and outside it. Try as they did, residents found it difficult to move on. "We just accept it and try as best we can," noted former Clifton worker Ibera Holt in the 1990s. "But you can't forget something that's happened, once it's happened. It's like driving a nail in a board. You can pull that nail out, but that hole is going to be there."

For the TWUA, its failure to secure a large number of new southern members would have been less important if it had been able to hold onto the precious bargaining gains it had made during the late 1930s and World War II. In fact, the union continued to lose members in the strike wave of 1945–50, and in the spring of 1951 it launched a doomed general strike across the region that hurt it dearly. In an effort to close the continuing gap between southern and northern wages, the TWUA sought a 12 percent wage increase across the region, as well as increases in benefits. It called its members out in order to secure these demands, but the walkout soon collapsed at the large Dan River Mills, the biggest southern plant that the union had under contract. Dan River management resolutely refused to buckle, and with many workers realizing that the union lacked the power to enforce its demands, they began to trickle back to work. TWUA leaders were forced to call off their walkout and accept a humiliating defeat. "The 1951 southern strike," writes Clete Daniel, the TWUA's chief historian, "was an unmitigated disaster, one that wreaked permanent devastation on the TWUA in the region that was the key both to its institutional viability and to the future of textile unionism in the United States."

Emboldened by Dan River, other unionized southern mills subsequently took a harder line with the union. Following the dispute, managers of the Virginia company themselves refused to provide a checkoff clause in the contract, destroying the financial strength of the union local. As was the case in 1934, the union also lost credibility in the region because of its rapid defeat. In addition, the strike destroyed the TWUA's ability to influence southern wages, ensuring that the wage gap between southern and northern mills, which had narrowed immediately after the war as employers tried to keep unions at bay, widened again. As a result, unionized northern mills continued to shut down at an alarming rate, reducing the financial strength of the TWUA. The strike had also been influenced by a political battle between TWUA leaders Emil Rieve and George Baldanzi, who were both anxious to prove their mettle in the South. The fight proved costly as Baldanzi eventually led over 20,000 southern TWUA members into the rival UTW, initiating a bitter raiding battle that neither union could really afford. In retrospective accounts, TWUA leaders admitted that the 1951 strike was a calamitous defeat. "It exposed so many weaknesses," noted TWUA official Ken Fiester, "it showed us, and it showed the companies just how strong we were down there. . . . The union was exposed really as a paper-tiger, because we not only got whipped, but whipped in a hurry."

By the early 1950s, as unions fought defensive battles to hold onto the few southern members they had, their hopes of making major organizing gains in the region had long since been dashed. Operation Dixie, in particular, had clearly failed, torpedoed by rising corporate opposition to unionism that had been encouraged by an increasingly conservative political climate. The failure of the drive greatly weakened organized labor, not just in the South but across the country. In 1954, a year after the CIO had finally abandoned its southern efforts, U.S. union membership began to decline, a slide that has continued steadily over the next fifty years. Rather than leading to breakthrough in labor's last frontier, the drive's collapse actually marked the end of the national period of union growth that stretched back more than twenty years.

The drive's failure also meant that conservative Democrats remained in political control of the South, dashing organized labor's hopes of forcing southern political leaders to be more responsive to them. Southern Democrats formed a conservative bloc within their party and were consistently antiunion; in 1947, for example, they provided the margin necessary to override President Truman's veto of the Taft-Hartley Act.

If unions had been able to establish a greater presence in the South, they would have been a force pushing these politicians to moderate their views. In the immediate postwar years, increased political activity by unionized southern workers highlighted the potential power of the labor vote. In 1946, textile workers in northwest Georgia provided critical support to Henderson Lanham, the only southern member of the House to vote against Taft-Hartley. Millworkers from Rome and Dalton worked hard to unseat entrenched Congressman Malcolm Tarver, a major achievement considering the fact that he had won reelection nine times. In Dalton, Tarver's hometown, Lanham secured 58 percent of the vote despite the attempts of the local paper to claim that the town's textile workers were being duped by the CIO's "communistic" leaders. The CIO's PAC was successful in increasing voter registration in unionized towns such as Dalton, where organized textile workers managed in 1947 to replace the town's antilabor administration with a coalition of workers and prolabor politicians.

In other towns where unions had made gains, they also began to influence local politics. In Memphis, increasing numbers of organized workers began to pay their own poll taxes and become increasingly independent of the entrenched political machine controlled by Mayor Ed Crump. In 1948, union voters mobilized by the CIO combined with business and civic reformers to hand Crump his first major election defeat since World War I. Crump was beaten to a Senate seat by Estes Kefauver, a liberal Democrat who had spoken out against Truman's Loyalty Bill and had been one of only two Tennessee representatives to vote to overturn the Taft-Hartley Act in Congress.

At the same time, however, even in locations where southern union members were politically active, it was clear that they were not willing to wholeheartedly follow the CIO's national agenda, especially when it came to the race issue. In some locales, the PAC, which aimed to encourage union members to vote for labor-friendly candidates, was successful at securing gains at the local level, but the race issue made it difficult to influence higher-level campaigns. In Rome, TWUA Local 689 increased voter registration among union members and helped to secure the election of friendly city, county, and judicial officials. When it came to gubernatorial and senatorial elections, however, union members supported the race-baiting Herman Talmadge, despite his poor labor record. In the 1950 Democratic primaries, blue-collar voters across the South repudiated CIO-backed candidates when their opponents used racial propaganda against them. As southern PAC director Daniel Powell wrote, "The introduction of the race issue by those who desired to maintain the status quo in the South . . . frustrated . . . efforts to focus the attention of the voters on the authentic issues[,] . . . the economic and social conditions of the South and its people."

American unions emerged from World War II in a position of unprecedented strength. In the immediate postwar years, they built on this platform, using their muscle to win steady improvements for their members at the bargaining table. Unions in these years, writes labor historian Robert H. Zieger, "exuded success." Success hardly captured organized labor's experience in the South, however. Here, the key battle was to organize new members rather than to service existing ones. In the ten years after the war, major assaults on the South yielded few results. Scattered gains were hard fought, and even then they were often subsequently undermined by corporate fightbacks. Although there were elements of continuity between the experience of southern workers and those elsewhere in the United States, especially as liberal groups across the country were hurt by an increasingly conservative political climate, the South remained much more nonunion than other regions. As the 1950s began, almost 40 percent of American manufacturing workers belonged to unions, but in the South fewer than 17 percent did so.

3

Split Wide Open

Black and White Workers in the 1950s

Despite the failure of Operation Dixie, organized labor was still a force to be reckoned with at the start of the 1950s. Nationally, these were years when workers prospered, helped by a growing economy and strong, stable unions that delivered steady improvements at the bargaining table. America's key mass production industries—coal, steel, rubber, meat-packing, and autos—were between 80 to 100 percent organized, and unions consistently used their considerable bargaining power to win a string of wage and benefit increases for their members. Over the course of the 1950s, basic wage rates for industrial workers rose by 56 percent. Benefits also improved substantially, with auto workers even winning automatic wage increases to compensate them for rises in productivity or the cost of living.

In the 1950s, the experience of southern workers had both similarities and differences with this national pattern. In these years, southern workers also experienced rising wages and an improving standard of living, especially as some firms increased wages in order to head off unions' continued organizing efforts. Southerners also shared in the national move toward home and car ownership, with many companies selling off housing to their employees, particularly in the textile industry. The breakdown of the close-knit, company-owned village changed the region, as many employees now chose to live farther away and commute in.

Few unions, though, were truly stable in the postwar South. As some companies continued to try and drive organized labor from their plants, unions in the South found themselves fighting more defensive battles to hold onto their members than they did in other regions. Although union strategists never managed to launch another southern campaign on the scale of Operation Dixie, organizing also continued to be particularly important in the region. Labor leaders remained acutely aware that the presence of the largely nonunion South threatened the living standards of their members in the North. In the 1950s, the economic growth of the southern states, much of it based on runaway northern firms, exacerbated this problem, yet union organizing efforts met determined resistance. Although southern workers' wages increased, a regional differential persisted, and the vain efforts of labor leaders to close it achieved little.

In the 1950s, the rise of civil rights protest by southern blacks also caused unique problems for southern labor unions. In May 1954, the U.S. Supreme Court's landmark decision in *Brown v. Board of Education* declared that segregated schools were unconstitutional. The following year, the Court issued its implementation order mandating public-school desegregation "with all deliberate speed." In December 1955, African Americans in Montgomery, Alabama began a thirteen-month boycott against the city's segregated bus system, the first successful direct action protest by a southern black community. The *Brown* decision and the launching of the Montgomery bus boycott led to increased racial tension across the region, especially as much of the white South mobilized to resist integration. White workers took part in the move toward "Massive Resistance," with many union members complaining about the funding that their leaders gave to civil rights organizations. As a result, union leaders in the South spent a great deal of time monitoring racial tension and trying to ward off potential secession movements by their white members.

In the workplace itself, the legal racial segregation that was unique to the region ensured that blacks and whites used a wide range of separate facilities. The two groups performed their daily routines, such as clocking in, changing clothes, and eating, separately. Work was also strictly segregated, with both workers and management understanding clearly which jobs were "black" and which "white." In some industries, blacks were represented by separate unions that only had jurisdiction over a limited number of unskilled jobs, while in other cases social custom and practice similarly confined them to menial work. Over the course of the 1950s, there was little change in segregated job assignments. Executives, who bore the ultimate responsibility for racial job assignments, continued to argue that their white employees would strike or riot if integration occurred. Despite the start of civil rights protest, workplace integration would not take place for at least another decade, illustrating the joint determination of white workers and management to uphold the racial status quo. Inspired by the start of civil rights protest, some African American workers did speak out against the lack of change, but their efforts met solid white resistance.

In the early 1950s, relations between the AFL and CIO improved following the deaths of former leaders William Green and Philip Murray. With the 1952 election of a Republican president, labor leaders also realized that they lacked a friend in the White House and could ill afford to continue fighting one another. In December 1955, following lengthy talks, the two organizations formally merged to create the AFL-CIO. The new organization was keen to apply its resources to southern organizing. In 1957, AFL-CIO leader Ben Segal wrote his colleagues that, "No one will deny that the South today, as it was 15 years ago, is organized labor's number one regional problem." Two years later, the AFL-CIO held its first national organizing conference and devoted particular attention to Dixie. "The need for more organizing effort in the South has never been more pressing," concluded the conference. "If an unrelenting program of organizational effort is not maintained there by the American labor movement, resulting finally in successful widespread organization, our labor movement will weaken." Following the conference, the AFL-CIO's Industrial Union Department, which was set up in 1955 to assist individual unions in fighting against recalcitrant companies, launched a campaign in Spartanburg, South Carolina that pursued a deliberate strategy of trying to organize southern branch plants.

Despite recognizing the need to organize the South, however, unions made little progress in the region. In the decade and a half after the end of the war, employers continued to slowly gain the upper hand; in 1946, "no union" won 24 percent of southern elections, but this increased to 35 percent in 1950 and 49 percent in 1962. The no-union vote was also considerably higher in the South than in other parts of the country, illustrating the peculiar difficulties that unions faced in the region.

Virulent opposition from employers and their community allies was the major reason for these difficulties. As had been the case during Operation Dixie, the opponents of unionism were able to draw on a wide variety of strategies to defeat organized labor. They continued to kill campaigns by launching intensive preelection campaigns where they used their unilateral access to their employees to drive home the message that voting for the union would be a mistake. They played on workers' fears of job insecurity by arguing that the union would lead to lengthy strikes and even plant closures. In campaign after campaign, they also frequently insisted that organizers were only after dues money and tried to reinforce workers' sense of identification with their employer.

Few southern companies shied away from conflict with organized labor. Even in industries where unions were strong, southern executives refused to bow to them. In the construction trade, which was highly organized outside the South, companies such as Brown and Root and Daniel became embroiled in long-running labor battles. The Texas-based Brown and Root fought the AFL building trades unions for almost two decades after World War II, using legal actions and injunctions to stall organizing efforts. Although the company was found guilty of violating the NLRB, its position was supported by Texas courts, which issued a series of anti-union decisions. In another protracted case, both AFL and CIO affiliates failed in repeated efforts to organize Calcasieu Paper Company, located in the company town of Elizabeth, Louisiana. The case vividly highlighted how virulent employer opposition gradually strangled workers' enthusiasm for union representation. In 1947, the CIO's International Brotherhood of Paper Makers (IBPM) had won an election at the plant but the company simply refused to sign a contract, pushing the IBPM to withdraw. Five years later, the union won another election, but when workers struck in an effort to secure a contract, the company obtained an injunction and began a campaign of violence, shooting into houses and assaulting pickets. In addition, fifty-seven families were evicted from company houses and many more were threatened with the same treatment. Calcasieu's harsh tactics caused support for the union to collapse, and despite organizing efforts that continued into the 1960s, workers were too afraid to support it again.

Through the 1950s, anticommunism also continued to hurt labor's organizing efforts. Although labor leaders had moved to head off charges of communist infiltration by expelling their left-led affiliates, in the 1950s unions continued to be viewed by many Americans, especially southerners, as outside the strict anticommunist consensus that prevailed at the time. In 1955, efforts to organize the growing chenille industry in Dalton, Georgia led manufacturers and the press to accuse local Holiness preacher Don West, who was leading the campaign, of being a communist. In the McCarthyist climate, the TWUA's national leaders, who had earlier purged all communists and radicals from their organization, were afraid to endorse West, and their efforts consequently suffered. In many towns, community support for anticommunism also undermined existing local unions. In Dalton, previously one of the most prolabor towns in the

South, the local textile union had been in existence since 1933 but was increasingly forced to defend unionism as "American." "McCarthyism," notes historian Douglas Flamming, "dealt a mortal blow to the town's labor unions."

As had been the case during Operation Dixie, many companies also fought unions by granting their workers wage and benefit increases. Following the demise of unions, in particular, some companies voluntarily maintained the same wages and benefits in order to deter their revival. At the huge R. J. Reynolds complex of plants in Winston-Salem, North Carolina, the company continued to give its staff many of the benefits that the FTA local had secured for them before it lost bargaining rights in 1948. Reynolds was careful to keep its wages slightly higher than its organized competitors, as well as continuing to pay benefits negotiated by the union and agreeing to an informal seniority system. These tactics helped to ensure that Reynolds, one of organized labor's prize gains in World War II, remained outside the union fold. In the 1950s, carpet manufacturers in northwest Georgia also increased wages and benefits in order to keep the union frozen out of a growing sector of the textile industry. The carpet mills carefully monitored conditions in Georgia's few organized mills in order to ensure that their employees did not feel mistreated. On other occasions, firms responded to specific organizing efforts by increasing wages. In 1955, the Tufted Textile Manufacturers Association in northwest Georgia gave workers in the growing chenille industry a 7 to 10 percent pay raise just as a TWUA campaign was announced, even announcing the increase on the same day that the union tried to call its first meetings.

Union efforts to extend their presence in the basic textile industry continued to be particularly unsuccessful. Between 1955 and 1957, the TWUA concentrated a wage campaign on the large Burlington Mills chain, hoping to close the North-South differential. Following its defeat in the 1951 strike, this pay gap had widened because the union was no longer able to pressure southern textile manufacturers into following increases it had won in the North. Realizing how weak the TWUA was, southern companies simply ignored its calls for higher wages and refused to grant any hikes for more than four years. At the end of 1955, the first company to break this pattern was the nonunion Burlington chain. Following this move, the TWUA unsuccessfully petitioned Burlington executives to up southern wages further, as they still lagged behind northern levels. The declining textile union also engaged in a half-hearted effort to organize several of the company's mills, yet it lost all the elections that it contested.

Worse, however, was yet to come. In 1956, the TWUA suffered a major setback when the Deering Milliken textile company decided to close its mill in the small South Carolina town of Darlington after workers there had narrowly voted in favor of the union. Mill owner Roger Milliken, a steadfast opponent of collective bargaining, refused to change this decision even after receiving a petition signed by 400 Darlington millworkers. If the mill stayed open, they pledged, they would revoke their union membership cards. Milliken also ignored a personal visit from the mayor of Darlington, who was anxious not to see the town's largest employer close. Within two months of the election, the plant had been closed, its machinery removed or sold at public auction. Although the NLRB found the company guilty of shutting the mill in order to avoid collective bargaining and ordered it to rehire the workers, Deering Milliken appealed the decision, asserting that they had an absolute right to go out of business. For the next twenty years, the case stayed before the NLRB and the federal courts before ending with an empty victory for the union.

By this time, of course, the damage to the union's cause had already been done. Workers across the South had learned the lesson that threats to close unionized plants, which companies had frequently used as a central part of their preelection campaign, were not idle. In the postwar era, the increasing prominence of chain companies also made it easier to transfer production between mills. "With their plants widely dispersed throughout the South," noted *Fortune* magazine, "these firms, if they lose one mill to the union, can simply shut it down and transfer its operations to another mill." The TWUA quickly found that the Darlington case hurt its organizing efforts; in 1958, for example, it abandoned a campaign at North Carolina's Cannon Mills because it was unable to secure support in all of the company's plants and was afraid that individual mills would be shut down if they were unionized.

Workers' fear that organized plants would be shut down was part of a broader apprehension about the risks of union membership. Many understandably worried that organized labor lacked the power to defend and reward them. By the 1950s, workers' memories or awareness of countless union defeats in the region, including the 1934 and 1951 strikes, added to these fears. As the 1950s progressed, textile unions suffered high-profile defeats even at mills where they had seemed to be well established. In the late 1950s, workers across the South watched as a well-publicized strike at the Harriet and Henderson Cotton Mills in Henderson, North Carolina led to the destruction of the union in one of its few southern strongholds.

The Henderson strike involved more than 1,000 workers and marked a further blow to textile unions' already-battered hopes of organizing the South. The strike was a disaster for the cash-strapped TWUA, which spent more than $1 million over a two-and-a half-year period. Workers struck to maintain a grievance arbitration provision in their contract, which they valued because it gave them some control over workloads and protection against arbitrary treatment by supervisors. After three months, the company upped the stakes by replacing the strikers with nonunion labor recruited from surrounding counties along the North Carolina–Virginia state line. The move triggered violence, including a bombing campaign that both sides blamed on each other. The bombings attracted national press attention and provided ample ammunition to support employers' claims that unions brought only discord and violence.

The strike, like many others in the textile South, failed not because of lack of support from workers, but because their determination was not enough on its own to prevail. The rank and file certainly did not lack militancy; even after Governor Luther Hodges deployed the state national guard to reopen the mills, many refused to give in, and the walkout was eventually called off by the international union. Two of the TWUA's few local unions in the Tarheel State were lost as a result. Despite their solidarity, the strikers were defeated by determined mill owners, who were able to introduce an alternative labor supply with the full backing of local and state authorities. In the wake of the dispute, the small town of Henderson remained divided, and the mills were still running on a non-union basis some thirty years later.

The Henderson defeat, which was widely reported across the South, hurt organizing efforts at other plants. In 1959, the TWUA launched an unsuccessful campaign at J. P. Stevens' mills in Roanoke Rapids, which were located about fifty miles to the east of Henderson. Explaining the union's defeat, staffer Joe Pedigo reported that Stevens had mounted an intensive campaign just before the election, utilizing the violence in Henderson to discredit the TWUA. "The mills here were plastered with pictures of alleged bombings of cars and houses in Henderson," he reported. When it came to the election, many workers who had pledged themselves to support the union instead refused to mark their ballots. It was, as Pedigo put it, "a scared vote rather than an anti union vote."

Not surprisingly, these repeated setbacks took their toll on textile union leaders. By the late 1950s, they exhibited little of the optimism that they had brought to earlier campaigns. Facing what seemed like overwhelming corporate opposition to unionism, they questioned whether the South could ever be organized, something they had refused to admit, at least publicly, during Operation Dixie. By the start of the 1960s, the TWUA had just 150,000 members, having lost 60 percent of its supporters over the previous ten years. Scaling back expensive organizing efforts, the union increasingly sought government solutions to shore up its declining membership base. Changing direction, TWUA leaders pressed for labor law reform to strengthen the NLRB and overturn the Taft-Hartley Act, tariff barriers to protect the industry from overseas competition, and government investment to revitalize economically vulnerable New England mills.

In the course of the 1950s and 1960s, the threat that the largely nonunion South posed to the living standards of unionized northern workers actually increased as a growing number of "runaway shops" located to the region. In these years, southern political and economic leaders made intensive efforts to attract outside industry, and the region's economy consistently grew at a faster rate than that of the United States as a whole. Many states issued municipal industrial development bonds for the construction of plants that were then leased to private companies, an approach pioneered by Mississippi's Balance Agriculture With Industry program. Southern states also led the way in granting long-term tax exemptions to new manufacturing plants. After 1950, local industrial development corporations became commonplace, spending vast sums on advertising and recruitment and offering loans and other inducements to outside companies.

Many of the firms attracted South had recognized organized labor in the North, but came to the region precisely because they could escape the costs of unionization. In the textile industry, firms such as the New England-based J. P. Stevens company began to relocate to the Carolinas shortly after World War II, setting up a large number of nonunion plants. Many apparel companies also headed South for similar reasons; in the two decades after 1950, the influx of runaway shops more than doubled the number of southern apparel workers. Along the Gulf coast, the petrochemical industry also grew considerably in the 1950s, and by 1957 the South was home to 36 percent of the nation's chemical plants, the vast majority of them nonunion. The growth of all these industries weakened

U.S. unions, as southern growth contributed to a steady decline in the overall proportion of organized workers.

As well as conventional organizing activities, unions also tried other tactics to protect the jobs of their northern members from nonunion southern competition. In the clothing industry, the ACWA launched "union-label" programs that aimed to stop the growth of unorganized southern shops by encouraging consumers to buy union-made products. Interestingly, the campaign, which was initiated in the 1950s and continued in subsequent decades, initially featured advertisements that focused on the traditional and domestic role of women, despite the fact that around 80 percent of apparel workers were female. Advertisements claimed that ACWA-made suits increased men's sexual attractiveness; as one put it, "ninety-nine point ten percent of women prefer men with Amalgamated Union Labels in their suits." Such slogans, which were thought up by the male-dominated leadership of the clothing union, reflected traditional gender models in a decade when the "June Cleaver" domestic ideal was widely upheld.

Across the South, the racial status quo remained firmly in place in workplaces throughout the 1950s. Despite the start of the civil rights movement, job opportunities for southern blacks were extremely restricted. Black and white workers were strictly segregated from one another, with blacks confined to lower-paying jobs that were often physically demanding. Blacks were also kept out of supervisory positions unless they were in charge of other blacks. While employment discrimination was clearly not confined to the South, it was considerably worse in that region than elsewhere. In 1960, black income in the South was only 40.2 percent that of white, compared with 73 to 75 percent in other regions. Outside the region, 10 percent of employed blacks worked in clerical jobs, but in the South just 3 percent did so. Between 1950 and 1960, the black percentage of white income in the South actually declined by 4.7 percent, highlighting that the region's rigid patterns of job segregation showed few signs of abating. In 1960, southern blacks held almost all the household jobs and nearly half of all laboring positions in both industry and agriculture. "In the South," concluded one 1960 report by the Southern Regional Council, an Atlanta-based civil rights group that carefully monitored race relations, "Negroes have not shared equitably in the rapid industrial expansion of the past two decades."

African Americans received few of the jobs that new plants brought to the South in the postwar years. In the apparel industry, for example, most jobs were still reserved for whites. In a typical recruitment effort, one company that located in South Carolina shortly after the war specified that it wanted "500 white women as soon as possible" to run the plant. Black women who did gain jobs in the burgeoning industry were restricted to the pressing department, where they prepared clothes for sale after they had been sewn by white women. The black pressers were paid less than the white women sewers or the white men responsible for repairing the sewing machines. Black women continued to be almost completely barred from the textile industry, while their male counterparts remained a tiny proportion of textile workers, confined to "outside" laboring jobs or janitorial work. The chemical firms then locating along the Gulf Coast also hired few blacks, even though they often built their facilities near politically weak black communities. Since black women were excluded from even the small range of jobs given to their male counterparts in southern industries, they were forced to crowd into low-paying domestic work where they continually depressed wages and working conditions.

National companies that located in the South carefully followed segregated hiring patterns, asserting that they had to operate their facilities according to the culture of the area they were located in. The big automakers epitomized this deference to southern customs. "When we moved into the South, we agreed to abide by local custom and not hire Negroes for production work," explained the manager of a General Motors plant in Atlanta that opened in 1957. Ford Motor Company, which was a major employer of black labor in the Midwest, also refused to challenge southern customs, apparently fearful of a reaction from white workers and community leaders. At its Atlanta plant, only 1.3 percent of all workers were black in 1957, compared to 33.4 percent in its Chicago plant and 15.2 percent in Detroit. This small group was restricted to traditional "black" jobs. In the late 1950s, GM actually employed more blacks in the South than Ford, while Chrysler had no plants in the South.

Although they often claimed that they were merely bowing to the preferences of their workers and the broader community, many native southern employers openly fought efforts to change the racial status quo. Employers' mobilization against unions immediately after the war reflected their broader desire to prevent interference in the workplace. Like many other white southerners, company executives especially disliked the way that the federal government had intervened in the labor market during

World War II, feeling that it had encouraged both civil rights activism and unionization. Fear of a permanent FEPC became a major issue for the "Dixiecrats," conservative white southerners who formed the States' Rights Democratic Party in 1948 with South Carolina's Strom Thurmond as their presidential candidate. Job segregation allowed southern employers to depress wages, and they were keen to hold onto these economic advantages. They also saw the FEPC as an outside agency that would dispatch federal agents to the South to interfere with management's right to hire and fire. As the Alabama Chamber of Commerce put it, the proposed FEPC would "strike at the fundamental rights of an employer in the selection of his employees in the operation of his own business." Painting apocalyptical visions, employers regularly exaggerated the FEPC's proposed provisions. "Should any Negro be denied the right to room in the best hotel or to a meal in the best restaurant," warned *Southern Textile Bulletin* publisher David Clark, "a heavy fine or imprisonment would confront the proprietor or manager of the hotel or restaurant."

Employers also consistently argued that blacks lacked the skills and qualifications to perform skilled jobs, frequently asserting that they were innately suited to unskilled work. As one company executive claimed, unskilled lumbering work was "something [that black workers] grew up with and knew how to do well." Black workers, added a steel executive, "did not possess the necessary educational background and knowledge" to perform skilled jobs. Railroad employers similarly claimed the "Southern Negro has never gone to school or . . . has never gone far enough to absorb more than the bare rudiments of writing." As a result, the "knowledge needed to run an engine" was "beyond the mental powers of a Southern colored man."

In reality, however, African Americans did not receive equal opportunities to learn the same skills as whites. They attended poorly funded, segregated schools, usually relying on books cast off from the better-funded white schools. Job segregation was also maintained by the vocational training system, which only provided classes to blacks in occupations in which they had traditionally worked. In Atlanta, Smith-Hughes School, the white vocational and technical facility, offered courses in many skilled trades, including electronics, tool and die design, plumbing, instrumentation, refrigeration and air-conditioning, and iron-working. None of these options were available to African Americans attending the Carver Vocational School, which instead offered industrial sewing, commercial and short order cooking, shoe repair, auto mechanics, tailoring, bricklaying, dry cleaning, and practical nursing.

Less formal mechanisms also ensured that blacks entered the workplace less qualified for skilled jobs. In textile communities, for example, white youngsters had much greater opportunities to learn production work as they were growing up. In the industry's early days, children often saw production jobs being performed when they entered the mills to take food or messages to family members. Later on, many mills loaned to white high schools or training colleges the textile machinery that was not similarly loaned to their black counterparts. White children often lived with parents who worked in textiles, went to churches with textile workers and supervisors, and attended schools with their children. When white youngsters left school, their contacts often helped them to get work in the mills, especially as local companies often had an open preference for hiring relations of existing employees.

Within manufacturing industries, black men continued to find themselves channeled toward heavy, labor-based jobs. Many were specifically selected for their physical strength, with some employers deliberately recruiting heavily built, black youngsters from farming backgrounds. In the lumber industry, blacks worked the heavy physical jobs on logging crews, wading through swamps where they cut down trees with hand-powered crosscut saws. Hours were long, as workers toiled on what one called the "can't to can't shift." "[Y]ou can't see when you go; can't see when you get off," explained North Carolina lumber worker Orie Tyson. In the rapidly expanding southern paper industry, many black men also processed raw lumber by hand or worked in so-called "bull gangs," crews of laborers chosen for their strength who toured the mill site performing heavy work. "Everybody knew it as Bull Gang," recalled Otis Walker, a former worker at St. Joe Paper Company in Florida. "Because all of the work was physical, we had no machines to do the work. . . . The Bull Gang have caught the blues at St Joe Paper Company, and we, oh shuck, we've had to work sixteen hours straight, and I'm talking about not just on the clock man, I'm talking about physical labor, working. We've had situations where we had to sandbag, build dams, or 'they can do it, they're black, they can handle it.' That was the attitude of the supervisor." African American men similarly provided sheer muscle power in the sugar mills and refineries located near New Orleans, moving raw sugar into the plants and carrying heavy sacks of refined sugar onto railcars.

Across the Jim Crow South, African American men were disproportionately exposed to heat, dust, and danger in the workplace. In the steel mills of Birmingham, Alabama, they worked in laboring jobs close to the blast furnaces, where temperatures reached 150 degrees. "It was a man-killer," recalled one worker responsible for directing the flow of molten iron. "You'd be wet from the time you hit the clock." At the Aluminum Company of America's plant in Badin, North Carolina, blacks were con-fined to unskilled jobs in the searing pot room. Walter Smith, who worked at the mill in the 1950s before going to college, remembered that the jobs took their toll on blacks, with many dying prematurely. "My fa-ther, when he was 55, my age, looked like an old man. I think the fumes generated in that plant killed people."

The same problems affected African American men in other southern industries. In the rubber tire industry, blacks were restricted to the hot, dirty compounding room, where they mixed together natural and syn-thetic rubber with chemicals. The small number of black textile workers was often exposed to large amounts of dust, particularly in the opening room, where they loaded raw cotton by hand. At the end of their shift, opening room workers were often covered from head to toe in cotton dust and lint. African American men who worked in the tobacco industry were largely confined to the dangerous job of casing and cutting, while white men were responsible for fixing and operating machines and supervising the workforce. Conditions in the casing room were very poor, as men crowded together without air-conditioning and used their feet to pack the tobacco together tightly. "It was so hot," recalled Winston-Salem worker Lonnie Nesmith, "sometimes you couldn't catch your breath. When I'd come down from there and walk to the restroom, you could trail me from the water coming out of my shoes. . . . I had to lay down many night after I come out of that place. All that stuff was in my nostrils, and I was so sick I'd just gag. I couldn't even take a drink of water." As well as coping with strong smells, workers toiled in the dark, as managers hung aprons or bags over the windows in order to protect the tobacco from direct sunlight.

African American workers were also often exposed to more immediate dangers. In the paper industry, many worked in the wood yard, where they labored in close proximity to heavy machinery that prepared raw wood for the paper-making process. Some lost fingers or hands carrying out these jobs, while the noise of heavy machinery often contributed to hearing loss in later life. African Americans who toiled in southern coal mines were also concentrated in the most hazardous areas. "Black miners often worked in the worst areas of the mine," explained former miner Robert

Armstead. "These included headings with low ceilings or water and areas with bad air that needed to be cleared and ventilated often, causing dead time, or time without pay."

It was in the lumber industry, however—one of the largest employers of black labor in the South—that workers suffered the highest numbers of disabling injuries. In 1945, logging workers suffered ninety-two disabling injuries for every million hours worked, and fatalities were not unusual. Racial classifications also corresponded closely with injury rates, with blacks performing the most dangerous logging work while whites clustered in less hazardous occupations. Most firms classified the dangerous job of "tong setting," for example, as "nigger work." "Setters" were responsible for securing fallen trees to cables that then dragged them to the skidder. Their job required them to communicate when the log should be pulled out, but when signals got confused, setters were often killed or badly injured, frequently being dragged along by moving logs.

With jobs divided strictly along color lines, and often represented by segregated unions, African Americans were acutely aware of what tasks they were allowed to perform. Work, many proclaimed, had a color. Matthew Davis, who was employed at Firestone's Memphis plant, asserted, "Whites had a job and blacks had a job." Added another, "They had white jobs and black jobs . . . and all of the blacks naturally had the lowest-paying jobs, the hardest jobs, the nastiest jobs." Promotional opportunities were extremely restricted, even though experienced black workers often possessed skills that they passed onto inexperienced whites, who quickly moved up the line. Across the region, blacks complained bitterly about this practice. "What I never could understand," reflected Florida paper worker Cleveland Bailey, "how could they hire a man, yes sir I should have understood it, off the streets, and you got blacks working on the job, and he pretty well knows that job. Why they wouldn't allow him the opportunity, a lot of blacks the opportunity, to learn the job, they could hire white and bring them in there, and then he had to learn the job. Well, because I know, the color of their skin, that's what made it all work in."

Being forced to train inexperienced whites highlighted the authority that any white person brought into the segregated southern workplace. Explained Memphis worker Clarence Coe, "I have seen the time when a young white boy came in and maybe I had been working at the plant longer than he had been living, but if he was white I had to tell him 'yes sir' or 'no sir.' That was degrading as hell. I had to live with it. . . . And you spent all of your good life fooling with petty stuff like this." In a wide variety of industries, workers had similar experiences. "Let me put it to you point blank," commented one lumber worker to an interviewer. "Everybody up there with a white face was your boss. What ever they tell you to do, you had to go and do it. If you didn't you would get fired." For African American women working in the tobacco industry, this authority brought extra problems, as they frequently had to cope with sexual abuse from white foreman as part of the broader indignities of segregation. "You were just Jim Crowed all around," asserted former tobacco worker Ruby Jones. "He didn't regard you as much as an animal. The foremen didn't respect you unless you done their dirty work or went with them."

In the Jim Crow workplace, African Americans were subjected to many other daily indignities, such as having to buy their own work clothing while seeing it provided to their white colleagues, or being forced to clock in outside while whites carried out the same duty protected from the elements. In many plants, blacks also had to use outdoor toilets and were not allowed to use the cafeteria, eating on the job instead. At the J. P Stevens textile mills in Roanoke Rapids, North Carolina, a black worker recalled, "we was upstairs on the second floor, but when the blacks was ready to go to the bathroom—rain, snow, or shine—we had to go to the bathroom outside." Shower facilities were also frequently "white-only." "They had a place to take a shower, I guess eat whatever, you take your shower when you get home, black did," recalled black paper worker Sammie J. Hatcher, who worked for many years at a Mobile plant. Outside the workplace too, company-sponsored social facilities were often all-white. At the Armstrong Tire and Rubber Company in Natchez, only whites could play on the company-sponsored softball team. At the Union-Camp paper mill in Savannah, the city's largest employer, blacks were similarly excluded from the Union Bag Athletic Association (UBAA), a social club located on company property. Despite this, blacks helped support the UBAA through the money that they spent in Union-Camp's cafeteria, which itself had segregated seating areas.

Facing such pervasive discrimination, and aware that they could easily be fired, black workers found alternative ways of protesting in the Jim Crow era. "Beneath the veil of consent," asserts historian Robin D. G. Kelley, "lies a hidden history of unorganized, everyday conflict waged by African American working people." In the tobacco factories of North Carolina, black stemmers used songs that reinforced their sense of collective identity and reminded them of a life without the drudgery of industrial work. In many factories, blacks also feigned illness to secure time off, engaged in slowdowns to control the pace of production, carried out sabotage to counter speedups, and launched short-term strikes to win redress of specific grievances. "We had to use all kind of techniques to protect ourselves and the other workers," asserted one.

Black workers did also lodge formal appeals with unions. In the 1930s and 1940s, many had been enthusiastic recruits to the emerging unions, hoping that they could be used as a way of advancing civil rights. "You didn't have any trouble explaining unionism to blacks," recalled one organizer, "with the kinds of oppression and conditions they had. It was a question of freedom." During the war, black workers in Winston-Salem, Fort Worth, and other industrial centers had tried to use their unions to address civil rights issues, but their efforts were ultimately hindered by a lack of white support and the broader postwar backlash against organized labor. Unions offered, however, one of the few opportunities for black workers to voice their complaints about discrimination, and in the 1950s their appeals to labor leaders did continue. In 1958, for instance, African Americans employed at the Atlantic Steel plant in Atlanta sent a typical petition to the USW's national leaders. "All the undersigned," they complained, "are employed at the Atlantic Steel Company plant in Atlanta, Georgia, and are members of the Steelworkers Union. For many years we have been denied the right to be upgraded and promoted . . . all the colored workers are kept in laborer jobs while the whites with less seniority are promoted over us." Despite such appeals, the situation failed to change, as USW leaders remained reluctant to alienate their majority-white membership. Like blacks elsewhere, the Atlantic Steel workers would have to wait several more years before racial job assignments began to be changed.

Local autonomy remained the key to explaining why unions did not do more to tackle segregation. AFL and CIO affiliates gave considerable independence to their members in the South, and job assignments and seniority were both negotiated locally. This autonomy ensured that there was often a considerable gap between national unions' nondiscrimination policies and actual racial practice in the South, where whites usually outnumbered blacks. This gap was especially noticeable among CIO unions, whose national leaders did give strong support to civil rights. During World War II, CIO president Philip Murray, who was also the president of the USW, declared the cause of racial equality to be a "holy and a noble work . . . that all right-thinking citizens should dedicate themselves to." Throughout the 1940s and 1950s, several labor unions gave funding to civil rights organizations, including the NAACP. Like the members of the Atlantic Steel local, however, black USW members across the South felt that their local leadership was ineffective in challenging segregation. Clyde Cook, a black USW member in Badin, North Carolina, recalled that the union helped "in the wages, but they had a division line, a color line that was well understood between the company and between the union, certain lines that they held for white, and certain they held for blacks. At that time there weren't even any blacks could go in for crane operators or truck operators or nothing of that kind."

A similar situation prevailed in other industries. The leadership of the United Rubber Workers, for example, supported civil rights at the national level and refused to charter segregated unions in the South. Leaders also gave considerable autonomy to these local unions, however, and many became strong opponents of integration. Despite the union's national stance, black union members at a Goodyear plant in Gadsden, Alabama had to pursue litigation that went all the way to the U.S. Supreme Court before the local union would process their grievances that it was cooperating with Goodyear to uphold a discriminatory seniority system.

The color line was especially obvious to workers who belonged to segregated local unions. Several AFL unions, including the IBPSPMW and the Tobacco Workers International Union (TWIU), chartered such unions in the South, arguing that they were the most effective way of organizing whites and blacks. Black locals, however, were generally outnumbered by white unions and were ineffective at changing the racial status quo. Leroy Hamilton, who belonged to a segregated local of the IBPSPMW in St. Marys, Georgia in the 1950s, recalled that the black union was only effective if it did not challenge segregation: "The blacks, we all went together in the negotiations, but very little that we could get because jobs, we had one thing we could do and that was it. We couldn't cross the line, we couldn't go where the money was. We was definitely the lowest paid job in the mill, they called it the yard service. . . . We fought for it, but we couldn't change it because there wasn't enough of us. See maybe, it was about, in our union, 616, there probably was 100 maybe, or 90 something, and over, the whites had, the maintenance had a union, the electricians had a union, the papermakers had a union, pulp mill had a union, and we was outnumbered. We didn't have too much of a voice, they outvote us, just a little handful of us you know." Some members of black unions became disillusioned by repeated setbacks. "The union wasn't going to battle for you, you could forget about that," asserted lumber worker

John Oatis. "When they negotiated they gonna give the white more than they do the black, anyway."

Others, however, recognized that segregated unions still provided them with some protection from arbitrary company treatment, especially within all-black jobs. Many recalled the time before they were organized, when supervisors had reigned supreme and had been able to send blacks home without pay on a whim. Some union members took advantage of this protection and spoke out against discrimination. In Natchez, Mississippi, African American paper worker Sidney Gibson recalled that unionized workers from the International Paper Company plant took the lead in protesting against Jim Crow: "One of the reasons that we took top positions in the civil rights movement was because we were unionized and they couldn't fire us. . . . We participated more openly than a lot of people because of our protection we had on our jobs down there by being union." In other cases, activists admitted that they initially disliked the fact that the union was segregated but soon realized that it nevertheless offered one of the few avenues available to express black demands. "I didn't think I should join the black union when I first went there," recalled one, "but I found out that was the only way I could do a little pushing, so I got in it." In both tobacco and paper plants, the leaders of black unions frequently used their positions to voice black demands for equal job opportunities.

Whether they belonged to segregated locals or not, black union representatives also had to suffer from the indignities caused by segregation. Across the region, it was common for black representatives to be forced to enter separate entrances and to have to stay in inferior "colored" accommodations. Contract negotiations were themselves often held in corporate personnel offices. As salaried staffs were exclusively white, most of these buildings lacked "colored" bathrooms, forcing black union delegates to go outside in order to find one. When negotiations were held in public places, black delegates faced similar problems. In 1948, staff at the Peabody Hotel initially refused to allow George Holloway, a UAW officer at the Harvester plant in Memphis, into their premises. A black man, they asserted, should not be allowed to challenge a white's word by participating in negotiations. When talks switched to another hotel, Holloway was admitted, but only in a freight elevator where garbage fouled his clothing. Holloway's white UAW colleagues offered him little support, failing to object to the company calling him a "nigger" during grievance meetings and refusing to second any motion by him.

While African American men could often turn to unions to offer them some assistance, very few of their female counterparts had the same opportunity. In the postwar South, African American women still performed the vast majority of domestic work, a sector of the economy that was completely unorganized. Around 45 percent of all wage-earning black women were domestics, raising families on less than half the amount paid to white women in industry. In textile towns, the mills steadfastly refused to hire black women, leaving them with few other employment options. Katie Geneva Cannon, who grew up in the mill community of Kannapolis, North Carolina, in the 1950s, recalled how it was common for local black women to work in the houses of white mill workers: "The first work I did was as a domestic, cleaning people's houses. The interesting thing was that all the white people we worked for were mill workers. Black women were not allowed to work in the mill then, so the only jobs available to black women were as domestics or teachers, and there was only one black school in Kannapolis. They only needed about thirty teachers, so that was very limited. All the black women I knew worked as domestics and all the black men I knew worked in Cannon Mills in the low-paying menial jobs." In textile communities, the domestic labor of black women made it much easier for large numbers of white women to hold down jobs in the mills. Within black families, however, the mother's absence meant that children had to take on responsibility at an early age. Cannon recalled that black girls learned how to clean and cook when they were very young because their mothers wanted to return to a tidy house after spending all day working at somebody else's. "There is nothing that would irritate a black woman more than to clean a white woman's house all day long and then come home to a dirty house," she explained.

Relationships between black maids and their white employers could be exploitative, but on other occasions they were close and affectionate. While many black women resented the indignities that they had to suffer on a daily basis, such as having to enter white homes through the back door, they also claimed that their employers helped them and that they became emotionally close to them. Winnie Hefley, who worked for a white family in Mobile from 1942 to 1972, spoke fondly of her employers: "I really stuck with 'em and they did me, too. She would send me Christmas presents. She'd send me money all along anytime that she felt like that I needed ten or twenty dollars or something. I'd always have a little surprise." Such memories were not unusual. "She was a wonderful woman," recalled domestic Sallie Hutton in describing her employer, "and she wanted to see, if you were working for her [and] you were nice to her, she wanted to see things better for you. She would try to look out for you."

Not all domestics had such positive memories. Many disliked having to neglect their own children in order to look after those of their white employer. Others resented being forced to use separate facilities and having to eat leftover food in the kitchen. Aletha Vaughn claimed that whites "treated animals better than they treated black servants. In fact, the animals get treated better than the servants. Plenty of 'em let the cat sleep in the bed with 'em!" "A lot of time I felt like spitting in their food," she added, "but I didn't. I would just go on and say: 'Well, they'll get theirs. This is their heaven, I suppose.'" Others also carried personal wounds; some bitterly recalled being barred from using the family china, while most remained acutely aware of racial divisions despite their personal relationship with their employer.

Most black women put up with these problems because they realized that they had few other options. "The onliest thing then was for a black girl to do was to get domestic work," recalled former domestic Essie Favrot. Unable to complain to unions, many kept their resentments to themselves. In addition, domestic workers coped with exploitation by changing employers or using subtle resistance strategies. Some, for example, deliberately called in sick when their employers had dinner parties or ruined some of the food so that they could take the rest home to their families. Others pilfered clothes or quit shortly before important social events, when their services were needed most, a strategy that relied on others refusing to take their place.

Whites also stressed the close bonds that they shared with their maids and often refused to acknowledge racial and class divisions. "I never really remember thinking too much about the way maids were treated," recalled Eugenia Bowden, who was raised in rural Louisiana. "I was just brought up with it, the way it was." Many insisted that the relationship between white families and black domestics was not exploitative. "[T]he white people took care of their servants," asserted Corinne Cooke of Pensacola, Florida. In retrospective interviews, some romanticized the past, insisting that there had been a mutual respect between the two sides that no longer existed. "I think now we don't respect the servants in the same way, because they don't respect us or themselves or their work," commented Louise Webster, a native of black-belt Alabama.

In the mid 1950s, southern blacks frustrated with the slow pace of racial change began to take matters into their own hands. Across the South, the *Brown* decision had raised black expectations, yet both the workplace and broader society remained as segregated as ever. In December 1955, blacks in Montgomery, Alabama began a thirteen-month bus boycott to protest against segregated seating arrangements that forced them to ride at the back of all buses. The successful boycott led to the emergence of Reverend Martin Luther King Jr. and secured nationwide press attention. A few months later, black student Autherine Lucy broke the color line by enrolling at the University of Alabama, provoking a white backlash that eventually forced her to withdraw.

The rise of the civil rights movement created new problems for organized labor in the South. Both the *Brown* decision and the Montgomery bus boycott made it much more difficult for unions to contain the segregationist views of many of their southern members. At the same time, national labor leaders threw their authority behind integration. In 1956, as many southerners were supporting a strategy of "massive resistance" to *Brown*, the AFL-CIO Executive Council issued a strongly worded resolution supporting the decision. Federation leaders also criticized the white citizens' councils that were fighting to uphold segregated schools as a "new Ku Klux Klan without hoods," and they subsequently publicly supported President Eisenhower's 1957 decision to send federal troops to protect black students attempting to attend Central High School in Little Rock, Arkansas.

Watching these events, many southern white unionists became ever more determined to maintain segregation. Union members from local plants participated in the riots that occurred following Lucy's enrolment, and across the region union leaders described the tension among the white rank and file. "Organizers attached to the AFL-CIO," reported a nervous union leader in March 1956, "and the national and international unions told me 'off the record' that they have never seen the membership of the local unions so stirred over any issue as they have been by the racial crisis in the South. The union members eagerly follow the Dixiecrat demagogues . . . and have joined the White Citizens Councils by the thousands." Surveys carried out by the AFL-CIO's Civil Rights Department indicated that large numbers of white southern union members favored state plans to put public schools under private control in order to circumvent *Brown*.

On some occasions, white workers used their unions to spearhead and organize their opposition to school integration. In Front Royal, Virginia, a small town located about sixty miles west of Washington D.C., no public high school admitted blacks at the time of *Brown*, forcing African American pupils to attend school outside the county. When a court order demanded that twenty-two black students be admitted, Warren County High School closed instead. The largest employer in the area was the American Viscose Corporation, whose workers were represented by Local 371 of the TWUA. With around 2,000 members, over 1,800 of whom were white, the local was one of the TWUA's largest in the South. Following the school closure, the white members of the local organized their own segregated private school and voted to use their union dues to fund it. A checkoff raised $1,600 per week to build the school, and the local also used its treasury to commit $8,000 for construction and $500 for an annual scholarship. Union member Julian Carper, who was the only white Viscose worker to openly criticize the action, remembered being ostracized as a result: "The emotions were so high that for three years every time the phone rang in my Richmond office I would expect it to be that my home had been destroyed or my family injured."

The local's action delighted segregationist politicians such as South Carolina's Strom Thurmond, who praised the Virginia unionists in a speech on the floor of the Senate. Southern segregationists such as Thurmond and Virginia Senator Harry Byrd felt that the Front Royal workers were standing up to outside union leaders who did not understand the true interests of working southerners. The TWUA's leaders, who had endorsed *Brown*, were not so pleased. They placed Local 371 under trusteeship, freezing its assets and removing its leaders from office. Still defiant, the local's leaders defended their actions on the floor of the TWUA convention, insisting that elected officers had a right to spend local union funds on what the membership wished. "We have too much pride," declared local union officer William Lillard, "to bow and kneel to anybody when the people that are earning the money and paying the dues tell us they want to do something with what they have left in their own communities. And we intend to always do what that membership stresses and tells us to do." As the high-profile fight dragged on, it became, in the words of the *Washington Post*, "painfully embarrassing" to labor leaders who supported civil rights. Although the local's defiance did draw some cheers and applause at the convention, the TWUA's leaders ultimately got their way. Following the local's suspension, the segregated high school declined and white enrolment at the public high school gradually increased as the years went by.

The Front Royal case highlighted the depth of many white southerners' commitment to maintaining segregated schooling. With feelings running high, conflict over the race issue hurt the labor movement in the South in a number of ways. Unions' ongoing efforts to sign up new members in the region were certainly affected, as nonunion workers made it clear that did not want to fund an organization that supported school integration. In the mid 1950s, organizers engaged in the TWUA's efforts to organize the Burlington Mills chain reported that workers "don't like the big boys at the top trying to force them to send their children to school with negroes. Won't have their dues going to NAACP." Companies also encouraged such reactions by repeatedly publicizing organized labor's support of civil rights. At the height of the school crisis, for example, the International Union of Electrical, Radio, and Machine Workers (IUE) narrowly lost an NLRB election at the Ncco Company in Bay Springs, Mississippi, after the company circulated a photograph of union president James Carey dancing with a black woman, an African delegate, at an international labor conference.

Labor's efforts to hold onto the members they did have were also affected by the rise of "Massive Resistance." Across the region, rank-and-file members did withdraw in protest at labor's national support of civil rights, often weakening already-vulnerable locals. Contributions to unions' political funds also fell, and relations between local and international unions were frequently embittered and strained. Emory Via of the Southern Regional Council, who spent much of the late 1950s monitoring southern workers' reaction to the growing civil rights movement, wrote that the "dissipation of energies over the race issue and fear of it" had brought organized labor in the South "to a point of near immobility." In Louisiana, as in most southern states, the labor movement was rife with racial tensions. "As far as I can judge," noted Louis J. Twomey, a student of the labor scene in the Pelican State, "union men are split wide open over this problem."

Throughout the "Massive Resistance" era, the main worry of union leaders was that white southerners would quit their unions en masse over the race issue, depriving organized labor of the fragile base it had worked so hard to establish in the region. In the wake of *Brown*, many union members, appalled at the AFL-CIO's support of civil rights and donations to the NAACP, threatened to set up independent unions. In 1956, a group of USW members from Birmingham wrote AFL-CIO president George Meany, "If we have to choose between staying in the union or see our segregated way of life being destroyed we will pull out and form our own union." In the mid and late 1950s, labor leaders anxiously monitored any potential secession movement, but in reality the independent union movement faced a number of impenetrable obstacles. Unions that seceded usually gave up rights to their property and assets, as these were held in the name of the international body. If they broke away, local unions also had to overcome the opposition of both employers and established unions in order to win bargaining rights over, a huge task. Faced with these hurdles, the infant Southern Federation of Labor, which dissident activists tried to organize in the summer of 1956, never really got off the ground. Much as they disliked the AFL-CIO's support of civil rights, many southerners were also reluctant to give up the benefits that union membership brought them, particularly protection against arbitrary discharge and good wages and benefits. Joe McCullough, a local union officer at the Union-Camp paper mill in Savannah, the Georgia city's largest employer, recalled that in the *Brown* era many whites were "as mad as hell" but they did not abandon organized labor in large numbers because "they needed the unions as bad then as they ever did."

What many white union members did do, however, was complain bitterly to their local leaders. Across the South, these leaders recalled heated arguments and exchanges with the rank and file over the issue of integration. At the Alcoa Aluminum plant in Badin, North Carolina, union official Carlee Drye related that many whites responded to the USW's support of civil rights in the 1950s by complaining repeatedly to him. "I was castigated not only by the rank and file," explained Drye, ". . . but by management and everybody except my wife." These local union officials often tried to shore up their positions by sympathizing with their members' feelings and trying to persuade them not to leave, but these tactics did not always assuage grassroots anger.

The AFL-CIO's representatives in the South became particularly unpopular, especially when they took a strong civil rights position. Victor Bussie, the leader of the state AFL-CIO in Louisiana, was subjected to death threats and harassing phone calls after he opposed efforts by Louisiana officials to shut down the state's public schools rather than comply with *Brown*. At the height of the school crisis, a bomb also exploded outside Bussie's house. In Mississippi, Bussie's counterpart was Claude Ramsay, a former Gulf Coast paper worker. A strong advocate of civil rights in a state with a reputation as the most racially intolerant of all, Ramsay received regular death threats. Undeterred, the union leader let it be known that he was armed at all times, as well as privately training his children how to use firearms.

While most black workers were struggling to secure a fair share of job opportunities in the 1950s, the living standards of their white counterparts were gradually improving. Wages were steadily rising, and many working people were also moving away from the basic company housing that had been commonplace in southern industry. At the end of World War II, for example, the vast majority of workers in the South's largest industry continued to live in company-owned mill houses. These structures were constructed between the 1850s and the 1930s and had allowed mill owners to draw on a steady supply of labor, especially as most mills were located in small towns or rural locations. "No textile development," commented manager William D. Anderson, "could have taken place in the South without the mill village."

The mill houses themselves were generally simple structures with three or four rooms. Although improvements had been taking place, even after World War II some of the houses lacked indoor plumbing, and bathing was usually carried out in tin tubs using water heated on the stove. Lacking underpinning, mill houses were propped up by brick pillars and were consequently difficult to heat in the winter. Richard Thorpe, who grew up in a North Carolina textile mill village in the 1940s, recalled that, "Many times I've heard my dad say, 'It would take a direct pipeline from hell to heat a cotton mill house!'" Textile workers also lived without air-conditioning, sweating through the South's hot, humid summers.

In the decade after the ending of World War II, a major social change took place across the textile South as most companies sold their mill houses to their workers. In 1945, some 185,000 South Carolinians (17 percent of the state's white population) lived in mill villages, but within ten years most companies in the Palmetto State had sold their houses. This move was part of the national trend toward increased home ownership in the postwar era. From 1940 to 1970, the home ownership rate in the United States increased from 43.6 percent to 62.9 percent, yet this rise was even more marked in southern textile states such as North Carolina and Georgia. In Greenville County, South Carolina, located in the heart of textile country, the rate shot up from 28 percent to 67.4 percent over the same period.

Other factors also drove the sale of the houses. Workers who had served in the military during World War II were frequently keen to break free of the mill villages that they had grown up in, and car ownership was now making it possible for them to do so. In the postwar era, locally owned mills were increasingly replaced by large corporations based in big cities, and these companies were less interested in owning and maintaining housing stock. In 1956, for example, J. P. Stevens bought a complex of mills in Roanoke Rapids, North Carolina, quickly selling off the houses and recreation centers that had been built by a locally owned textile firm. The decline in child labor, a central feature of textile employment until the 1920s, also reduced the need for company-owned housing.

Mill owners also sold off housing because they feared that the isolated mill villages could foster militancy and create a negative image of textile employment. In earlier strikes, executives argued, union supporters had been able to exert more pressure on their coworkers because they were mill village neighbors. Selling off the houses was a better way of recruiting good employees and distributing them among the broader population, reducing the chances for worker protest. As one North Carolina textile promoter put it: "When you get a lot of people living in one community, living in one mill village, they're naturally objects of concern—and, of course, exploitation—by labor unions. But scattering these people out all over the county turned out to be a very healthy concept." Union organizers had found it hard enough to sign up workers who lived in the mill villages, but now they would have to travel large distances to recruit supporters. Selling the houses therefore was partly a reflection of southern textile executives' long-standing and deep-seated antiunionism.

Textile workers themselves often felt that the sale of the company houses had broken down close-knit communities. Although companies frequently had extensive control over mill village life, particularly when communities were unincorporated, former residents also stressed that there were strong social bonds in the mill villages. Life was certainly not the unremitting misery that some outside observers of mill life described; workers felt a close bond with each other and used a variety of strategies to mitigate against management domination, including informal negotiation and quitting. In particular, the tradition of promoting rank-and-file employees into lower-level management positions ensured that workers usually knew their supervisors and could often persuade them to be lenient in their enforcement of company rules.

In many respects, the sale of the houses contributed to the long-term social decline of these close-knit and vibrant mill villages, as company schools, stores, and recreational facilities all closed soon afterwards. As increasing numbers of workers commuted into the mills from other communities, older residents bemoaned that they no longer even knew many of those who toiled in the mills. Prior to the sale of housing, southern textile workers had lived so near to their work that companies used whistles to awaken workers and signal shift changes, but once workers drove to work, life in the mill villages no longer followed the rhythms of the mill in the same way.

Some looked back nostalgically on the close communities that company housing had helped to foster, yet they also accepted that selling the houses had helped to reduce prejudices about textile workers. "Though changes on the mill hills are definite improvements, many of the things we remember so fondly aren't around anymore," reflected Richard Thorpe. "Gone are the mill company houses that rented for 30 cents a room. Gone is the company store that was in walking distance of the home. . . . However, also gone is a lot of the prejudices toward all of us 'lintheads!'" The mill village sales were in fact generally popular with workers, many of whom welcomed the chance to buy their homes. Many properties were sold at below-market prices, and some new homeowners were able to make a quick profit by reselling them soon after purchase. Others were keen to personalize the houses and improve them, often remodeling and installing air-conditioning. Most houses were indeed sold just at the time when window air-conditioners were becoming available to ordinary southerners.

The benefits of home ownership came more easily to white textile workers than to their black counterparts. Prior to the sale of the textile mill houses, black employees had been excluded from many of the benefits of mill village paternalism, unable to swim in the company-owned pools or play on the baseball teams that competed proudly in local leagues. In many southern textile communities, restrictions against black residents leaving their segregated neighborhoods also proved resistant to change. "See, back a time," recalled one Roanoke Rapids resident, "the colored folk couldn't even go into Roanoke Rapids." Housing was strictly segregated, and this remained the case even after companies sold off the mill villages. The deeds of some mill houses decreed that the homes could only be sold to whites, and although in 1948 the U.S. Supreme Court ruled racial restrictions in property deeds to be unenforceable, they persisted in southern textile communities until 1960. Mill village housing was sold on a segregated basis, and it was not until after the civil rights legislation of the 1960s that African Americans were able to gain access to houses in the former white mill villages.

In the postwar period, African American workers in other southern industries often continued to live in dilapidated, substandard housing. This housing had usually been hastily constructed near to industrial plants, ensuring that African American communities were disproportionately exposed to environmental pollution and noise. In Winston-Salem, North Carolina, African American tobacco workers lived in three-room apartments in an area of the town known as "Monkey Bottom." The community had grown up in the 1920s, and most blacks rented the substandard buildings, which were located within earshot of the Reynolds' plants. "In the cold wintertime you could sit in the house and look through the floor," recalled resident Robert Black, who also remembered leaking roofs and rat paths. "You wouldn't believe it, living in a country like America, that people would have to live under those conditions."

The situation was very similar in other southern industrial cities. In Birmingham, for example, African Americans often lived in small rented homes located right next to the city's steel and iron plants, many of them subdivided so that they could accommodate two families. Retired black steelworker Hosea Hudson recalled the cheaply constructed homes well. "[T]hem houses wasn't sealed but just outside weatherboarding with no sealing inside. Anybody pass along on the outside can hear you talking on the inside." Companies also invariably provided blacks with housing that was inferior to that of whites. In Kannapolis, the company even built a separate mill village for its black employees that was some distance from white housing. "The Negroes' homes generally appear smaller and not as well maintained," noted a *Wall Street Journal* reporter who visited the community.

In the coal and lumber industries, companies had also traditionally provided workers with housing. For both blacks and whites, conditions in these basic dwellings were primitive. "Throughout the coalfields," recalled former miner Robert Armstead, "miners lived in look-alike houses built and rented out by the local coal company. Rows and rows of these single and duplex houses, called coal camps, dotted the hillsides and valleys surrounding the mine. Beneath the startling, shrill train whistles and clanging bells, we heard the constant rumble of 'skips,' or railroad cars, bumping into each other." As in the textile mill villages, however, former residents stressed the community cohesion that existed in these towns. "It was just one big family," recalled one resident of an Appalachian coal-mining town. "All of the houses were sort of close together. Everybody knew each other." Neighbors borrowed food from one another, banded together at harvest time, and made sure that the elderly and infirm were cared for. At the same time, they were acutely aware of the complete corporate control over their lives. "If you or a member of a coal miner's family misbehaved, you became a community problem and were removed from the community," related another.

In the postwar years, coal companies also sold most of their housing to workers. Like their textile counterparts, many miners were anxious to live farther away from work, and firms were usually keen to be free of the costs of maintaining the houses. Home ownership was in fact generally popular with miners, but they could not enjoy it for long, as by the early 1950s employment in the coal industry fell. Across Appalachia over the course of the 1950s, mechanization and the declining demand for coal halved employment, leading to steady depopulation that continued over subsequent decades. "It's not the same kind of population I grew up with," reflected one resident of an eastern Kentucky town in 1980. "Just about every house then had father, mother, and a group of children. Now about every third house is a widow whose children have gone to Ohio or Michigan to get a job. Most of 'em would like to come back if they could make a living. Our elementary school in Blackey covers the first eight grades. Seventy percent of the hundred twenty students are eligible for free lunches. That tells you somethin' about the town. It's just heartbreakin'." As mechanization reduced union membership, coal operators increasingly took on the United Mine Workers (UMW), a union that was no longer the dynamic force it had been under CIO founder John L. Lewis in the 1930s. In the postwar years, the UMW was led by an ageing and increasingly isolated Lewis, who had taken the union out of the mainstream labor movement. The miners' union was also hit by the declining importance of coal to the national economy, and in Appalachia it had effectively collapsed by the end of the 1950s.

In the 1950s, similar problems affected the lumber industry. In communities such as Chapman, Alabama, and Elizabethtown, North Carolina, where lumber companies had built housing after World War I in order to secure a steady labor supply, the sale of homes occurred just at the time when the industry was declining. Home ownership was popular with the predominantly African American workforce, who felt a strong desire for "a place of their own." As houses were sold off, many workers moved them on flatbed trucks to new plots of land farther away from the original town, establishing new African American communities and commuting to work by car. Within a few years, however, employment in the lumber industry declined dramatically, forcing many to sell up and search for jobs elsewhere.

To a certain extent, southern workers in the 1950s were affected by many of the same problems as their counterparts in other parts of the United States. Across the country, an increasing proportion of workers became homeowners, and many left established working-class communities and began to commute to work from new suburbs or outlying small towns. Racial discrimination in employment was also not uniquely southern. Although the differential between black and white incomes outside the South was smaller than it was in Dixie, African Americans who had migrated to the Northeast and Midwest also found themselves disproportionately concentrated in unskilled work. In northern steel plants, for example, many blacks, excluded from higher-paying and cleaner work, performed the hotter and dirtier jobs.

At the same time, however, the South also remained distinctive. Despite union efforts, the region was lower paying and less unionized than other parts of the country. In 1953, for example, almost 40 percent of American manufacturing workers held union cards, but in the South less than 17 percent did so. While workers across the country were affected by the rise of the civil rights movement, this was especially true in the South, where protests were actually occurring. Although black workers in the North were often confined to unskilled, menial jobs, many whites, especially newly arrived immigrants, also held these positions, whereas in the South strict racial classifications permanently reserved such work for blacks. White workers in the South therefore derived particular economic benefits from segregation that they would fight hard to defend. The segregation of work was particularly severe in the region, where jobs were formally delineated as "white" or "black" and often represented by segregated unions. "I realize that civil rights represent the great unresolved social problem of the whole American society," commented NAACP Labor Secretary Herbert Hill at the start of the 1960s, "but there can be no doubt that in the Southern states there currently exists the most extreme, rigid, and systematic pattern of employment discrimination to be found anywhere in the United States." In the 1960s, this systematic segregation attracted particular attention from both the federal government and civil rights groups such as Hill's NAACP, and they gradually succeeded in pushing companies and unions to abandon Jim Crow and begin integrating jobs. This process of integration was both complex and lengthy, and it consumed the energies of southern workers and union officials over the next decade.

4

Civil Rights Struggles

In the 1960s, major changes in race relations affected southern workers, both on the job and in wider society. At the end of the 1950s, segregation remained firmly in place in all areas of southern life. Despite the beginnings of civil rights protest, whites had successfully fought to maintain the status quo, while the federal government had not taken the lead and passed strong civil rights legislation mandating the end of Jim Crow. Within the workplace, executives—even those from national companies with little direct interest in segregation—remained unwilling to challenge southern "customs" and hire blacks in nontraditional jobs. In the 1960s, however, the system of racially separate job assignments came under concerted pressure for the first time. In 1961, President Kennedy's Executive Order 10925 strengthened nondiscrimination standards for companies with government contracts, while three years later Title VII of the Civil Rights Act formally abolished discrimination in employment, creating the Equal Employment Opportunity Commission (EEOC) to monitor compliance.

The legislation was partly a response to mounting civil rights protest. In February 1960, four African American students sat down at a white-only lunch counter in Greensboro, North Carolina, initiating the direct action phase of the southern civil rights movement. The students were protesting against the fact that black customers at southern department stores were able to buy goods but were not allowed to sit at the in-store lunch counters. Their protest struck a nerve, especially with a new generation of young Americans increasingly frustrated with the slow pace of racial change after *Brown*. Within two months, similar sit-ins had taken place in fifty-four cities in nine southern states. Soon after, young activists formed the Student Nonviolent Coordinating Committee (SNCC) to coordinate future civil rights protests by southern students. Student activism convinced leaders of Martin Luther King's Southern Christian Leadership Conference (SCLC) to embrace direct action protest, and in the early 1960s they led campaigns in a variety of southern cities, including Albany, Georgia, Birmingham, Alabama, and St. Augustine, Florida. In 1963, civil rights protest played a key role in pushing President Kennedy to introduce a comprehensive civil rights bill, and following Kennedy's assassination President Lyndon Johnson used the mood of national mourning to secure a speedy and unadulterated passage for the bill. The protest by the Greensboro students occurred on February 1, 1960, and it set the tone for the decade that was to follow. The 1960s were to be dominated by the struggle for civil rights, and this struggle had profound implications for southern workers.

The 1964 Civil Rights Act has often been viewed as the culmination of the civil rights movement. Between 1960 and 1964, a series of direct action campaigns by the SNCC and the SCLC targeted segregated public facilities. As the Act abolished segregation, the movement had achieved one of its major goals. In the southern workplace, however, the Civil Rights Act was just the start of real change in race relations. Over the next five years, in particular, black and white workers, together with company, union, and government officials, struggled to work out the law's mandate. The Act's implications were profound: the southern workplace had been structured around racial discrimination, and now huge changes had to take place. All segregated facilities had to be abolished, separate unions had to merge, and traditional job segregation could no longer be tolerated. Many white workers resisted integration, and they were often encouraged in their actions, at least tacitly, by both union representatives and company officials. Even at the end of the decade, many black workers in the South remained mired in traditional, menial jobs. Frustrated with the pace of change, African American activists brought class action racial discrimination lawsuits under Title VII of the Civil Rights Act, and the body of litigation that developed slowly forced both companies and unions to move toward providing equal job opportunities. Just as black protest in the streets pushed politicians to begin to address their demands for equality, so black activism in the workplace prodded companies and unions to gradually change.

This activism reflected the way that the civil rights movement had radicalized many African Americans across the South. Following the passage of civil rights legislation prohibiting the segregation of public space and strengthening black voting rights, civil rights leaders, including King himself, further encouraged this activism by becoming increasingly interested in economic issues, especially the racial disparity in incomes. Improved job opportunities, they argued, were crucial to the civil rights struggle because blacks needed to have the economic resources to take advantage of their new found access to public facilities. As the civil rights leader put it, "Of what advantage is it to the Negro to establish that he can be served in integrated restaurants or accommodated in integrated hotels, if he is bound to the kind of financial servitude which will not allow him to take a vacation or even take his wife out to dinner?" Through the 1960s, many working southerners asked themselves the same question. "We were just more or less protesting because there wasn't much integration, you know social integration," recalled Mississippi paper worker and civil rights activist Sidney Gibson. "I always advised against that. I said, 'Well we can go to the Newark hotel if we want to, can't anybody stop me, but when we get there, who's going to pay the bill?'"

From the mid 1960s, King and other SCLC leaders became increasingly supportive of unionization, arguing that it was one of the most effective ways of raising black incomes. In two of the South's leading cities, Memphis and Charleston, the SCLC worked closely with groups of predominantly African American workers who were striking for better wages and union recognition. These two high-profile campaigns, however, had very different outcomes.

Over the course of the 1960s, job opportunities for African Americans did begin to improve. By the end of the decade, court settlements in Title VII cases were breaking up the system of job segregation that had long prevailed in the region, especially as increasing numbers of workers were banding together and bringing class action suits. Looking back, Julius Chambers, the NAACP Legal Defense Fund attorney who represented black plaintiffs in a wide variety of cases, insisted that Title VII litigation was "extremely important for that time period" because it had helped to improve black opportunities at a time when he felt that industries would not have changed voluntarily. As they watched this litigation, in fact, many companies hired more black workers into nontraditional jobs in order to avert Title VII charges. Blacks made steady progress into more production jobs; between 1966 and 1969, for example, the percentage of operators' jobs held by black men in the South increased from 16.61 percent to 21.31 percent, with gains occurring across a wide range of industries. In the tobacco industry, for example, the proportion of operators' jobs held by blacks increased from 14.7 percent to 17.3 percent between 1966 and 1968. By 1968, blacks had also secured nearly 14 percent of production jobs in the historically segregated aerospace industry.

Black women, who faced particular barriers to gaining industrial jobs, now began to finally make progress. Across the region, they put increasing pressure on companies to employ them for the first time, filing lawsuits and applying for jobs en masse. In 1960, women made up 43 percent of workers in the Carolinas textile industry, but there were twenty-seven times as many white women workers as black women. Through the force of litigation and black women's increased activism, this picture gradually changed. The U.S. Court of Appeals, for example, claimed that the 1966 case of *Lea et al. v. Cone Mills*, brought by a group of women against a North Carolina mill that had never hired a black woman, had "opened the way for employment of Negro women in the Cone Mills plant." Across the region, African Americans entered industrial jobs in larger numbers than ever before; between 1966 and 1969, in fact, EEOC data showed that black women's share of jobs in the South jumped from 9.37 percent to 13.39 percent.

African American women hired in industrial plants found that the jobs were a clear economic improvement compared to the work they had done before. "One of the things that the mill did was give me an opportunity to do some things I wouldn't have been able to do," reflected one worker in Kannapolis, North Carolina, where black opportunities in the textile plants improved following a major Title VII case. "While we don't make that much money, it gave me an opportunity to make more money than doing anything else in Kannapolis. It gave me a chance to give my kids a college education. They couldn't have gone to school if I'd still be working in that cafeteria." The greater availability of industrial jobs helped to reduce black women's dependence on low-paying domestic work. In South Carolina, the proportion of black female wage earners who were domestics fell from 48 percent at the start of the 1960s to 28 percent in 1970. Even in the textile and apparel factories, where wages were low by industrial standards, they were significantly higher than those paid to domestic workers. In the 1960s, black women in the Piedmont typically earned around $15 a week in domestic jobs. In the mills at the same time, entry-level jobs paid around $50 to $60 a week.

Despite these gains, both black men and women found it hard to obtain higher-paying jobs, especially white-collar positions, and they complained that integration was incomplete. While they did make gains, the long history of black exclusion from production positions meant that they were also still invariably underrepresented in these jobs in comparison to their proportion of the population. Many labored in low-paying jobs with poor working conditions, as subsequent labor struggles would vividly spotlight. In the textile industry, for example, the concentration of blacks in low-paying jobs was often striking, especially for black men who had traditionally been confined to such positions. In April 1969, black male employees at Dan River Mills, one of the South's largest textile companies, earned only $1.89 an hour, while their white counterparts made $2.35 an hour. A similar picture prevailed elsewhere; at the end of 1969, for example, black men working for J. P. Stevens made $2.08 an hour while whites earned $2.40.

Regardless of industry, in fact, African Americans found it much harder to penetrate higher-level jobs. As late as the end of the 1960s, no major southern industry employed more than 2.6 percent of its black workers in white collar occupations. In July 1967, only 5 of the 383 skilled craftsmen at Atlantic Steel Company in Atlanta were black, and over 98 percent of the firm's African American workers still held semiskilled or service jobs. In the petroleum industry of Louisiana, Texas, and Oklahoma, one study found that out of 395 employees holding craft positions in 1966, not one was black, while only 0.3 percent of white-collar jobs were staffed by African Americans. In July 1967, a survey of leading paper mills carried out by the American Paper Institute, an industry group, showed that only 1.6 percent of the better-paying paper machine jobs were held by blacks. "[T]hese results are not very good," noted the API bluntly.

African Americans faced many obstacles to securing higher-paying positions. Some companies gave open preference to applicants recommended by existing employees, who were overwhelmingly white. Executives also frequently continued to view blacks as less qualified than their white counterparts, seeing them as lacking in discipline and being more prone to absenteeism. It was true that many blacks lacked a tradition of working in skilled jobs, and this handicapped them as they tried to secure these positions. In the 1960s, African Americans entering the southern workforce were the product of inferior, segregated schools that usually equipped them poorly for skilled or even semiskilled jobs. Many companies, moreover, used employment tests as a basis for selection for promotion to higher-paying positions, and in court cases psychologists repeatedly argued that their educational and cultural background equipped whites to perform better on these tests.

Black workers, especially those who had worked in their jobs for many years, often knew how to perform "white" jobs from watching their co-workers, and they argued that practical experience, rather than abstract tests, should determine promotions. "I knew what they was doing," recalled one veteran black worker, "they wasn't hunting the area of qualification, they were hunting an area how to disqualify you." Collective bargaining agreements that required blacks to give up their seniority rights if they moved to another department were another hindrance, frightening experienced staff that if there were a layoff in their new job they would be among the first affected by it. Better to stay in an all-black area and retain protection against layoffs, many reasoned. While some pioneers were keen to break into new jobs, others who had spent all their working lives in a segregated job sometimes lacked the confidence to move into more responsible positions. In the early 1960s, black railroaders in Mississippi tried to dissuade James A. Reed, a young black employee who wanted to secure a job as an engineer. "Don't talk like that, don't even think like that," one warned him. "All you gonna do is cause problems."

Black progress into formerly "white" jobs was also thwarted by resistance from both workers and management. Across the South, when blacks did try to secure formerly "white" jobs, some whites refused to train them or did so reluctantly and poorly. In the steel mills of Birmingham, the job of craneman was one of the most prized, as cranes were essential to moving material around the plant. The job had been dominated by whites and was learned by the new trainee observing the driver in their cab for two weeks. At the Tennessee Coal and Iron mill, some whites refused to accept a black in the cab with them. "I'll retire before I train," commented one. Others fought change more covertly, accepting blacks but trying to sabotage their progress. As one white committeeman told several blacks, "no nigger is going to operate a crane at TCI." In many paper mills, blacks who were promoted into white jobs were often intimidated or trained poorly, pressuring them to "sign off" and return to their old positions. "They would totally harass you," recalled Horace Gill, a paper worker from Mobile, Alabama, "so ninety-five percent of the older blacks, and the records would show that, they signed off because they couldn't handle it because of the harassment, because they weren't shown proper training." On the southern railroads, whites fiercely resisted any black advance into nontraditional jobs. The mindset of whites, recalled one black worker, was "any time they would hire black that was taking a white man's job."

White workers had grown used to strict segregation that clearly marked all jobs as "white" or "black," and they struggled to adjust to the breakdown of these classifications. Unlike many black workers, who often felt frustrated with the lack of integration, whites recalled the 1960s as a time when rapid racial changes occurred. "It was an adjustment and there was nowhere to go to learn," recalled Joe McCullough, a retired white worker from the Union-Camp paper mill in Savannah. "The culture was moving faster than we could deal with it. . . . Things was moving so fast that we couldn't move up to it, things was changing, and the civil rights movement was moving so fast and there was a lag in the communities . . . we didn't know how to deal with it really. It was just an education."

Companies also held back from making rapid changes in racial assignments, arguing, as they had for many years, that abrupt change would only provoke white violence. Although executives often used this argument as an excuse for inaction, on some occasions their fears about the violent reaction of their white employees to job integration did prove to be justified. In the mid 1960s, efforts to upgrade blacks into nontraditional positions at the Armstrong Rubber Company in Natchez were fiercely resisted by whites, led by the local union, which had been infiltrated by the Ku Klux Klan. Several workers were assaulted outside the plant, and the president of the local NAACP was badly injured by a car bomb. In the worst incident, Wharlest Jackson, an NAACP leader and Armstrong worker who had recently been promoted into a "white" job, was killed by a car bomb in February 1967. Though the FBI investigated the murder, no arrest or conviction had been made more than thirty years later.

In other locations, whites organized workplace protests when blacks were upgraded. At the General Tire Company in Waco, Texas, disgruntled whites launched an illegal strike when the first black person was promoted to the position of tire builder, which had previously been an all-white position. At a Burlington Industries' plant, white workers also walked out when the first blacks were hired in production positions. Such strikes could be defeated, however, if companies refused to back down. At General Tire, for instance, managers kept the plant open and escorted its black pioneer to and from work until feeling subsided. In several other cases, racially motivated strikes by whites were crushed when managers fired the ringleaders.

At other plants, individual whites quit when jobs were integrated, but there was no collective protest. At the Vanity Fair apparel factory in Jackson, Alabama, for example, one white worker asserted that she had left when more blacks were hired because "it wasn't a nice place to work anymore." There were isolated incidents in many workplaces; at a textile mill in Columbia, South Carolina, a black worker's coat was torn up shortly after he was hired, while at International Paper Company's mill in

Natchez, angry whites wrote "KKK" in areas of the plant where blacks were hired. White workers also directed their frustrations at union leaders, blaming them for allowing too much job integration. These leaders remembered having to contain a great deal of white anger at union meetings. "It was just like walking on eggshells all the time," reflected one veteran of the civil rights era. "It wasn't an easy time, I can tell you that. . . . I mean threats were a normal occurrence, you just got them." At U.S. Steel in Birmingham, shots were fired into the home of the USW's Howard Strevel, while other labor leaders were hanged in effigy by disgusted rank and filers.

In many cases, however, integration did not result in as much violence and resentment as companies and union chiefs had previously warned. Some workers kept their resentments to themselves, aware that open opposition to job integration was unlikely to stop it. Many reasoned that they could not stand up to a federal law. Allen Coley, a white former local union leader in a Mississippi paper mill, remembered his members' reaction to the Civil Rights Act: "They didn't necessarily like it but ninety percent of them, ninety-five percent of them knew it was the law, and knew it was something they had to live by." When the first blacks were promoted into formerly white jobs, they also often came from other parts of the plant and were therefore known to whites. This undoubtedly helped overcome potential resistance. Herman Anderson, a white textile worker from Rome, Georgia, recalled that there was little trouble when jobs were integrated at his plant because "most of the black folks they put into the plant had worked somewhere or other in the plant, so you knew them. It wasn't like they'd go off on the street." Companies were careful to deter white reaction by upgrading well-known and popular blacks who were often well qualified for their new jobs. "You had a whole lot of blacks in the workforce that you could just move up," recalled one executive. "It wasn't a question of integrating the workforce, it was a question of integrating jobs. . . . We weren't naive about the risk involved, and when we started to integrate we would systematically seek people that were well recommended, good record in work. . . . Often it was someone's maid that you knew."

Union leaders often acted to head off resistance, telling their white members that the law had to be obeyed and that everyone had to "get along." In the steel industry, some union leaders, prodded by a national leadership more supportive of civil rights than that of many other unions, went further than this, telling workers that the law was morally right.

E. B. Rich, chairman of the grievance committee at the large Fairfield Steel plant in Birmingham, repeatedly told his members, "It is the law, it is right, it is fair." White attitudes did vary and some respected the courage of black pioneers and even covertly admired them. Virgil Pearson, a black worker fronting efforts to improve black opportunities at a Birmingham steel mill, recalled several white workers quietly telling him, "I can't support you publicly but you did the right thing."

The fact that integration occurred slowly and in a limited fashion also helped whites to accept a certain amount of change. Throughout the 1960s, whites retained most of the higher-paying industrial jobs in the South, so the black progress that occurred often failed to fundamentally challenge their racial privileges. Across the region, the most prized jobs were particularly difficult for blacks to secure. In many industries, for example, whites started out in lower-level production jobs in the hope of eventually working their way into supervisory posts. Such positions were almost impossible for blacks to secure, as Title VII cases clearly spotlighted. In January 1968, 27 out of 63 white workers at the American Tobacco Company's leaf plant in Reidsville, North Carolina, were supervisors, compared to only 3 out of 200 black workers. Thus, 45 percent of white workers held these lower-level management jobs compared to just 3.9 percent of blacks. In its 1973 decision, the U.S. District Court for the middle district of North Carolina noted that these figures "would chafe the conscience of this Court, even if objective criteria [for promotion to supervisory jobs] were fully in use, which has not been demonstrated. The lack of objective guidelines and written criteria are some indicia of discrimination." Rather than using objective guidelines, in fact, promotion to supervisory jobs across the region was often determined through access to networks or contacts with existing supervisors, who were overwhelmingly white and often former production workers themselves. The integration of supervisory positions was also hindered by cultural resistance to blacks being in charge of whites, a taboo which was particularly powerful in the South. "We were slow to really accept that black people could work their way up to supervision and stuff like that," admitted white textile worker Elboyd Deal, "and I know a lot of people that resented a black man being over them." Black underrepresentation in supervisory jobs was in fact worse in the South than in other regions; in 1968, blacks held only 1 percent of all white-collar jobs in the southern chemical plants, for example, a lower proportion than in northern factories.

Black activists were especially frustrated with the pace of change, complaining that African Americans were still not being hired and upgraded quickly enough. In 1970, the NAACP's Legal Defense Fund (LDF), which represented black plaintiffs in many of the Title VII cases, charged that "progress toward equal employment opportunity remains minuscule and snail-paced." Southern black workers, noted the LDF, were still confined to low-paying, dirty jobs, and black family income in the region was consequently little more than half the white average. In Pascagoula, Mississippi, State Stallworth, a local worker and NAACP LDF community aide, led efforts to get more blacks hired by local employers, particularly the Ingalls Shipyard. As the 1960s drew to a close, Ingalls employed around 15,000 staff, yet fewer than 1,000 of them were black, even though the local area contained roughly equal proportions of the two races. "We've begun to make a breakthrough into 'white jobs' but nothing significant," complained Stallworth. "When a Negro goes in, they have five or six bowlegged ways of hiring. If he didn't finish high school, 'go back and finish.' If he's finished, 'if you just had some college.' With college, 'Well, if you only had some experience.' But when we checked the records, we found they hire whites with less than an eighth-grade education."

The need for better job opportunities within black communities remained great. Throughout the 1950s and 1960s, continued poverty in the rural South pushed increasing numbers of blacks to look to industry to provide them a more secure living. By the end of the 1960s, however, the limited black progress into a range of industrial jobs had failed to alter fundamental patterns of poverty. Conditions were especially poor in rural, predominantly black areas such as eastern North Carolina or parts of the Deep South's "Black Belt," where whites still owned the majority of land, and a disproportionate number of African Americans continued to be tenant farmers. One study found that in 1969, 28.5 percent of black farmers were tenants compared to 14.4 percent of whites. Black tenants were also more often concentrated on small, less-profitable farms than whites. Whites in fact still dominated the county-level Agricultural Stabilization and Conservation Service committees, which determined both acreage allotments and conservation payments to individual farms. The federal Farmers Home Administration, which provided loans to small farms, also gave far more funding to white farmers than to blacks, arguing that its remit was to help those who could benefit most from the money. According to the 1970 census, 50.9 percent of black farm families fell below the poverty line of a $3,000 annual income compared to 18.8 percent of whites.

In several southern industries, blacks also found that just as their opportunities improved, companies began to decline and lay off staff. Across the South as a whole, African Americans remained disproportionately concentrated in declining industries. During the 1960s, for example, blacks made up over a third of the southern labor force in agriculture, saw mills, and personal services. On the railroads, employment levels began to decline just as blacks began to mount effective legal challenges to historic discriminatory employment practices. Between 1960 and 1968, the number of railroad jobs fell from 909,000 to 683,000. Hit by the expansion in automobile ownership, by 1965 only a third of the U.S. rail network was providing passenger service. The steel industry around Birmingham had also traditionally been a major employer of blacks, but in the 1960s a dramatic rise in imported steel caused employment levels to plummet. Between 1960 and 1973, global steel production increased from 345 to 697 million tons, and American producers were hit by rising numbers of imports from Europe and Japan. Between 1962 and 1966, employment at Tennessee Coal and Iron Company (TCI) in Birmingham fell from 13,000 to 10,000. Increasingly struggling to survive, the city's large Sloss-Sheffield furnace also shed staff before closing down completely in 1970. Smaller firms were also affected; at a local tin mill, black efforts to improve their opportunities were hit by a big layoff that cut employment from 2,300 in 1962 to just 170 in November 1965.

In a range of industries, traditional, labor-based black jobs were often the most affected by automation. In the southern coal industry, the effects of automation hit black miners particularly hard, as their jobs were disproportionately eliminated by the rise of mechanized mining. As one black miner explained, companies "always put them (machines) where blacks were working first." In particular, the rise of the mechanical loader gradually eliminated hand loading, a traditionally black job. In southern Appalachia, the number of black coal miners fell from 42,266 in 1930 to just 3,673 in 1970, while in Alabama, blacks made up 53.2 percent of miners in 1930 but a mere 11.4 percent by 1980. Black miners complained that companies were keen to use automation to eliminate their jobs, charging that they made little effort to train black workers on the new machinery. "They don't bother to train black men to operate the modern equipment," alleged a black miner in 1971. "[T]hey don't reach back and get the black man and say, 'I want you to learn to run it,' they just don't do it." As was the case in other industries, black coal miners battled to overcome negative stereotyping as less competent and unreliable. "From the beginning years of mechanization," recalled retired African American miner Robert Armstead, "the accepted thinking in coal mining was that black men could not learn or could not adapt themselves to the new techniques of producing coal. Company policies surrounding mechanization forced black miners to leave the industry as the machines took over. For machine jobs, mine superintendents sought coal miners who were loyal, dependable employees. Although many black miners were steady and reliable, the offers went to white men." Black miners were also not helped by the UMW, a declining union which actually supported mechanization in the hope that this would increase profitability and wage levels and ensure the industry's long-term survival.

As well as leading to changes in job opportunities, the 1964 Civil Rights Act also sounded the death knell for segregated facilities in the southern workplace. Prior to the 1960s, the complete separation of bathrooms, water fountains, locker rooms, and pay lines had allowed white workers to avoid any contact with their black coworkers. Again, some whites protested when change occurred. At the Armstrong Rubber Plant in Natchez, Mississippi, disgruntled whites launched a two-day strike when separate drinking fountains were abolished and boycotted the cafeteria when it was integrated. At several other plants, whites refused to line up with blacks when separate pay lines were eliminated. In a serious incident, a black worker who used a formerly "white" toilet at Gilman Paper Company in St. Marys, Georgia, had "white liquor," a water solution used to dissolve wood chips, thrown on him over a partition. The affected worker was left with first and second-degree burns to his head and scrotum, yet nobody was ever disciplined as a result.

Companies often failed to confront white workers' prejudice out of fear of provoking further conflict. They frequently moved slowly in integrating facilities, keeping them segregated into the late 1960s. In Atlanta, the Atlantic Steel Company kept its locker rooms, bathrooms, and other facilities segregated until March 1968, while at Albemarle Paper Company in Roanoke Rapids, North Carolina, the company refused to take down a plywood partition dividing black and white workers in its cafeteria. As late as 1970, some companies still maintained separate facilities. Even when managers removed "white" or "colored" signs, workers often carried on using the same facilities out of a combination of custom and, for black workers in particular, fear. At a Louisiana lumber mill, the company integrated toilets by cutting a door in the dividing partition, but blacks hung back from entering it, afraid that "the first black head that goes through it won't come back."

On the ground, integration was often enforced by representatives from federal agencies such as the General Services Administration and the Defense Supply Agency when they inspected plants for compliance with federal regulations. Throughout the 1960s, officials from these agencies traveled south from Washington to push for change. Under Executive Orders 10925 (1961) and 11246 (1965), firms carrying out work for the federal government were required not to discriminate. While recalcitrant companies dragged their feet, inspections did lead to some changes. Integration could, however, precipitate white boycotts of integrated facilities that persisted for many years. Both white and black workers vividly recalled such protests. "After we started going in the cafeteria, the cafeteria used to be almost full, but it fell off a lot, probably about 50% of the whites quit going there," recalled Leroy Hamilton, a black worker at a Georgia paper mill. White workers had similar memories. "They had separate bathrooms, had one for the black, and one for the whites," recalled one worker. "Well, when they integrated the bathroom, most of the whites just left their lockers and everything and didn't use the shower facilities. Stopped using them. I'd say ninety-eight percent of the whites quit using the bath facilities." At the Crown-Zellerbach paper mill in Bogalusa, Louisiana, white workers unhappy with the integration of the locker rooms even set up a private club and rented shower facilities on private land across from the mill. While this formal arrangement was unusual, many whites left the workplace and used bathrooms outside it during their breaks.

The fact that whites could continue to avoid social contact with blacks clearly helped facility "integration" to proceed. Companies again did their best to make the changes palatable to their white employees. They alleviated white fears about black cleanliness, for example, by providing paper cups when water fountains were integrated and often replaced seated cafeterias with anonymous vending machines, allowing staff to buy food and take it back to their work area, thereby avoiding social contact. As similar integration was occurring in society as a whole, many white workers were at least resigned to some degree of change, and over time most became increasingly used to the new ways.

The Civil Rights Act also had a big impact on the labor movement, especially as it led to the abolition of racially segregated local unions. Such unions were commonplace among AFL affiliates in the paper, tobacco, and long shore industries. Again, change progressed slowly, and many locals remained segregated in the late 1960s. At Scott Paper Company in

Mobile, for instance, white union members repeatedly refused to accept merger with the black local, and as late as 1970, six years after the Civil Rights Act, three members of the black union were refused entry to a "white" union meeting. Merger was not finally accomplished until 1972, and only after the international union had placed the white local in trusteeship. In both the paper and tobacco industries, national leaders accomplished merger by abolishing black locals, ordering them to surrender their charters. Black union officers sometimes opposed these moves, worried that their members would lose the automatic representation that a separate union had given them. They supported integration, but argued that the costs of change should also be borne by whites. These leaders had consistently fought to gain better job opportunities for their members, and they fought any move that they thought would jeopardize their efforts.

Blacks also struggled to gain equal rights within integrated unions. Across the South, blacks complained that they were outnumbered by white union officials and managers, who were reluctant to address black demands if they called for fundamental changes in the racial status quo. "Back in those days," recalled one black member of an integrated union, "you had to just take whatever they offered . . . you couldn't strike because you were outnumbered. So I guess you had to just go with the flow, just vote whatever they voted for whether you liked it or not." Blacks often struggled to get their grievances heard by white union officials. "When I went on that shop committee," recalled Fletcher Beck, a white textile worker in Rock Hill, South Carolina, in the 1960s, "I would hear language that . . . the blacks wouldn't hear by the all-white committee about some of the grievances: 'Well, you don't have to push that one too hard, they're black.'" Many whites especially resisted the introduction of integrated seating at union meetings. In Rome, Georgia, where the TWUA's main local contained both black and white members, whites resisted efforts to integrate seating and continued to sit separately in practice well into the 1960s. At the UAW's local in Atlanta, where the eight black janitors in the plant had been barred from membership in the union until the international insisted that they be admitted, workers similarly resisted integrated seating for many years. When a black worker tried to sit in the white section in 1962, an angry union member hit him over the head with a chair.

Across the South, white workers spoke out against the 1964 Civil Rights Act. Avoiding overt references to race, many claimed that the legislation marked excessive intrusion by the federal government into state affairs. Private enterprise, they asserted, should have unilateral control over the hiring and firing of its staff. In 1964, Georgia Power Company worker Bill Blaylock wrote, "with the passage of this bill, you are no longer a free citizen—you are now a slave of the federal government." As the legislation made its way through Congress, both manufacturers and workers harangued their political leaders, asserting that the South should not be told what to do by the federal government. In the words of one textile manufacturer, the Civil Rights Bill was the "Federal Dictatorial Bill."

Once the bill passed, many whites abandoned openly segregationist rhetoric and instead opposed integration more covertly. Most common of all, they argued that all employees should be hired strictly in accordance with their "qualifications." As two Georgia workers wrote to their local newspaper in 1964, they were "not saying that the Negroes are inferior, just that it isn't right for them to take jobs they are not qualified for." In retrospective interviews, whites repeatedly stressed that integration had led to many unqualified blacks being promoted. "Blacks couldn't really do the jobs that they was assigned to do," claimed one. This emphasis on qualification, however, overlooked the fact that black workers had not always had the same opportunity to gain the same skills as whites, especially as most had attended poorly equipped segregated schools.

Workplace integration also encouraged southern whites to abandon the Democratic Party, which had sponsored civil rights legislation. Although southern workers' disaffection with the Democratic Party had been evident for some time, this shift was especially noticeable in the 1964 presidential election, when many southerners voted for Republican candidate Barry Goldwater. In the textile mill town of Rome, Georgia, Goldwater gained the largest number of votes ever cast for a Republican presidential candidate in the mill village wards. Ignoring the advice of the TWUA's leaders, who supported Lyndon Johnson, one labor activist in Rome publicly backed Goldwater, despite the Arizona politician's anti-union views. The election marked the first time that a Republican presidential candidate had ever won in Floyd County, where Rome was located. In Georgia as a whole, Goldwater became the first Republican presidential candidate to win the state's electoral college votes. In all, Goldwater won five Deep South states and probably carried a majority of the white vote in every southern state except Texas and Kentucky.

In 1968 and 1972, many southern workers also supported George

Wallace, the strong opponent of civil rights who ran for president as a third-party candidate. In the 1968 election, Wallace won a majority of the votes cast by white southern manual workers. Although Wallace did have a reasonably positive record on labor issues, many were attracted by the Alabama politician's defiant support of segregation, which he had earlier claimed should exist "forever." During the 1960s, Wallace also adjusted to some degree of racial change, turning away from openly racist rhetoric and instead pitching his message in terms of a defense of the individual against the "eastern establishment." On the eve of the 1972 presidential election, the maverick third-party candidate was shot and badly injured, ending his bid for office. Following his withdrawal from national politics, many of Wallace's southern supporters did not return to the Democrats but instead began to endorse the GOP. The outspoken leader therefore played a key role in the shift of southern voters away from the Democrats and into the Republican Party.

The emergence of the Republican Party is a major theme of postwar southern politics. In 1945, all the governors, all twenty-two U.S. senators, and 118 of the 120 members of the House of Representatives from the eleven former Confederate States were Democrats, but by 1994, six of the eleven governors were Republicans, along with thirteen senators and sixty-seven representatives. Throughout the postwar era, the GOP has been most strongly supported by urbanized white-collar whites, particularly in suburban "Sunbelt" areas, but studies by political scientists highlight that it has also gained strong support from lower-income southern whites living in small towns and rural areas. The Republican Party's opposition to civil rights legislation was important in attracting this support, but its stance on gun control, abortion, and school prayer was also influential.

The civil rights movement also influenced the expansion of union membership among many public workers in the South. In the 1950s and 1960s, government employment expanded considerably across the country, and federal civil rights laws helped to ensure that increasing numbers of African Americans and women were brought into the labor force. Finding entrenched patterns of racial and sexual discrimination, these workers were receptive to union organization. The new generation of public employees was less reticent than their older colleagues. Whereas the previous generation often clung to the reputation of public employment as providing security and respectability, their younger counterparts were more assertive in demanding better pay and conditions. In 1969, the president of the firefighters' union in Tampa summed up this change in attitude when he declared, "Duty and service are two-way streets . . . [The] relationship in which the city plays the role of the benevolent Massa and its employees, his faithful servants, can no longer be tolerated."

Many of the key battles in the expansion of public unionism took place in the South, including the 1968 Memphis sanitation workers' strike and a major walkout in the following year by hospital staff in Charleston. These struggles both involved predominantly black, urban workforces, reflecting the broader pattern of black migration to southern cities. In 1940, 35 percent of southern blacks lived in urban areas, but by 1970 this proportion had increased to 67 percent. Leaving the declining farming sector behind, southern blacks migrated to the cities with the hope that they would secure improved economic opportunities, but many found themselves working in menial jobs as day laborers or service workers. The strikes were also influenced by the civil rights movement, which made blacks across the South more willing to fight for their rights.

In the spring of 1968, the strike by sanitation workers in Memphis received national attention after Reverend Martin Luther King took up the cause. The walkout began independently of King, however, having been called spontaneously on February 12, 1968, after supervisors sent black workers home without pay during a rainstorm while retaining whites at full pay. Black workers' anger was also fuelled by an accident where a malfunctioning garbage compactor had crushed two of their colleagues to death. In a larger context, sanitation workers' dissatisfaction with their poor working conditions had been accumulating for some time. Hardworking staff earned little more than a dollar an hour and had virtually no benefits. "At that time working conditions were terrible," recalled former sanitation employee Taylor Rogers. "We had all kinds of things to go through with the boss. Whatever the boss said was right. You didn't have no rights to speak up for nothin.'" The city of Memphis, like many other southern cities, banned public employee unionism and steadfastly refused to recognize workers' grievances. Consequently, gaining union recognition became a central demand of the strikers.

Above all, the Memphis strikers looked for the union to provide them with the dignity that they felt their labor deserved. "I Am a Man"—the slogan adopted by the 1,300 all-male strikers—struck a strong chord among black men who had always detested being called "boys" by whites. The African American sanitation workers were no longer willing to be treated as children by both their supervisors and the city administration and demanded a living wage and respect. "I Am a Man [meant] that they weren't going to take that shit no more," one recalled bluntly. Strike leaders focused particular attention on Memphis Mayor Henry Loeb, a segregationist who still referred to black Memphians as "his Negroes" in public addresses and who was seen as having a "plantation mentality." Striking against a city that had historically refused to recognize organized labor required a considerable degree of courage, and some were initially afraid to join the union. "To most people in Memphis, a strike against the city equalled rebellion," remarked one resident.

The strikers received a great deal of support from the black church, and this helped their fight to become a broad-based civil rights struggle. "We found," noted one minister, "that we were not only involved in a strike situation but that we had come face-to-face with an economic tradition, a racial tradition, a southern tradition." Emulating the tactics of earlier civil rights protests, the strikers based their movement around the local black church and mobilized support through marches and mass meetings. As the strike increasingly became a racial struggle, however, white sanitation workers became wary, illustrating once again the difficult task of building a truly interracial union in the South. "Early in the strike," recalled union leader Bill Lucy, "we had people telling us that 'I'll help you all I can, but if the NAACP becomes involved, you can forget about me.'" In this case, however, white workers were too few in number to significantly weaken the union's struggle.

Within five weeks, the Memphis strike had attracted the support of Reverend Martin Luther King, long a supporter of unionization as a way of raising southern blacks out of poverty. The civil rights veteran was also drawn to the walkout by the fact that it had many of the features of earlier civil rights protests, particularly broad, community-based support and church leadership. On March 18, King made his first visit to Memphis. "Our struggle," he told a large gathering, "is for genuine equality which means economic equality." Just over two weeks later, on April 3, the civil rights activist returned to the city. In a rousing speech, King told his audience that the ongoing struggle for racial justice, which he had headed for well over a decade, would eventually be successful. Although death threats were a constant worry for the black leader, King seemed particularly aware of his mortality as he spoke. "I may not get there with you," he warned his audience, "but I want you to know tonight that we as a people will get to the promised land." The next day, the civil rights leader was assassinated on the balcony of the motel where he was staying in downtown Memphis.

In the aftermath of King's assassination, city leaders were placed under a great deal of pressure to recognize the union. Soon after the shooting, President Lyndon Johnson, the Tennessee governor, and national labor leaders all expressed support for the strikers. On April 8, more than 20,000 whites and blacks from all over the country also flocked to Memphis to take part in a silent mass march through the streets. Facing this pressure, the city came to terms with the union, granting the checkoff of union dues and a pay raise. "We bargained with a gun at our head," complained the city's lead negotiator. "They had the ball game won." A key part of the agreement was the city's willingness to finally "recognize" the union, giving strikers the dignity they felt was crucial. As union leader James Reynolds recalled: "I Am a Man! They meant it. They wanted—for the first time—even though they were the men who picked up garbage and threw it in trucks—they wanted somebody to say, 'You are a man!' It was a real thing. We have got to get some recognition for these people; it's a basic matter of dignity."

Having lost their most eloquent spokesperson, however, the victory came at a considerable cost for the Memphis garbage men. Like many public employees, they had reluctantly agreed to a no-strike clause, and bargaining with the city's hardheaded leaders would never be easy. In the decades after the strike, Memphis suffered from deindustrialization and much of the black community remained mired in poverty, especially those laid off from industrial plants such as the Firestone tire factory, which closed its doors in 1983. In the strike's aftermath, however, the sanitation local became the largest union local in the city, fighting to secure steady improvements for its members. The union's success also sparked the growth of other public employee unions across the South, especially among sanitation workers. In Memphis itself, unionization spread to other city employees in subsequent years, including the police, firefighters, and hospital workers.

In the aftermath of the Memphis strike, sanitation workers in St. Petersburg, Florida, also walked off their jobs. The overwhelmingly black workers were protesting against a pay cut implemented by the city, although they also, as in Memphis, wanted to be treated with more respect. Many members of the African American community in St. Petersburg felt that the city government was not responsive to their needs, and local officials, like their counterparts in Memphis, did take a hard line against the strike. They were led by city manager Lynn Andrews, who had earlier described the sanitation workers as ignorant and illiterate and not deserving of higher wages, claiming that they had been "goofing off" in order to collect overtime. As in Memphis, the strike attracted the support of outside civil rights leaders, including the NAACP heads and Reverend A. D. King, brother of the slain civil rights activist. Without Martin Luther King's unique presence, however, it proved harder to exert the same pressure on St. Petersburg's leaders as had been necessary to secure the Memphis settlement. Marches continued through the summer of 1968, but the city resolutely refused to settle, backed up by white public opinion, which was overwhelmingly hostile to the strikers. At the end of August, the two sides agreed on a settlement that fell well short of what the union wanted. The city did agree to rehire the strikers, but it refused their demands for a pay raise. Although the workers could not claim victory, the walkout did lead to increased black participation in city government, partly by activating a core of black leaders. In succeeding years, these leaders pushed St. Petersburg's elected officials to adopt both a fair housing ordinance and a new city charter that dropped references to racial segregation and white primaries.

In early 1969, African American hospital workers in Charleston also forged an alliance between the causes of labor and civil rights. Historians Leon Fink and Brian Greenberg have termed the Charleston hospital strike, waged between March and June 1969, "one of the South's most disruptive and bitter labor confrontations since the 1930s." The 113-day walkout indeed led to nearly 1,000 arrests, cost millions of dollars, and secured widespread media coverage. Like many other southern workers, the Charleston strikers were unable to establish a permanent union despite their best efforts. Charleston's city leaders were as vehemently opposed to organized labor as their counterparts in Memphis and St. Petersburg, and in a battle that occurred more than a year after King's assassination, they ultimately won the day.

Like their Memphis counterparts, the Charleston hospital workers were poorly paid public-sector employees. At the time of the walkout, all of the 510 strikers were African American, and only twelve were male. In the late 1960s, black hospital staff formed part of a new, low-wage service sector, toiling for wages of $1.30 an hour and receiving few benefits. In Charleston, black economic conditions as a whole had improved little in the 1960s, and at the end of the decade 40 percent of black families lived below the poverty level, while another 10 percent existed just above it. In the Medical College Hospital of the University of South Carolina, job assignments were still overwhelmingly segregated, with blacks filling all of the nurse's aide and service worker positions, while all physicians and nurses were white. All bed and waiting room assignments, as well as restrooms, were similarly divided along racial lines.

After initial efforts to improve conditions were fiercely resisted by the hospital administrators, the Charleston workers appealed to Local 1199 of the Hospital Workers' Union in New York City, a new union that had successfully organized in the Big Apple a decade earlier. Administrators continued to rebuff the workers, however, with hospital president Dr. William McCord telling them that he was "not about to turn a 25 million dollar complex over to a bunch of people who don't have a grammar school education." Consequently, on March 20, 1969, hospital staff struck, demanding union recognition and the rehiring of twelve fired colleagues. The hard stance taken by hospital administrators was matched by state political representatives, particularly Governor Robert McNair, who was reportedly keen to prevent organized labor from increasing its profile in his state. Labor unions, feared the governor of one of America's least organized states, might jeopardize his efforts to attract outside industry.

Faced with such intransigent opponents, the Charleston workers fought back by forging bonds with the civil rights movement. The hospital workers' union had strong ties to the Southern Christian Leadership Conference (SCLC), which Martin Luther King had led until his assassination. King's wife, Coretta Scott King, was honorary chair of the union's national organizing committee, and the SCLC leadership was keen to get involved in the dispute. Since the mid 1960s, the SCLC had shown a particular interest in improving black economic conditions, and they had attempted to highlight the existence of continued black poverty during their 1968 Poor People's Campaign. On March 31 1969, new SCLC leader Reverend Ralph Abernathy, who had been King's faithful understudy for many years, visited Charleston and told strikers that his organization would be at their "beck and call." Promising to "sock it" to city leaders, Abernathy and SCLC colleague Andrew Young worked through the black churches and, in the historic downtown area, arranged mass demonstrations of "people's power" designed to secure publicity and put increased pressure on state and local officials to settle. The frequent demonstrations alienated many white residents of a city that was proud of its genteel image. "It was horrible, absolutely horrible," one recalled. "Why even today when I go downtown I can still see all those colored people marching around and singing and praying and everything."

Tensions indeed escalated, especially after Governor McNair responded to scattered violence by declaring martial law. The move, however, actually helped the strikers, as press coverage of the dispute increased. National civil rights and labor leaders rushed to Charleston to express their support, many of them taking part in a Mother's Day march that drew 10,000 participants. At the protest, local strike leader Mary Moultrie taunted the governor: "You thought we'd just die out after a day or two of marching. You thought we'd say 'Sorry boss' and put those handkerchiefs back on our heads. Sorry about that governor, but we just had to disappoint you." Moultrie's determination was typical of the predominantly female strikers, many of whom endured long spells in jail after public-order arrests. As was the case in other disputes, women's activism led to traditional gender roles being reversed. "Many times my husband performed many of the duties that were mine as a wife and mother," reflected former striker Claire G. Brown, "and at times became quite upset, but beared with me." Although acknowledging that the long struggle had sometimes left her "depressed," Brown, like other activists, generally looked back fondly on the strike. The spring and summer of 1969 was, as Brown put it, "one of the most exciting, hardest, and important periods of my life."

Called off without the union being formally recognized, the Charleston strike nevertheless secured some gains; as in Memphis, it left a legacy of activism in the local black community, and black representation on the city council increased significantly in the decade following the dispute. The *New York Times* agreed with a union leader who claimed that the strikers had won "recognition as human beings" and stressed that their protest had shown that unions and civil rights organizations, which had often been viewed as having conflicting interests, could work together effectively.

Although the strikers had secured outside publicity and support, hospital administrators and state politicians continued to stand firm together. The involvement of outside figures, particularly civil rights activists, alienated many white Charlestonians, who sprang to defend the governor's position. The strike also failed to have a real economic impact, as hospital officials coped with the walkout by cutting capacity and hiring temporary replacements. Under little immediate pressure, hospital negotiators steadfastly refused to recognize the union, and once the national spotlight had faded they undermined an earlier commitment to grant workers a grievance procedure. The SCLC, meanwhile, lost several of its high-ranking leaders in the early 1970s and entered a period of decline. Without King, who had acted as a unifying figure, the civil rights groups' leaders increasingly wrangled among themselves. Like many southern labor disputes, the Charleston hospital strike highlighted the militancy and determination of southern workers, but it also showed that these were ultimately insufficient to overcome the intransigence of employers and politicians who were determined to oppose organized labor.

In February 1968, the South's important role in the history of public employee unionism was further highlighted when Florida's teachers initiated the first statewide teachers' strike in the country. The walkout, which involved a predominantly female workforce, illustrated the way that teachers' unions had been transformed by the influx of new staff less beholden to traditional notions of deference and professional respectability. Although the teachers' strike was not as influenced by the civil rights movement as the Charleston and Memphis walkouts, it did mobilize both black and white teachers, who had merged their previously separate organizations two years earlier. Strike meetings were in fact the first integrated public gatherings that many staff had ever attended. Unlike the Memphis and Charleston strikes, however, the Florida Education Association's predominantly white leadership did not seek links with civil rights groups. Despite this, opponents of the strike often viewed the teachers' walkout as a reflection of the protest culture that the racial struggle had introduced into American society.

On February 20, 1968, over 27,000 teachers in the Sunshine State walked out. Reflecting the broader restlessness of teachers with their low-wage status in a growing economy, the Florida strikers called for adequate funding, retirement benefits, tenure procedures, and the right to bargain with state officials. New FEA leader Phil Constans, who was determined to make his organization more outspoken and assertive, voiced these demands. The union leader, however, was confronted by a Republican governor who was bitterly opposed to the strike. Casting himself as the champion of traditional family values, Claude Kirk compared teachers who walked away from the classroom with parents who abandoned their offspring. "Please don't desert your children," he pleaded. In response, the teachers argued that they were striking to improve the quality of education, insisting that their action was consistent with "the highest ideal of professional service."

Occurring at the height of the Vietnam War, the teachers' action was seen as selfish and unpatriotic by many state residents. "What would become of our country if all the boys in the service should strike?" asked one. "I am sure they do not have the wages or working conditions that the teachers have here at home." The walkout occurred at a time when many white Americans were growing tired of social protest and were instead embracing the conservatism of emerging presidential candidate Richard Nixon. Reflecting this mood, many Floridians, encouraged by the press and their governor, viewed the strike as a classic example of the excesses of 1960s protest. The walkout was also undermined by a lack of support from many teachers themselves, especially older staff who found it difficult to throw off their profession's traditional deferential posture. Only twenty-two of Florida's sixty-seven counties closed all their schools, and the strike was only partially observed in another four counties. By the third week of the dispute, the number of striking teachers had dropped to just over 19,000. The strike eventually fizzled out by the middle of March 1968, with none of the teachers' major demands being met. To make matters worse, some who had walked out lost their jobs due to a state law that prohibited strikes by public employees. The teachers had attempted to address this by submitting their resignations, but this did not stop many being fired, blacklisted, or forced to pay fines in order to be reinstated. The largest labor action in Florida history had ended in a clear defeat, although sporadic organizing efforts did continue in subsequent years.

In many respects, the public workers' strikes seemed to represent a new departure in southern history, as previously unorganized groups demanded union recognition. At the same time, older continuities were apparent in these disputes, especially in the way that southern city leaders resolutely refused to recognize their workers' prerogative to bargain collectively for their rights. Just like their counterparts in earlier strike waves, the central issue in the disputes was union recognition, something that was still deeply controversial in the southern states. Many of these walkouts also highlighted the ongoing economic disparities between black and white southerners. While it was increasing, at the end of the 1960s black family income in the South still stood at around half that of whites. African Americans in the South also continued to be worse off than they were in other regions, earning around 20 percent less. As the 1960s came to a close, many Americans felt that the civil rights movement had ended, but black workers' struggle for equal job opportunities was far from over.

Southern Workers in the Sunbelt Years

In the 1970s, the national media discovered the Sunbelt south. After political strategist Kevin Philips characterized the region as a "Sunbelt" that the Republican party should pursue in order to ensure its continued political success, the term was further publicized by journalist Kirkpatick Sale in *Power Shift* (1975), a revealing analysis of the South's economic emergence. Sale described a growing South that had gained "enormous economic importance," a region that had changed in a short space of time from "pleasant little backwaters and half-grown cities into an industrial and financial colossus." The term was taken up by the media and came to describe a burgeoning region that was growing economically and throwing off its racist past. "Sunbelt" was often used loosely, stretching to encompass states as far removed from the southeast as Oregon, yet for many observers it conjured up an image of an economically prosperous and racially progressive region that had successfully thrown off its legacies of poverty and racism. As historian John Boles has written of the era, "One could hardly pick up a magazine without finding pictures of smiling whites and blacks working together in an Atlanta 'too busy to hate,' with the reflective-glass skyscrapers in the background a not-so-subtle suggestion that Henry Grady's New South had finally arrived."

The Sunbelt image failed to accurately reflect the lives of many southern workers in the 1970s. Despite all the headlines about economic growth, for example, the South had its fair share of declining industries. Steel, lumber, and coal were all steadily laying off workers, and although it continued to dominate the region's economy, it was in the 1970s that the textile industry began its long-term decline. The Sunbelt image also disguised the fact that the South was still the poorest region in America, with many of its African American citizens, in particular, mired in poverty. The media was also too quick to suggest that the South had thrown off the legacies of segregation. In fact, in many southern plants meaningful integration did not begin until the 1970s, and it was hindered by the fact that both white executives and white workers often clung to traditional notions of "white" and "black" jobs.

Much of the economic growth that did occur in these years caused particular problems for the American labor movement. In particular, many union shops continued to shut down in the North and move South specifically because of Dixie's low wages and lack of unionization. The South was indeed sold to outside firms by its political and economic leaders precisely because of the "benefits" of lower wages and weaker unions. Georgia, noted the Peach State's Chamber of Commerce in a typical brochure from the era, had an "ample supply of workers . . . of proven ability and loyalty." The state had been "one of the first" to enact a right-to-work law, and incoming companies could expect "local-level resistance" to "union rules" and "unwarranted disturbances." Increasingly worried about low-wage foreign competition, textile and apparel companies led the way in moving South. In the 1950s and 1960s, the percentage of U.S. apparel produced in the South had increased from 17 to 40 percent, with southern apparel workers earning only two-thirds as much as their organized northern counterparts.

Unions responded with some high-profile attempts to organize southern workers. Many of these battles, such as lengthy campaigns against the J. P. Stevens textile company and the apparel-maker Farah, reflected unions' ongoing efforts to organize the South and stem the threat that it posed to their membership in the North. The battle with Stevens—which had moved virtually all of its operations from New England to the South after World War II—became the defining labor struggle of the 1970s. In 1976, the giant textile-maker earned national publicity after the union launched a national boycott of their products, part of the first "corporate campaign" used by an American union. These efforts ultimately yielded mixed results. The union did succeed in winning a 1974 election at Stevens' plants in Roanoke Rapids, North Carolina, but at other Stevens' plants that it tried to organize workers held back, scared off by the company's willingness to fire or harass union supporters.

Retired textile workers did not hold these fears of job loss, and in the 1970s they challenged their powerful industry over the issue of occupational health. Southern textile mills had always been dusty, and workers had for many years complained of breathing problems, especially in later life. With both medical professionals and companies denying the existence of any occupational disease, most seasoned millhands had refused to blame the mills for their health problems. In the 1970s, however, growing awareness of bysinnosis, or brown lung disease, led to a change of attitude, as groups of retired workers began to organize to seek compensation and force the industry to clean up its facilities.

Over the course of the 1970s, black southerners did continue to make economic strides. The passage of civil rights legislation, in combination with the willingness of black activists to keep the pressure on companies through Title VII litigation, clearly led to improved job opportunities. Some of the benefits of the expanding southern economy also reached southern blacks. Between 1970 and 1974, the median income of southern black families increased by 28.8 percent, in contrast to a 13 percent increase in the northeast. Over the same period, the traditional pattern of black migration to the North reversed. This change was partly caused by the economic decline of large northern cities to which blacks had traditionally migrated, but it was also linked to the broader dismantling of the Jim Crow system, which had pushed blacks North.

Across the South, African Americans made significant gains into public sector jobs as firefighters, police officers, and civil servants. Affirmative action, in combination with the rapid growth of the southern economy, also opened up new opportunities in the corporate world, in banks, and in law offices. In manufacturing industries, too, blacks made progress as federal legislation and fear of litigation prompted companies to change. As blacks were hired, they in turn made it easier for others to follow. By the end of the 1970s, African Americans held around 25 percent of all jobs in the southern textile industry, while in the paper industry they began to make isolated breakthroughs into previously "white" production positions as paper machine operators and millwrights. Blacks also made progress into the apparel industry. In 1966, around 8.5 percent of apparel workers were black, but by 1978 this figure had risen to over 15 percent, with the South containing the largest concentration of African American apparel workers. White southerners who had grown up under segregation were especially conscious of these changes, as blacks began to appear in a host of nontraditional jobs. Some whites, such as Duke University President Terry Sanford, proudly boasted that their region was making more progress in race relations than any other area of the country.

There was, of course, also another side to the story. Gains into public sector jobs such as police work need to be weighed against the fact that African Americans were usually confined to working in black neighborhoods. The growth of the black middle class also has to be contrasted with the parallel increase in the size of the black underclass, men and women who were unemployed or working in low-paid, insecure jobs. Black poverty continued to be a reality, even in many of the Sunbelt cities whose prosperity was repeatedly cited by the media. In archetypal Sunbelt cities such as Atlanta and Houston, many blacks still lived in crumbling shacks located just outside the gleaming office blocks of the New South. In the late 1970s, one visitor to Houston noticed that "literally in the shadow of the tall buildings . . . are black slums straight out of the heart of Mississippi. They are so antiquely southern, they're not even urban." Southern cities indeed contained a higher percentage of residents below the poverty line than their counterparts in other regions.

Sunbelt growth did little to help most southern blacks, because the new high-tech jobs put a premium on skills possessed by whites, the vast majority of them the products of better-equipped, segregated schools. Hoping to avoid racial "conflict" and believing that blacks were more prone to join unions, incoming companies also generally located in predominantly white areas, often filling many posts with staff from outside the region who relocated with their employer. Companies found that they could fill their best jobs with whites and lacked incentives to promote African Americans or push for better training programs. Federal aid to the poor failed to increase in the Sunbelt era. While they supported agricultural subsidies and increased federal defense spending in the region, prominent southern politicians led the opposition to federal welfare programs, arguing that they would produce dependency. Like their voters, these politicians opposed welfare spending partly because they understood that blacks were disproportionately poor and would be the main beneficiaries of these programs.

Despite progress, entrenched patterns of job segregation also lingered into the 1970s. In manufacturing industries, changing historic patterns of job segregation was not quick or easy. As Title VII cases vividly illustrated, some employers continued to be particularly tardy in embracing equal employment opportunity. At Savannah Sugar Refining Corporation in Savannah, Georgia, for example, the U.S. Court of Appeals noted in a 1974 decision that the company "has had a history—which has continued to the present time—of confining black employees to lower-paying, less-skilled positions within the refinery." It was not until 1968 that Savannah Sugar, one of the Georgia city's largest employers, made any attempt to change its system of complete job segregation, and these belated and half-hearted efforts were criticized by the court. In textile plants, black workers—especially men who had traditionally been confined to labor-based jobs—were getting hired in larger numbers, but they continued to earn much less than their white counterparts. Many older staff, in particular, remained clustered in traditional, labor-based positions. In April 1973, black men at the huge Dan River Mills earned $2.36 an hour, 41 cents less than whites. Black women, who had not been hired in the industry before the mid 1960s, were still the most likely to be turned away by companies who often believed that white women, with their long tradition of textile employment, made better workers. Between 1969 and 1975, only 10.9 percent of black female applicants at J. P. Stevens' plants were hired, compared to 28.9 percent of black men, 36.3 percent of white women, and 53.5 percent of white men. Complaints of discrimination helped ensure that blacks supported the union's campaign at Stevens much more strongly than their white counterparts.

In other industries, traditional racial assignments proved just as resistant to change. African American truck drivers found it especially hard to overcome their longstanding debarment from lucrative over-the-road positions, which were reserved for whites. In the 1970s, African Americans who applied for over-the-road positions were given a variety of excuses, often being told that they could not be given the job because there were "no places for blacks to eat or sleep on the road." Black applicants for over-the-road positions, many of whom had acquired truck-driving experience in the U.S. military, were also told that they could only become a long distance employee if a black partner could be found to travel with them. As was the case in several other southern industries, collective bargaining agreements in the trucking industry often compounded job segregation because they recognized departmental seniority, thereby requiring blacks who wanted to transfer to all-white departments to surrender all their seniority with the company, meaning that they would be the first to be laid-off in the event of job cuts.

In a wide range of industries, white workers continued to harass or intimidate blacks who transferred into previously "white" jobs. Over time, many whites had accommodated themselves to some black progress within lower-paying production positions, but they still resented blacks taking more high-paying posts. Herman Autry, one of the first blacks in the South to secure a job as a railroad engineer, encountered constant harassment and resentment from his white coworkers as he battled his way through the ranks. "It was very, very difficult," he recalled, faced as he was by whites who "did everything they could to get me fired." In the mid 1970s, Willie Ford, an Alabama paper worker, became the first African

American in his mill to receive the job of millwright, a well-paid and prestigious position. A highly skilled worker, the millwright was responsible for maintaining and repairing the costly paper machines. Ford, who received the job partly through the efforts of a federal inspector, recalled that many whites refused to accept him, contributing to his eventual decision to take early retirement from the mill in 1984. "The problem I had, they didn't really want me to be a millwright because I was the only black," he recalled. "I had a hard time with them white folks over there, sure did. . . . Them fellas rode my back until I left there, sure did, in '84. . . . You don't feel free when folks are on you like that. . . . I tell you what, I felt so scared I thought some of them would come to my house and try to kill me, that's the kind of way I felt, because they didn't want me to have the job."

Like many whites, Plez Watson, who worked in Alabama's paper mills throughout the 1960s and 1970s, acknowledged that it took years for him to adjust to integration. "No man should be denied having the same pay for the job that he's working on," he reflected in the 1990s, "and nobody should be denied going into a restaurant or into a motel or the other things that people were denied. . . . All those things were wrong, but it took me a lot of years to actually see how wrong it was, to be honest with you, it took a long, long time. . . . It took me a long time to accept some things that should have been accepted right off." This process of adjustment was what civil rights attorney Julius Chambers, who represented plaintiffs in many Title VII cases, really stressed in looking back on the integration of the southern workplace. Chambers noted that integration required a complete change of values, especially for whites: "I saw people, thirty, forty, fifty years old, who all they had known was a segregated society, and I watched them as their schools were integrated, their workforces were integrated, and in many instances their social life was integrated. . . . So that's what stood out more with me than the law or the cases."

Over the course of the 1970s, the integration of women into many southern industries also moved forward at a slow pace. Again, litigation forced some change, but lingering notions of what constituted male or female work continued to hold back true equality. In the 1970s, the federal government and the courts forced municipal governments to open firefighters' jobs to women. Members of a profession with a close work culture that celebrated brotherhood and physical strength, many firefighters vigorously resisted women being hired. "We're still trying to fit in after sixteen and a half years," noted one female firefighter in Tampa, where women were first hired in 1978. Holly Biggs, another Tampa firefighter, also stressed the slow pace of change. "The young men that are coming on now with the women, they're more accepting," she explained in the 1990s, " . . . and then once they get on the job they may not be so accepting anymore because . . . you've got the old guard that brainwash the younger ones." A cadre of women proved that they could work as firefighters, yet they remained underrepresented in the workforce; a decade after first gaining entry to firefighting jobs in Tampa, women made up just 3.4 percent of all firefighters in the Florida city.

Women also faced a hard time penetrating heavy manufacturing industries that had traditionally been dominated by men. The experience of Gladys Harvey, who in 1978 became the first female production worker at BASF's large chemical plant near Baton Rouge, Louisiana, illustrates well the barriers facing women who tried to secure jobs in previously male environments. Frequently requiring physical labor, jobs in chemical plants had been reserved for men, and Harvey encountered hostility and suspicion when she was first hired. "It was awful," she recalled. "The men were very close-minded, in the beginning. . . . They had an old man had been there about thirty-five years, and he just looked at me and said, 'Can't no damn woman do my job.' It was kind of tough, and then I got the wolf-whistles and all the good stuff that goes with being the only woman around." Even after over twenty years on the job, Harvey still did not feel completely accepted by her predominantly male colleagues: "I'm still on the outside. There's a non-solidarity there when it comes to interpersonal work relations because I'm female." In the summer of 2000, only eight of BASF's 500 workers were female, a fact that Harvey attributed to the hostile climate that women still faced in a male-dominated industry.

In industries where women were accepted in larger numbers, they were kept out of the better-paying jobs. The apparel industry had a long history of employing women, but they were confined to low-paid sewing machine work, while men carried out the higher-paying cutting positions. Women, it had long been believed, had nimble fingers that made them most suitable for repetitive sewing jobs. As the struggle of predominantly female workers at the Farah Manufacturing Company's plants in Texas spotlighted, conditions in the apparel industry were poor. In March 1972, the union's struggle with Farah began after twenty-six women at the company's El Paso plant walked off their jobs to protest low wages and poor working conditions. Management refused to discuss workers' grievances and fired both the El Paso activists and colleagues at a plant in San Antonio who had joined the protest in sympathy. Like many southern business executives, Willie F. Farah, the fifty-three-year-old son of the founder and company president, insisted that his company would never be unionized. Regularly patrolling his vast sewing operations aboard a motorized bicycle, the maverick owner asserted that his staff were already well treated and argued that higher wages would make his operations uncompetitive. The business magnate also treated strikers roughly, ordering the use of unmuzzled dogs against pickets and giving short shrift to claims that they were injured by his seventy-six-year-old mother as she drove at high speed through the gates of one of his giant plants.

By the time of the strike, the union had filed a variety of unfair labor practice charges against Farah, accusing the company of firing its supporters and monitoring organizing meetings. Willie Farah remained unrepentant; interviewed six months into the strike, he dismissed the strikers as "communists" and "boozed up Latin Kids" and was confident of beating the union. "We have 'em whipped and we're going to keep 'em whipped," he declared defiantly. The son of a Lebanese immigrant, Farah had previously boasted that no foreigner had ever worked at his company and he had been reluctant to hire greater numbers of Latino staff until required to do so by a court order.

Farah's opposition to workers' rights encouraged the union to devote substantial resources to the strike, which became a symbolic test of the ACWA's efforts to organize Latino workers in the Southwest, a growing sector of the industry. Within two months, around 4,000 employees had walked off their jobs, and their battle had secured national headlines. Farah himself continued to believe that his staff, who were paid slightly more than the federal minimum wage and had hospitalization benefits, did not need a union, but the strikers insisted that they wanted a greater voice in the workplace, particularly a grievance procedure and more clearly defined job classifications. Above all, they wanted to be treated with more dignity. "I didn't like what I saw in the shop," explained striker Rosa Flores. "They treated people like machines. They pushed you around to get you to produce more. And they didn't even pay you for it." During the 1970s, the number of Latino women employed in the Texas apparel industry had increased by 40 percent, and many of these new recruits viewed Farah as paternalistic and arbitrary. In particular, operators objected to a company personnel policy that allowed it to dismiss anybody it judged to be an undesirable influence on others. As historian Dorothy DeMoss has written, for Latino workers and their supporters the Farah strike "became a crusade against the entire patron system which they believed had existed in the southwestern United States for centuries."

The ACWA built on these feelings by portraying the walkout as a struggle for Latino dignity. They sent Spanish-speaking organizers to work with the strikers and launched a broad-based boycott of the company's products that publicized the struggle of the predominantly female and Mexican-American labor force. These efforts secured a great deal of publicity. The strikers were particularly strongly supported by both the local Catholic Church and by prominent Catholics such as Senator Edward Kennedy and Congressman Thomas O'Neill. Many other public figures, including Bayard Rustin, Cesar Chavez, Esther Peterson, Nelson Rockefeller, and Arthur Schlesinger Jr. also backed the union's position. During the 1972 presidential campaign, Sargent Shriver even came to El Paso to join the workers in shouting "Viva la huelga!" A wide range of national organizations endorsed the boycott, including the NAACP, the NFL players' association, and NOW. "This is no ordinary labor-management conflict," explained Democratic Senator Gaylord Nelson in September 1972. "The issues in this strike are basic to our democratic process. At Farah, the issues are not only decent wages and working conditions. The issues are human decency—the rights of American citizens [and] the continuing struggle of Mexican-Americans to overcome the prejudice and repression that keep them vulnerable to exploitation."

On December 11, 1972, which the union declared as "Don't Buy Farah Day," an estimated 175,000 pickets protested outside retail stores that still carried the company's clothes. An ACWA leader claimed that the boycott was "without [a] doubt, the most successful such campaign in American labor history." Such claims were not empty; the boycott clearly had bite, contributing to the $8.3 million loss that Farah suffered in 1972. Even Willie Farah himself admitted that the long-running dispute had cost him sales, although he was keen to blame sabotage by union militants rather than the boycott. By early 1974, with the giant apparel-maker forced to shut two plants and running a three-day week at its other factories, the two sides finally reached a settlement that gave the union full recognition.

Given Willie Farah's pledge never to recognize the union, the settlement represented a clear victory for organized labor. The ACWA's use of a consumer boycott was innovative and highlighted that unions could find alternative methods of bringing recalcitrant companies back to the bargaining table. The clothing union had also shown that it could success-fully organize Latino workers, who were becoming an increasingly com-mon sight in apparel plants. Labor leaders were jubilant. AFL-CIO presi-dent George Meany claimed that the settlement would "give new impetus to efforts to organize nonunion workers," while ACWA president Jacob Sheinkman asserted that the victory allowed Mexican Americans "to enter the mainstream of economic life" in the Southwest. In the wake of the settlement, Sheinkman confidently predicted that his union would now make real progress in the South, where it had previously struggled.

There was, however, also a down side to the agreement. Despite win-ning several NLRB decisions and a contract, some former strikers felt that the national union had pushed them to end their walkout and had left local activists out of the negotiations. The costs of victory were consider-able, as the ACWA had spent over $5 million on a campaign to secure just over 5,000 new members. As a result, the union lacked the funds that it needed to carry on additional intensive organizing work in the South, and many nonunion manufacturers remained confident of still being able to resist their efforts. The union also did not hold onto its new members for long; despite the ACWA's efforts to avert plant closings, within a decade of the dispute most of Farah's U.S. plants had shut down. By the end of the 1980s, the apparel company had slashed output in Texas and had shifted over 60 percent of production to factories in Mexico, Hong Kong, and Ireland. The strike itself had helped to highlight the availability of work-ers in Mexico, as Farah imported over 2,000 replacements from South of the Border. In the 1980s, many Mexican border towns had unemployment rates of over 40 percent, and firms such as Farah were able to move their factories to these impoverished communities and pay staff as little as 30 cents an hour.

Given the subsequent rise in the amount of apparel imported into the United States and the broader decline of the industry, these plant closings would probably have occurred anyway, but companies subsequently used the example of the Farah boycott to strengthen their argument that unions caused plants to shut down. During the campaign to organize J. P. Stevens, for example, the company publicly asserted on several occasions that the union had hurt Farah and had cost workers their jobs. In 1977, Stevens executive E. M. Palmer attributed layoffs and declining produc-tion at Farah plants to the union boycott. Boycotts, he asserted, "put people out of work." Stevens' managers were able to argue that the Farah boycott indicated that unions cared little for workers' job security and that their employees were better off casting their lot with their employer, who had their true welfare at heart. The boycott weapon, even if it did help to produce a settlement by reducing profits, could therefore damage unions' subsequent efforts to recruit new members.

The TWUA entered the 1970s having endured more than three decades of largely unsuccessful efforts to organize southern workers. The failure of these efforts, combined with the economic decline of its northern base, had hit the union hard. In 1947, the TWUA had 325,000 members, but by the early 1970s this had dropped to little more than 100,000. In the South, where many northern plants had relocated, organizing the region's largest employer remained a high priority. Even in the 1970s, the size of the industry eclipsed all others in the region; in 1973, textile plants employed close to 700,000 workers in the South, while more than 420,000 southerners worked in the related apparel industry. No other industry in the region employed more than 275,000 workers. Millworkers were, as a *New York Times* journalist noted in 1973, "the bedrock of the Deep South's economy, religion, politics, industry."

Realizing that the South had to be organized to try and protect its dwindling northern base, the TWUA continued its efforts in the region. Employers again vigorously resisted these campaigns, but there were a few successes for the union, especially when it was able to mobilize its allies in the broader community. In 1973, the TWUA won a six-month strike at Oneita Knitting Mills in Andrews, South Carolina, after an election victory had failed to secure a contract. The victory came at a plant whose workforce was 85 percent black and 75 percent female, helping the union to draw on support from both the civil rights and women's movements. In May 1973, Oneita strikers joined with women's activist Gloria Steinem and civil rights leader Bayard Rustin in a march through the center of New York City to the headquarters of J. C. Penney, one of Oneita's main customers. The Oneita workers, most of whom earned $1.60 an hour, struck primarily to secure better wages and benefits. "What can you do for your family on $1.60 an hour?" asked striker Mary Lee Middleton. "When these kids get sick I can't afford a doctor. When they get a toothache, I can't afford a dentist. . . . This strike is for my babies and I'm not going back until we win a decent contract."

Middleton eventually secured her wish, as the strike settlement gave workers a 75-cents-an-hour wage increase, as well as a company-paid pension plan and improvements in fringe benefits. Many of the Oneita strikers felt that they had proved that women could organize. "Now we felt great," reflected local union activist Laura Ann Pope, "because the majority of us was ladies and we really held out and we tried to do everything we could to win, and we did." For organized labor, the victory was particularly pleasing, because the company was a "runaway shop" that had moved from Utica, New York, to South Carolina in order to reduce its wage scales and avoid the union. In the aftermath of the strike, the Oneita local became one of the TWUA's strongest in the South.

For the entire duration of the 1970s, most of the union's efforts in the South were concentrated on J. P. Stevens. The Stevens campaign actually dated back to 1963, but it was in the 1970s that the struggle between the two sides became a national story. The New York–based company bitterly resisted the union, epitomizing the way that firms relocated to the South in order to avoid organized labor. In response, the TWUA fought back with an innovative campaign that succeeded in attracting national publicity to its cause and contributed to the company's decision to finally agree to a truce.

In January 1963, the TWUA and the AFL-CIO's Industrial Union Department (IUD) selected J. P. Stevens as its key "organizational target." Starting in 1961, IUD organizers had journeyed South in an effort to organize southern textile plants, but they were beaten back by determined corporate resistance. Tired of securing organizing victories only at small mills, the IUD selected Stevens because it was large and profitable, running a range of southern plants that provided jobs to over 40,000 employees. Union leaders hoped that if they could organize the burgeoning textile giant, others would follow suit. "A victory against J. P. Stevens," asserted TWUA leader Sol Stetin, "holds the promise of breaking the backs of the anti-union companies of textile owners in the South. It can be the largest contributor to realizing the dream for which textile workers have fought for generations." Both sides indeed saw the fight as crucial in determining the fate of efforts to organize southern textile workers, and the company became the "standard-bearer" for antiunion southern textile executives. Sticking doggedly to their guns, the TWUA and Stevens became embroiled in a brutal twenty-year-long battle that had enormous costs for both.

The campaign began slowly, as union leaders tried to avoid the excessive publicity that had afflicted Operation Dixie. Stevens soon seized the initiative, launching a vigorous offensive against the TWUA's efforts. The strength of this opposition surprised the union, which had managed to organize most of the company's northern plants during World War II.

Stevens, however, had relocated most of its facilities to the South in order to drive down costs, and it worried that union demands would make it uncompetitive. CEO Robert Stevens, reputedly "upset that the union thought he was a patsy," led the opposition, determined "to prove himself." Consequently, managers began firing and intimidating prounion workers, as well as delivering captive audience speeches that berated unnecessary third-party interference in the direct relationship between the company and its employees. Unions, workers were told, brought only plant closings, violence, and bitterness.

From the outset, Stevens' management repeatedly showed a willingness to violate federal labor laws. Between 1963 and 1975, the NLRB filed fifteen suits on behalf of Stevens' workers and brought five contempt citations against the company. In the majority of cases, the federal courts found against Stevens, earning the textile firm the label of the nation's "number one labor law violator." In one major case, the Court of Appeals for the Fifth Circuit found that the company was "engaged in a massive multistate campaign to prevent unionization of its southern plants." "The evidence found in the present record," it added, "fails to dispel [the] impression of corporately designed lawlessness." These legal victories, however, took time, and while the various cases inched their way through the courts, many Stevens' employees became increasingly afraid that they would lose their jobs if they supported the union. In this sense, the company's campaign was effective, as the TWUA struggled to sign up enough workers to secure elections or lost votes when they did take place.

Although the TWUA had discussed closing down the campaign, Sol Stetin, a tough activist elected president in 1972, was determined to maintain the fight. The long-term future of textile unionism, he argued, ultimately depended on establishing a greater presence in the South. In 1976, the TWUA merged with the ACWA to form the Amalgamated Clothing and Textile Workers' Union (ACTWU). One of Stetin's main goals in forming ACTWU was to mobilize a more powerful organization to take on J. P. Stevens. Indicating the union's total commitment, the merger agreement specifically stipulated that ACTWU should carry on with the campaign until the company was brought to its knees. The union continued to view organizing Stevens as the key to making inroads into the whole South, and the struggle was reported as "The Battle of the Sunbelt" by both the press and Stevens' management. Executives, in particular, were keen to argue that the union really cared little for Stevens' workers, but were more concerned with broader organizing goals. J. P. Stevens, claimed a company executive, was the "first wedge of the AFL-CIO 'Operation Sunbelt,' the announced purpose of which is to organize the entire textile industry and, following that, other industries in the Southern States."

In early 1976, ACTWU leaders set about achieving their goal by launching what was to become the best-known aspect of the Stevens campaign—a national boycott of the company's products. In high-profile advertisements, potential customers of the company's sheets were warned: "Don't sleep with J. P. Stevens." The boycott drew support from other unions, as well as from church leaders and civil rights and women's activists. Despite these endorsements, it struggled to hurt sales, partly because much of the cloth made by the company went into products that were not sold direct to the consumer. In 1979, at the height of the boycott, Stevens managed to earn a record $47.7 million on revenues of $1.8 billion. Even the union estimated that the boycott had only a mild impact on sales, but it had always been envisaged primarily as a public relations weapon, and here it was clearly effective. Largely because of the high-profile boycott, the Stevens campaign had become, as textile historian Clete Daniel has noted, "organized labor's cause celebre during the late 1970s."

Alongside the boycott, the union initiated other innovative tactics, including a "corporate campaign" that was headed up by Ray Rogers, a young, energetic staffer. In order to attract attention to the dispute, Rogers took activists to the company's annual meetings, where he led picketing and put prolabor resolutions on the agenda. In March 1977, Coretta Scott King was among the union supporters who attended the company's annual meeting, defiantly telling the audience that "an abundant and secure life is unattainable for working people except through trade unions of their own choosing." Rogers also identified outside directors on the Stevens board, some of whom were in charge of companies with union links. Highlighting that Avon chairman David W. Mitchell sat on the Stevens board, Rogers linked sales of Avon products to women with Stevens' opposition to the unionization of its female employees, pushing Mitchell to resign. The ACTWU also financed Southerners for Economic Justice, a lobbying effort that attracted support for the campaign, and successfully capitalized on the popularity of the movie *Norma Rae*, which was loosely based on the Stevens struggle. The real-life Norma Rae was in fact Crystal Lee Sutton, a Stevens worker from Roanoke Rapids, North Carolina, who ACTWU sent on a well-publicized national tour in the wake of the Oscar-winning movie.

In addition to these efforts, the union also continued its ongoing struggle to organize Stevens' plants, most of which were located in the Carolinas and Georgia. The company again harassed and fired union supporters and threatened workers with plant closings if they did vote the union in. Between 1967 and 1975, the NLRB found Stevens guilty of illegally firing 289 workers and ordered it to pay more than $1.3 million in back pay awards. The company devoted huge resources to fighting the union. Wherever they went, union organizers were watched particularly closely. In Wallace, South Carolina, the company was implicated in the bugging of an organizer's motel room telephone, while in Milledgeville, Georgia, the mayor and police chief spied on union meetings and passed on their information to Stevens officials. The manager of the Milledgeville Holiday Inn, where union meetings were held, conveniently rented the police a room above that of the organizers, giving them a vantage point to observe union activities and record the license plates of all those attending. When a union meeting was held at another building, the police were still able to carry out surveillance effectively by requisitioning a sixteen-year-old prisoner from the local Youth Development Center and stopping and questioning him while an officer recorded the license plates of cars parked outside the meeting. In a subsequent court case, Milledgeville Mayor Robert Rice admitted that the surveillance activities had helped to destroy ACTWU's campaign. It became, he noted, "quite obvious from the way attendance had dropped off at meetings that we had been successful in our surveillance work and that union activities had stopped."

Given Stevens' record of spying on, harassing, and firing union supporters, it is not surprising that organizers working on the campaign consistently described worker fear as their main obstacle, not just in Milledgeville, but in every location. As organizer Eddie Nichols reported from a campaign in Rock Hill, South Carolina, the "major problem" that he faced in trying to recruit supporters was "fear that Co. will fire them or out them on a less desired job." Supervisors further encouraged this fear by increasing the workloads of union supporters and spreading rumors of plant shutdowns. There were other problems as well; in many communities, local merchants refused to rent the union a meeting hall, making it difficult to give the campaign a focus. Across the South, organizers also labored to overcome a history of union defeat and failure of which many workers were all too aware. In addition, the organizer's job itself was demanding and poorly paid, and turnover among ACTWU staff was high.

The union also found it difficult to build interracial support for its campaign. Labor leaders generally welcomed the influx of African Americans into the southern textile industry, believing that they were more prone to join unions, but they failed to realize that organizing an interracial workforce posed new challenges. In many locations, overworked staffers repeatedly complained that it was particularly difficult to get both black and white workers to unite together. African Americans, who still faced discrimination in textile plants, usually joined first, causing whites to steer well clear of what they perceived as a "black union." As organizer Henry Mann reported from Allendale, South Carolina, the main problem in many campaigns was "Putting black and white together."

While organizing efforts faltered, the union was successful at keeping Stevens' name in the national spotlight through its boycott activities. Although the boycott only had a mild impact on sales, it was successful in generating poor publicity for the textile giant, particularly in the northern press. Rogers' "corporate campaign" was also able to force the resignation of two Stevens directors from the boards of other corporations. Eventually the pressure on the company told. By 1980, Whitney Stevens, the great-great grandson of the firm's founder, wanted to end the negative publicity. On October 19, 1980, following private settlement talks with ACTWU leaders, the two sides announced an agreement granting two-and-a-half-year contracts at the three sites where the union had won elections. Under the terms of the deal, ACTWU won promotion by seniority, a checkoff for union dues, better grievance procedures, and arbitration of disputes. In return, they agreed to call off both the boycott and their broader corporate campaign against the company. Stevens also agreed to pay around $3 million in wage increases that had been withheld from its Roanoke Rapids employees in the lengthy bargaining period since the 1974 election victory.

The Stevens settlement ultimately represented a partial success for the union. The agreement covered just ten of Stevens' eighty plants and only 3,500 of its 32,000 production workers. Viewed negatively, the union had expended huge resources to secure very limited results, especially as the settlement did not lead to other company mills becoming organized. While agreeing to a truce with ACTWU, the company had clearly not renounced its general opposition to unionism, and the barriers to organizing the southern textile industry remained as formidable as ever. After the settlement, Stevens successfully fought the union by keeping wages at its unorganized plants on a par with those in Roanoke Rapids, telling its nonunion employees that their counterparts in the North Carolina town were getting nothing in return for their costly dues payments. Soon after the campaign had ended, the increasing economic problems of the southern textile industry also gave new potency to management threats to close down plants if workers organized. As was the case at Farah, the economic decline of the southern textile industry quickly took the shine off any union breakthroughs. In the mid 1980s, Stevens itself began to lay off workers at its southern plants, and in 1988 the company disappeared as a corporate entity when it was bought and divided into three separate textile firms.

At the same time, the campaign against J. P. Stevens succeeded in securing a considerable degree of support and publicity for the union, as well as highlighting the continuing resilience of textile unionism despite the multitude of barriers it faced. Given the company's virulent opposition to organized labor, ACTWU had won a point of principle by securing a contract at J. P. Stevens, especially as former CEO James Finley had said that he would never accept either a dues checkoff or the arbitration of disputes, both of which the union had secured. Many southern newspapers recognized that the union had made a breakthrough. The *Charlotte Observer* saw the contract as "clearly a victory" for ACTWU. While it had only won "a toehold," it was "a toehold in a large mountain in an extensive range." The contract was also widely celebrated by workers in Roanoke Rapids, who viewed it as a reward for their years of effort. "Everybody stood up, held both hands, and was waving and yelling," recalled ACTWU supporter Gladys Wright. The tactics that Ray Rogers pioneered in the Stevens campaign also became a blueprint for many other unions over the next twenty years. Rogers himself was involved in other corporate campaigns, and while not all of these efforts were successful, they did highlight labor leaders' recognition that in order to exert real leverage against powerful employers, they had to move beyond traditional bargaining tactics and link up with their allies in the broader community. The economic problems of the textile industry were also not as apparent when the union won the contract as they would become later. At the time when the union secured its election victory in Roanoke Rapids, the textile industry still dominated the South's economy, accounting for one quarter of all jobs in five southern states. As late as 1979, in fact, investigative journalist Mimi Conway described textile plants as "the bedrock of the southern economy."

As the South continued to grow economically, however, any gains that organized labor did make were undermined by the continued influx of nonunion plants. Many firms, including foreign companies, were specifically attracted to the region because they wanted to run nonunion operations. By the early 1970s, the South was claiming half the annual foreign investment expended in the United States, with many European firms looking to the region as an opportunity to set up their first nonunion operations. In 1974, for example, Michelin Tire Corporation selected Greenville, South Carolina, as the site for its first American plant. In the Greenville area, which had traditionally been dominated by the textile industry, only two percent of workers were organized. Michelin executives, while keen to deny that they were running away from unions, admitted that they liked South Carolina's "first generation, off-the-land workers." By moving into a low-wage, nonunion area, corporations such as Michelin could pay their staff more than other proximal employers, ensuring that jobs at their plants would be highly prized, yet still maintain a cost advantage over their competitors' union operations in the northern states or in Europe. Worried that union plants would push up wages and make it hard to staff local plants, community leaders and local firms themselves often stipulated that incoming companies should not be organized. In 1977, for example, the economic development commission in Person County, North Carolina, voted to welcome a beer bottle plant that wanted to locate in the area only if it was nonunion.

In the 1970s, unions also struggled to make progress in efforts to organize the furniture industry. In the early twentieth century, furniture manufacturing had developed alongside textiles, slowly growing to become an important part of the southern economy by the post–World War II period. Utilizing the good quality lumber and cheaper labor supply available to them, southern manufacturers gradually made inroads into northern markets. North Carolina led the nation in the manufacture of wooden furniture, with around two-thirds of all southern-made furniture being manufactured within a 125-mile radius of the Piedmont town of High Point, the industry's hub. Like their counterparts in the textile industry, furniture manufacturers paid their employees poorly. Shortly after World War II, for example, average earnings in the industry were still less than $1 an hour. Organized labor was also fiercely resisted by furniture executives, most of whom belonged to the influential Southern Furniture Manufacturers' Association. In the 1940s and 1950s, sporadic efforts by unions to increase their presence in the industry yielded few results.

In succeeding years, the lack of unionization continued to hold furniture workers' pay levels down. In 1978, North Carolina's 80,000 furniture workers made $3.88 an hour, compared with a national manufacturing average of $5.36. Unionization continued to be bitterly resisted by manufacturers, who repeatedly scared their employees that the union would threaten their job security. In the late 1970s, an organizer with the United Brotherhood of Carpenters and Joiners of America claimed that furniture workers were afraid that if they joined the union, they would be called out on strike. As a result, workers were more likely to simply quit if they were dissatisfied. There were many similarities with the textile industry, where the ability to change jobs had traditionally acted as a safety valve for dissatisfied workers confronted by managers bitterly opposed to organized labor. Over the course of the 1970s, unions repeatedly lost elections at furniture plants or found that their support fell away before they could even set a date for a vote. At the Singer Company in Lenoir, employees originally asked the union to begin organizing, but company opposition gradually reduced support and the campaign got nowhere. Organizers were left feeling understandably frustrated with their failure to make more progress. As one asked in 1978, "People here have got a right to have their own union, to have higher wages. Why in the world can't they see that?"

As was the case in the textile industry, winning an election at a furniture plant did not mean that a secure union could be established, especially as manufacturers often acted in concert to isolate organized plants. In June 1978, the United Furniture Workers of America (UFWA) did win a close vote at Phenix Chair Company in West Jefferson, North Carolina. Following the election, however, Phenix managers would only agree to a weak contract that gave their staff lower pay than nonunion furniture workers. The plant was the only organized facility in North Carolina's furniture belt, and orders also fell after workers voted the union in. Lee Lewis, a Phenix employee, told the *Winston-Salem Journal* that his colleagues blamed the UFWA for losing them orders from other furniture companies. "After the union came in, (the contract orders) seemed to dwindle away," he explained. "We weren't really getting anywhere, and we were in the neighborhood of a dollar (an hour in wages) behind the other Thomasville plants." In November 1982, it was no surprise when Phenix workers voted the union out.

For decades, many southern textile workers had feared that if they supported unions, they risked losing their jobs. Retired workers did not share these worries, however, and in the mid 1970s successfully organized to publicize the fact that many of them suffered from the disease byssinosis, or brown lung. Brown lung, which was contracted by inhaling cotton dust over a prolonged period, had been discussed in medical literature since the early eighteenth century. The British government began compensating victims in 1940, but it was not until 1968 that the U.S. government, held back by lack of research and resistance from the industry itself, formally recognized the disease. Exposure to cotton dust was widespread; in the late 1970s, for example, over 25 percent of the approximately 400,000 textile employees in the Carolinas breathed cotton dust on their jobs, and at least 10,000 worked in levels that could kill.

Spurred by growing recognition of the disease, retired and disabled workers mobilized into the Brown Lung Association, which at its peak in 1981 had fifteen chapters in five southern states and thousands of members. The BLA was modeled after the success of the Black Lung Association, which had previously been effective at publicizing the problem of black lung (pneumoconiosis) among coal miners. The BLA found that it was able to recruit retired or disabled workers who were not worried about losing their houses or jobs if they became active. By providing free screening clinics, the BLA was able to raise awareness of the disease and recruit new members at the same time. Like most sufferers, Louis Harrell, a former North Carolina millworker who became a BLA activist, had known little about the disease until he went to a screening. "I've got what they call byssinosis," he stated in the late 1970s. "Brown lung. It comes from breathing cotton dust too long. The first time I ever did hear it named that was last year when this here Carolina Brown Lung Association set up that health clinic. . . . They tested me at the clinic and found out I had a 63 per cent breathing capacity. . . . You know, back before we heard what was wrong with us, people thought they just had asthma or something." The symptoms of the debilitating disease included chronic breathlessness, tightness in the chest, and coughing. "My chest feels like it's gonna bust," explained Harrell. "And you know how your arm feels when they take your blood pressure? Well, mine feel exactly like that."

Following the screenings, the BLA encouraged sufferers to file for compensation as a group, a tactic that attracted a great deal of media attention and gave many former textile workers their first experience of collective protest. In the late 1970s, BLA members also traveled to Washington to testify before hearings held by the Department of Labor's Occupational Safety and Health Administration. At the hearings, which were designed to establish a cotton dust standard, textile workers from across the Piedmont described how they had been exposed to large amounts of dust. "The dust would fly in your face, your eyes, and everywhere," explained one. "You could taste it." Workers related how they had received little support from supervisors, who told them that they should stay where they were because the dust would not harm them. Carolina BLA chairperson Lucy Taylor explained that as well as helping sufferers, her organization was determined to prevent future cases of the disease as well: "We want to do something that will make sure that our organization never gets too big: We want to clean up the dust in the mills. We are not technical experts, but we are experts in experience and in telling the truth about our lives. We are sick, but fair and honest." Other witnesses were equally determined. "I have designated what little life I have left to doing everything I can to stop brown lung in the textile plants," noted one defiant sufferer.

Among those most affected by brown lung disease were African Americans, who had traditionally worked in some of the textile industry's dirtiest jobs. Since the mills were first constructed, one of the few textile jobs available to African American men was that of "clean-up man," a laborious position which involved sweeping up cotton dust off the mill floor. Walter Jones, who worked at a mill in Roanoke Rapids for over thirty-five years, explained in the 1970s how he had been exposed to copious amounts of cotton dust in this position: "They had me as a clean-up man, sweep-up floor man. . . . The cotton on the floor, I'm telling you, was six inches deep sometimes. The whole job that I done for thirty-five years was in the biggest of the dust. You couldn't see across the room. That's just the way it was." Like many former clean-up workers, Jones eventually developed bysinnosis, joining with black and white fellow sufferers in fighting to obtain compensation and raise awareness of the disease.

The BLA's activism did produce results. In South Carolina, the association helped to secure the passage of a compensation bill, whereas before it had been organized, no successful claims for the effects of the disease had ever been made in the Palmetto State. In neighboring North Carolina, by 1986 over $24 million had been awarded to 1,600 claimants, whereas just thirty-six claims had been upheld prior to the BLA's organization. In 1984, the association's efforts also influenced the enactment of a federal cotton dust standard. Throughout the country, the BLA had undoubtedly increased public awareness and medical acceptance of the debilitating disease.

Despite these achievements, however, many sufferers still did not re-

ceive any compensation. By 1980, fewer than 10 percent of those estimated to have the disease in the Carolinas had secured successful claims.
As the *Charlotte Observer* pointed out in a series of Pulitzer Prize–winning
articles, many obstacles prevented brown lung sufferers from securing
adequate compensation. Some doctors still remained ignorant of the disease, receiving little instruction about it at medical school. "[W]e really
don't teach (byssinosis) as such," admitted Dr. Frederic Eldridge, profes-
sor of Medicine at the University of North Carolina's School of Medicine.
"We don't have enough time." In some small towns in the Carolinas, doctors also acted as consultants for textile companies and were anxious not
to offend the biggest employer in town.

Even if the disease was diagnosed, the Industrial Commissions in both
North and South Carolina took so long to investigate claims—an average
of twenty-six months in the Tarheel State—that many brown lung victims
died before they received any compensation. Even if a payout was
awarded, the average settlement of around $13,000 was usually not
enough to cover sick workers' lost wages and medical expenses. Many
sufferers unfamiliar with the legal process also accepted low payments in
return for forfeiting all future claims against their former employer. "I
didn't know anything about the process," admitted one worker who ended
up with a settlement of $450 after working in the mills for forty-three
years. "I just took what they gave me." Not surprisingly, many ended up
feeling that the system had failed them. Len Haskett of Lincolnton,
North Carolina, who was disabled with brown lung, told the *Charlotte
Observer*: "I just want the mills and government to do their jobs right.
When I was workin', I had to do mine."

The cotton dust standard itself was not always enforced, partly because
inspections by the understaffed Occupational Safety and Health Administration (OSHA) were rare. Sufferers regularly complained about the inef-
fectiveness of the federal safety agency. "That OSHA," charged one,
"they take their time inspecting, and when they do go in and catch them,
they put a fine on them of six or eight dollars." This was an exaggeration,
but companies such as J. P. Stevens, which had sales of close to $2 billion
a year, were given penalties of around $400 by OSHA, which was clearly
not enough to be an effective deterrent. Industrialists also frequently refused to cooperate with OSHA inspectors. As they had highlighted in
their opposition to the FEPC and the NLRB, most southern textile executives resented any outside intrusion in their business. In South Carolina, William Pitts, the owner of Hermitage Cotton Mills in Camden,

spent over five and a half years using the appeals procedure in order to refuse to reduce dust levels or pay fines awarded by the state Department of Labor. Pitts justified his actions by claiming that there was too much government intervention in business. "If you give in to socialistic laws that are eroding your freedom, you're a damn fool," he asserted. Pitts' case was not unique; in February 1980, about 40 percent of the South Carolina mill owners cited for OSHA violations had challenged the inspections and the dust standard. Industry groups, who had previously blocked research into the disease by refusing access to their premises, argued that they needed more time to clean up their mills. They also tried to shift the blame for brown lung from cotton dust to smoking. "Doctors know," claimed one industry ad, "that the vast majority of lung disease is related to cigarette smoking."

Just as awareness of occupational diseases increased in the 1970s, many Americans also became more conscious of the environmental costs of rapid economic growth. Across the country, environmental groups grew, especially after the first Earth Day in April 1970 encouraged grassroots activism. At the same time, many Americans continued to reason that pollution was an acceptable trade-off for economic rewards, an argument that carried particular weight in the South. Throughout the post–World War II period, most southern states had placed a higher emphasis on attracting jobs than on protecting the natural environment. Both were all too aware of the traditional poverty of southern states and reasoned that pollution was a small price to pay for good-paying industrial jobs. In North Carolina, state regulators allowed a paper mill to use the Pigeon River as an outlet for its effluents in the interest of preserving jobs, while in postwar Louisiana, the Steam Control Commission granted permits to petrochemical companies that wanted to dump toxic waste in the Mississippi River. By the 1960s, more than two million acres in Appalachia were covered with coal waste, as many mining companies had simply ripped out as much subsurface coal as possible before leaving communities with the mess, taking advantage of inadequate state laws that failed to require more effective cleanup. In Savannah, Georgia, the large Union-Camp paper mill, for many years the city's largest employer, was even given legal protection by local boosters against litigation that might result from the plant's pollution. By 1969, 80 percent of the industrial contamination in the historic Georgia city could be traced to Union-Camp, as the company poured oxygen-depleting wastes into the Savannah River, decimating plant and animal life.

Despite this environmental damage, workers and political leaders continued to stress the economic benefits that industrial jobs had brought them. In southern paper mill communities, workers brushed off the distinctive egg-like smell that permeated their communities by calling it "the smell of money." Political leaders were similarly blasé. "When a paper mill was constructed in a little Alabama town some 20 miles from Montgomery," wrote journalist Marshall Frady in 1970, "it tinged even the Capitol's corridors, on especially muggy mornings, with a vague reek: [George] Wallace, who was then Governor, would note on such mornings, 'Yeah, that's the smell of prosperity. She does smell sweet, don't it?'" Some southerners, particularly college students, participated in the 1970 Earth Day protests, but the rise of environmentalism did little to change the region's patterns of economic growth. In 1972, one survey found that Louisiana and Mississippi ranked forty-sixth and fiftieth respectively in a ranking of states' pollution control programs, concluding that "most southern states are interested in recruiting industry instead of scaring them with strict pollution control regulations."

These attitudes were partly conditioned by the fact that employment opportunities in the agricultural sector continued to decline. Throughout the post–World War II era, steady mechanization reduced the number of jobs available on the land, creating a dire need for industrial work. Agricultural decline was particularly apparent in the Sunbelt era; over the course of the 1970s, for example, North Carolina lost 32,546 tobacco farms. Most of those thrown off the land were African Americans, and prior to the 1970s many had responded by migrating to take industrial jobs in the North. Now, however, blacks were able to land a greater range of jobs in the integrated factories of their home areas.

In the 1970s, public employee unionism continued to expand across the country, driven by changes in the workplace that gave government workers genuine grievances. Seeking to keep down taxes, hard-pressed governments increasingly sought productivity improvements from their employees rather than hiring more staff. Across the country, activism was also encouraged by new, more outspoken labor leaders. Previously genteel functionaries were replaced by more assertive figures such as Jerry Wurf, a tough activist who took over the presidency of the American Federation of State, County, and Municipal Employees (AFSCME) in 1965 and was determined to bring "power to the public worker." By 1973, Wurf's AFSCME had grown to 500,000 members. Nationally, union membership among government workers rose from under 400,000 in

1955 to over four million in the early 1970s, as police officers, firefighters, nurses, civil servants, and postal employees all signed up in record numbers. President Kennedy's Executive Order 10988 (1962), which made it a federal policy to encourage union membership among government workers, was crucial in facilitating this upsurge. Similar laws were also often passed at the state level, but they were largely resisted in the South, where city governments consistently refused to recognize their employees' right to bargain collectively.

The state of Florida was the exception to this pattern, as it was the only southern state to pass legislation protecting public employees' right to union representation. Encouraged by the 1974 law, many public workers in the Sunshine State organized successfully. Prior to the passage of the act, Florida had one of the lowest rates of unionization among public employees, but by 1987, 38.3 percent of the state's public workers were organized, compared to 21.2 percent of their counterparts in the rest of the region. At the same time, Florida also had around two-thirds of all collective bargaining contracts between state and local governments and public workers in the South.

Despite hostile state laws, public workers in other southern states continued to show an interest in unions. Like their counterparts in other areas of the country, many southern teachers increasingly demanded union representation. In the 1970s, the American Federation of Teachers (AFT) grew considerably in the South, the region becoming what the union called a "Hot Bed" for teacher unity. Between August 1971 and June 1974, AFT membership in the South increased from 6,023 to 25,667, while the number of chartered locals rose from thirty-one to fifty-six. Florida again led the way, but the AFT also established state federations in Tennessee and Louisiana. By August 1974, Arkansas was the only southern state without a single AFT local union. At the same time, the National Education Association, previously a bureaucratic organization, began to function as a bona fide labor union and also grew in the South, abandoning its no-strike traditions.

Other southern public workers became increasingly militant. "Throughout the Carolinas," noted the *Charlotte Observer* in 1976, "public employees from policemen to street cleaners to clerks are getting organized." Inspired by the Memphis strike, sanitation workers in other southern cities, including Atlanta, Miami, Charlotte, Durham, and Raleigh, also organized unions. Police officers in several North Carolina cities also turned to organized labor after complaining that salaries of as little as

$6,000 a year forced them to moonlight or even accept food stamps in order to make ends meet. In several states, even prisoners tried to get a union off the ground.

Low pay was the principal grievance of southern public workers. In the 1970s, high inflation exacerbated the problem, yet state governments were reluctant to grant big increases because taxpayers, who paid public salaries, were also feeling the pinch. Like their counterparts across the country, many southern public employees also wanted improved fringe benefits and a grievance procedure to give them a greater voice in the workplace. As a worker in Charlotte's Landscape Department concluded, "They make their own rules down there, and it just ain't right. I think a union can stop that right fast." Organized public workers often spread the message that unions offered the most effective way of improving conditions. "It has helped show the public and city officials what the needs were and what benefits would come from what we were asking them to do," commented Martin Maynard, a member of the sanitation workers' union in Durham.

Frequently congregated in the lowest-paying jobs and subject to particularly arbitrary treatment from their employers, African American public workers often led the way in demanding better conditions. In the 1970s, growing numbers of African Americans were entering southern police forces, but they usually came in at the bottom and were confined to working in black neighborhoods. As the decade progressed, black officers frequently headed organizing efforts. Even domestic workers, traditionally among the most exploited in the region, began to unite for the common good. In Atlanta, maid Dorothy Bolton organized the South's first Domestic Workers' Union after being socked in the jaw one day by an angry housewife. At the end of the 1960s, when Bolton began her organizing efforts, the average pay for an Atlanta maid was just $8 a day. But after a decade of activism, Bolton had helped to raise this to $25, as well as to negotiate some fringe benefits. By 1982, Bolton represented more than 2,000 domestic and hotel workers from a cramped office in downtown Atlanta, where she screened prospective job applicants and employers, as well as training and counseling existing maids. Despite this progress, however, most maids remained nonunion, partly because they were often afraid to make job demands. Across the region, many domestics continued to work in private households without social security, vacation, or sick leave.

Many African American workers continued to be inspired to fight for their rights by the legacy of activism established by the civil rights movement. In a struggle that had strong parallels with the 1969 walkout in Charleston, black hospital workers at Duke Hospital in Durham, North Carolina, led the way in demanding union representation. Durham was a community with a long history of civil rights protest, yet this activism had failed to improve the economic condition of most African American residents. Black workers at Duke had traditionally been confined to cooking and cleaning, and in the 1970s they were still largely excluded from the better-paying jobs. In 1976, over 90 percent of staff members in the lowest pay scale were African American, with some earning so little that they qualified for food stamps. In addition to low pay, African Americans complained that they needed a clear grievance procedure and better benefits. Many also called for clearer job classifications, asserting that they were being treated like personal servants. "When I was a [nurse's] maid," recalled Helen Johnstone, "our second head nurse, Joan Ashley, she used to run me everywhere—uptown to get the immunizations and to put them in my refrigerator. She had me run to the library to return her books for her on work time."

Workers' efforts were fiercely opposed by Durham's largest employer, which harassed labor activists and used the presence of some communist organizers as an opportunity to red-bait the union. In November 1976, the AFSCME narrowly lost an election at Duke, a defeat it largely blamed on the NLRB, which had added white secretaries to the bargaining unit late in the campaign. Throughout the organizing drive, in fact, white workers were alienated by black activism and proved more difficult to mobilize.

When the union launched a second organizing effort two years later, the company stepped up its opposition. Using management consultants to run an intensive antiunion campaign, supervisors were transformed into a "management team" who used coffee hours to meet with workers and tell them the disadvantages of joining the union. The management consultants also circulated leaflets publicizing recent AFSCME election defeats and spotlighting the salaries of the union's top officers. In a well-financed preelection campaign that AFSCME was simply unable to match, Duke also repeatedly linked unions to strikes and violence and claimed that organizers were only interested in collecting dues—twin assertions that companies would use repeatedly in the 1970s and 1980s. Consequently, in

February 1979, the AFSCME lost a second election by more than 200 votes. While Duke's opposition was the central reason for the loss, the union was also hurt by growing pressure for cost containment in the health care sector and political infighting within its own ranks. In the wake of the defeat, staff had to cope alone as subcontracting and cost cuts increased workloads and led to more intense supervision. Nevertheless, their activism did lead to some improvements, including a company grievance procedure and pay raises granted by Duke in order to undercut the union's appeal.

While Duke workers were fighting for their rights, many other public workers also showed a willingness to protest in order to publicize their grievances. In 1976, firefighters and police in Memphis engaged in a simultaneous walkout. During the eleven-day strike, the National Guard enforced a strict curfew and uncontrolled fires caused millions of dollars worth of damage. In the same year, police officers in Asheville, North Carolina, staged a work slowdown provoked by their low pay, while in the spring and summer of 1978, public workers at the port authority in Wilmington, North Carolina, also stopped work. In other Tarheel cities, sanitation workers took to the streets to demand better pay and union recognition. Labor activism by government workers was opposed by most public officials, who repeatedly invoked traditional notions of "public service." In the South, in particular, state officials and city governments were fiercely opposed to the rise of unionism, often portraying strikes by public workers as inappropriate and selfish acts. In 1970, Florida Governor Claude Kirk claimed that strikes by public workers "brought to mind the vision of heaps of unsanitary garbage . . . menacing the health of the people . . . Of prisons without guards . . . Streets without policemen. Fires with no one to fight them. Complete chaos and an open invitation to anarchy. Clearly, public service is . . . above and beyond the ability to collectively bargain . . . which can only encourage illegal strikes." Several strikes, such as a 1971 walkout by sanitation workers in St. Petersburg, Florida, were broken by city governments hostile to organized labor. In North Carolina, where a state law prohibited state and local governments from collective bargaining with their employees, employers and their supporters proved particularly adept at minimizing organized labor's influence.

While public employment grew considerably in the 1970s, the South's economy continued to be dominated by the textile industry. In 1977, for example, the industry accounted for 39.3 percent of all manufacturing jobs in South Carolina and 35 percent in North Carolina. By the end of the decade, however, a dramatic rise in imported textiles was already leading executives to call for stricter tariffs. Ironically, the campaign to restrict imported textiles brought together both textile unions and manufacturers at a time when the two were engaged in bitter battles to organize southern plants. Both warned that the textile and apparel industries would disappear if action were not taken; in similar 1977 announcements, for example, ACTWU leaders claimed that textile and clothing workers were "an imperilled species," while North Carolina–based Burlington Industries warned that uncontrolled imports threatened "the potential destruction of two of this nation's most important industries." Opponents of import restriction, such as the U.S. State Department, replied by arguing that tariffs would be damaging to the nation's economy because other countries would retaliate, hurting exports. Led by the Consumers' Union, many public interest groups also opposed import controls, asserting that they would force up prices. President Carter proved receptive to these pleas and refused to grant the protection that both textile workers and manufacturers called for.

Even in the 1970s, working in a textile plant was not an easy way to make a living. Textile wages remained lower than those of any other manufacturing industry, ensuring that other executives viewed the textile industry as "a banished child." In the late 1970s, most southern textile workers earned between $2.10 (the minimum wage) and $4 an hour. Industry figures defended their wages by arguing that they were on the rise and asserting that the cost of living in the South was lower than in other parts of the United States. In 1979, Charles McLendon, a senior vice president of Burlington Industries, commented, "We think we've made great progress in the last 10 years in wages and benefits." Unions continued to press for higher wages, of course, but manufacturers argued that increasing foreign competition restricted their room for maneuver.

In some ways, textile jobs were improving. Textile wages, while low by U.S. standards, had enabled thousands of southerners to gain access to many of the fruits of the postwar consumer society. Many now owned their own homes, and most commuted to work by car. By the 1970s, air-conditioning also protected southern textile workers from summer heat, although it had also ensured that workers often labored in new, windowless plants rather than the naturally lit older mills. Jobs in the mills were still, however, physically arduous, especially for the unaccustomed, as workers operated fast-paced machinery with few breaks. "I had not expected to find physical work so demanding," admitted one northern jour-nalist who took a job in a southern plant in the mid 1970s. As foreign competition increased in the 1960s and 1970s, many firms responded by increasing workloads, causing repeated complaints about stretch-outs. With unions remaining weak, most southern textile workers continued to cope with poor working conditions by quitting rather than by organizing. Safety in the plants was often poor, and inspections were few and far be-tween. State lawmakers, indeed, consistently channeled funds into at-tracting new industry to the region rather than into tightening up health and safety laws in existing plants, publicly claiming that they did not have sufficient funds to investigate safety and working conditions. Across the region, workers were surrounded by fast-moving, noisy, and dangerous machinery, and many continued to breathe in large amounts of cotton dust. In broader southern society, moreover, the breakdown of the company-owned mill village had still not completely eradicated the industry's poor image, and its workers were still sometimes disparagingly referred to as "lintheads."

By the 1970s, southerners exiting textiles did have more options avail-able to them, as a range of new industries had moved into the region. The textile industry itself had diversified, with carpet production growing es-pecially rapidly. At the same time, continuing complaints about heavy workloads highlighted the persistence of familiar problems in the south-ern workplace. Into the 1980s, in fact, southern workers continued to fight for basic rights, such as better pay and a grievance procedure. Wages in the region remained lower than elsewhere, and unions weaker. While southern workers were used to fighting against the odds, in the last two decades of the twentieth century they faced a particularly hostile climate, as determined management offensives undermined existing unions and stifled organizing efforts.

6

Toward a New Century

Over the course of the 1980s and 1990s, important changes altered both the type of jobs available to southern workers and the composition of the southern labor force. For years, the textile industry had dominated the region's economy, offering steady work to successive generations. The pay might have been low and the conditions hard, but southerners could rely on textile mills for jobs. Even during the Great Depression of the 1930s, the mills had generally kept operating, partly in order to give people work. For over a hundred years, textiles had been the economic mainstay of the region, but this huge industry now began to decline precipitously. Hit, like textiles, by rising foreign competition, other manufacturing industries soon followed suit. The decline of these industries was part of a broader contraction of the manufacturing sector; nationally, manufacturing lost over 1.6 million jobs during the 1980s. Across the country, service industries did grow, and many southerners were able to forge new careers in this sector, especially if they were mobile and adaptable. Isolated in one-industry towns with few options available, many others were not so fortunate. Both whites and blacks were hit hard by layoffs, but job loss was an especially cruel blow for the many African Americans who had battled their way into industries just as they started to decline.

Over the course of the 1980s and 1990s, the composition of the southern workforce itself changed dramatically. In a wide range of industries, Hispanics became an increasingly important part of the labor force, especially in the region's burgeoning food-processing industry. The Latino arrivals changed many southern communities, and by the end of the twentieth century the new immigrants had established stores, radio stations, and even soccer teams in small southern towns. In the early years of the twenty-first century, Hispanic migrants continued to enter new southern workplaces, ensuring that they would continue to alter their adopted region. Like many white and black workers, however, Latinos often worked in hazardous jobs with low pay and poor benefits.

Through the 1980s and 1990s, organized labor declined significantly. While only a small proportion of southerners belonged to unions, the unions' emasculation affected most workers, especially as unorganized companies now had less reason to increase their wages in order to deter unionization. Organized labor's problems had been evident for some time, but in the 1980s the pace of union decline accelerated. Union membership fell precipitously during the decade, from 23 percent of the workforce in 1980 to 16.1 percent in 1991. "The 1980s," noted the *Boston Globe*, "were a disaster for the labor movement." Layoffs by manufacturing companies were a major cause of this fall, especially as organized labor had been strongest in the blue-collar sector. Unions themselves were partly responsible for their problems, especially as they had often been slow to organize outside manufacturing industries. At the same time, a conservative political climate and increased foreign competition encouraged companies to seek concessions at the bargaining table. In the South, where organized labor had always been weak, many companies were able to reduce or totally eliminate union influence in their plants. In many ways, it was southern employers who led the increasingly open antiunion offensive by U.S. manufacturers. Across the country, in fact, those who tried to resist the concessionary tide were often locked out of their jobs or permanently replaced by strikebreakers.

Like their counterparts in other regions, many southern workers held the president himself responsible for antiunionism. Ironically, in the 1940s Ronald Reagan had headed the AFL's Screen Actors' Guild. Almost forty years later, however, Reagan was determined to take a hard line against unions. Within a few months of assuming office at the start of 1981, the California Republican smashed a walkout by 13,000 air traffic controllers who, as federal employees, were prohibited from striking. As well as breaking their union, the Professional Air Traffic Controllers Organization (PATCO), the new president also banned its members from working for the federal government for life, sending a clear message to workers across the country. Like their counterparts across the United States, southern union members vividly recalled the PATCO strike and viewed it as a turning point that opened the way for attacks on unions everywhere. "I was at home in my living-room and saw the news on TV when Ronald Reagan disbanded PATCO," recalled Don Low, a union member from southwestern Louisiana. "I sat down in the middle of my floor and cried. And my wife wanted to know what in the world was wrong, and I said, 'He just gutted every union in the nation.'"

In addition to a more conservative political climate, in the early 1980s southern workers also faced a challenging economic environment. In late 1982, unemployment stood at 10 percent nationally and was even higher in the manufacturing sector, which was hit by falling exports, rising foreign competition, and technological obsolescence. With an economy in recession, many workers became fearful of losing their jobs, hindering union progress. In 1982, R. V. Durham, president of the Teamsters' Union in Greensboro, North Carolina, commented, "When you're going through this type of period, workers are more interested in trying to hang onto their jobs, rather than trying to improve them. The priority right now is staying employed." The effects of the political and economic climate combined to halt union efforts to improve conditions for their members. In 1983, Donald M. Cruse, southeastern regional commissioner of the Bureau of Labor Statistics, commented, "I don't remember any time where there have been concessions on contracts to this extent."

Across the South, bitter strikes erupted when union members resisted management's demand for wholesale concessions, especially since companies increasingly broke walkouts by hiring permanent replacements. Unlike temporary strikebreakers, who had traditionally been hired but let go at the end of a dispute, companies now took advantage of a loophole in labor law to permanently displace their striking employees. Between 1985 and 1989, for example, companies hired permanent replacements in around 20 percent of all strikes. Robert Reich, Secretary of Labor during the Clinton administration, later described the 1980s as "a decade characterized by a wave of labor disputes in which thousands of employees lost their jobs after they engaged in completely lawful strikes."

In small southern towns, the use of permanent replacements caused lasting community divisions, especially as union members often knew those who took their jobs. "We had one of the members of our local that committed suicide, a lot of it was due to the pressures of the strike, the financial burdens and things like that," recalled Johnny Sharp, a Louisiana worker who was one of the thousands who were permanently replaced in the 1980s. "It was a terrible deal. It's hard on communities, you had fathers against sons, cousins against uncles. . . . Back during that time, this was a poor community around here and people needed work. There was union people that were out on strike that had kinfolks crossed the picketline and went in and tried to get jobs, put in. And there's families to this day that still don't speak over that. I'm one of them." Wherever permanent replacements were hired, similar scars resulted.

Few southern unions were immune from the corporate onslaught. In the pulp and paper industry, previously one of the most unionized in the South, companies pursued union-avoidance strategies with increasing success. They pressured workers in unionized plants to surrender concessions, and labor relations became increasingly confrontational in an industry with a long history of peaceful bargaining. In the spring of 1987, managers at International Paper Company (IP), the largest in the industry, demanded that their employees accept a range of concessions, including the loss of premium pay for working on Sundays and holidays and the elimination of "cold shutdowns," or days when the plants were closed altogether. Claiming that the changes were necessitated by increased overseas competition, IP locked out its workers in Mobile, Alabama, when they refused to agree to its terms and permanently replaced over 2,000 employees at other mills who had struck in sympathy. Local unions were left reeling. "We still haven't recovered from it, we're trying," admitted Mobile local union leader Wayne Fisher ten years later.

The increasingly antiunion climate also affected organizing. Across the region, unions found it more difficult to bring their campaigns to votes, and when they did so they usually lost. In 1983, organized labor won less than 25 percent of the NLRB elections conducted in North Carolina, down from close to 40 percent in 1979. Even the few victories were all in plants employing fewer than 100 workers. "The climate right now is perfect for undermining the unions," admitted S. Eugene Ruff, an International Brotherhood of Electrical Workers (IBEW) business manager in Charlotte. "If things continue like this, you're going to see many unions fold up their tents and get out of the state."

In the 1980s, union decline was a national phenomenon, yet in many ways the South was at the forefront of corporate efforts to take on organized labor. Many companies had come to the region specifically because it was largely nonunion, and they wanted to keep it that way. When workers did try to organize, southern employers increasingly turned to management consultants for assistance. These firms have helped to ensure a marked drop in organized labor's success rate in NLRB elections. Located in the historically antiunion textile Piedmont, Greenville, South Carolina, and Charlotte, North Carolina, emerged as headquarters for the burgeoning union-busting business. By 1993, union avoidance was a billion dollar industry with over 7,000 practitioners. These consultants helped companies to initiate schemes designed to build employee loyalty and take away the need for a "third party." If there was a real threat of unionization, consultants also helped their clients to mount intense campaigns on the eve of elections, when they were usually willing to fight dirty.

As their employees were preparing to go to the polls, company propaganda repeatedly associated unions with violence, suffering, and community division. Similar preelection tactics had been used as early as Operation Dixie, but in the 1980s they became increasingly common and imaginative. Just days before an NLRB election at its High Point, North Carolina plant, J. P. Stevens brought a one-legged man into the plant and told workers that he had lost his leg in a strike. Another textile company mailed each of its employees a record of a fictional radio broadcast of a strike with gunshot in the background. The recording also featured speeches by local ministers blaming the union for dividing the community. Shortly before a 1985 election at Cannon Mills, company officials, aided by the prominent antiunion law firm of Constangy, Brooks, and Smith, produced their own film in which new mill owner David Murdoch told his employees that union-inspired "dissension" could make the plant unprofitable. Many consultants used "captive audience" sessions, permitted under the Taft-Hartley Act, to get their message across, often forbidding workers from asking questions. As one union organizer told a journalist in 1986, "There are a hundred ways they can either make your life miserable or make life easy. These consultants take a worker apart piece by piece over the course of workdays, months or years, almost using them as a behavioral psychology experiment. Eventually the workers cannot stand the pressure, and I'm not sure you could either."

Throughout the 1980s, union organizers claimed that companies were effective at deterring their efforts. "Fear is the biggest obstacle we have to overcome," declared Mike Black, an AFL-CIO organizer based in Charlotte. "If we could overcome fear, we could organize everything. . . . But most people believe if they start organizing, they are going to get fired." Many workers had similar complaints. Tonya Bristol, a rank-and-file union supporter at a large North Carolina plant, recalled management using captive audience speeches to help defeat a Teamsters' organizing effort. "They told the people, 'If you think you've been harassed now, wait until the union gets in,'" she explained. "They scared the people, just like they always do."

Consultants did not just advise employers on how to defeat organizing campaigns. A key part of their message, in fact, was that companies should undercut workers' need for representation in the first place. As the consultants frequently preached, vigilant managers could easily avoid unionization, especially if they could encourage workers to see themselves as part of the company "team." Management consequently rewarded the most productive with merit prizes such as "Employee of the Month," while "hotlines" to company officials assured staff that their input was valued and that they did not need outside representation. Companies also upgraded workers' job titles. At Nissan's flagship plant in Smyrna, Tennessee, for example, the company recast assembly line workers as "production technicians," while the expanding Wal-Mart chain famously called its hourly employees "associates."

The effort to organize Nissan's Smyrna plant was the highest-profile organizing campaign of the 1980s, but it ended in overwhelming defeat for the union. The loss was a disaster for the UAW, the largest union in the country, indicating that it would not be able to make any headway into the growing number of southern auto plants. Like other companies, Nissan was able to fend off the union through a combination of long-term efforts to build employee loyalty and extensive propaganda shortly before the election.

Nissan's arrival in Tennessee was a sign of the increasing diversification of the southern economy. At the start of the 1980s, the Japanese auto giant announced publicly that Smyrna, a small town located around thirty miles southeast of Nashville, would be the location for its first U.S. plant. As early as 1974, the company had begun looking for a U.S. location, but it eventually selected the 850-acre site in central Tennessee, citing the fact that it was very well placed to ship finished vehicles to the U.S. market. Frequently visiting Japan and corresponding closely with the company's top executives, Tennessee governor Lamar Alexander was instrumental in bringing Nissan to the Volunteer State. Like southern governors before him, Alexander was keen to attract outside investment by stressing Tennessee's "pro-business" climate, a term that was often a euphemism for weak unions. In informal correspondence, Alexander pointed out to Nissan president Takashi Ishihara that the Tennessee "work environment is superior to the Kentucky work environment." Tennessee, the Republican politician pointed out, had a right-to-work law, whereas their neighboring state, which was also vying for the plant, did not.

Nissan's decision to build the Smyrna plant was highly significant, representing the largest overseas investment ever made by a Japanese company in the United States. Most local residents of predominantly rural Rutherford County were delighted, but from the outset the company's relationship with organized labor was poor. Nissan decided to build its factory with nonunion workers, a move that angered local labor activists. Pointing out that Nissan had previously crushed the independent auto union in Japan, they insisted that the giant automaker was antiunion. In February 1981, state union activists staged a demonstration at Nissan's groundbreaking ceremonies, which were attended by Alexander. Around 1,500 demonstrators jeered at Nissan officials and forced Alexander to shout to be heard. As the governor and company executives struggled through the crowd to reach a Nissan truck that was to be used for the groundbreaking, they were pelted with rocks and found that three of the vehicle's tires had been flattened. Alexander also claimed that some of the demonstrators were armed with knives and smelt of whiskey, later recalling the incident as his "most embarrassing moment as governor." The demonstration ultimately backfired on organized labor, causing local and state public officials to rally around the Japanese company, much as they did in the subsequent UAW campaign.

Despite this bumpy start, the Nissan plant thrived, and was soon producing cars as well as the light trucks that company executives had originally envisaged. Relations between the company and organized labor, however, never recovered after the opening ceremony. Nissan executives continually spoke out against unions, asserting that its workers did not need them. Worried that the presence of a nonunion southern plant threatened the living standards of its northern members, the UAW nevertheless began organizing efforts in the early 1980s and gradually recruited support with a message that only a union could give workers a truly independent voice in the workplace.

In the summer of 1989, after a sustained organizing drive, an election date was set at Nissan. Union organizers went into the vote in an optimistic mood, having built most of their support from workers who complained about the relentless pace of work at the plant. In 1987, an article in the liberal magazine *The Progressive* argued that the plant had achieved high productivity not through sophisticated Japanese production methods but because of the old-fashioned speed-up. "You don't have time to unwrap a piece of chewing gum and stick it in your mouth until the line stops," claimed one worker. "You feel like you've done three days' work at the end of the shift," confirmed another. A Smyrna barber told journalist John Junkerman that he knew if he was cutting the hair of a Nissan worker because they always fell asleep in the chair. Disgruntled staff criticized managers, with some claiming that supervisors instructed them to restrict their intake of fluids so that they would not need to use the bathroom. "I actually saw a man wet his pants on the line," commented one. Nissan denied these allegations, although it refused to directly address claims that the plant had a poor safety record.

The company in fact vigorously fought the union's campaign, drawing on a variety of strategies. Prospective employees were carefully screened before they were hired, and few with a union background were taken on. Labor leaders indeed claimed that Nissan looked to recruit rural workers without industrial experience, because they would be less prone to join a union, and that the company was reluctant to hire African Americans, who were seen as more likely to organize. In addition to efforts to encourage their employees to identify with management, the company also undercut union support by matching the wage levels of organized autoworkers. Executives consequently insisted that their workers did not need the UAW. "Our employees are very happy and the vast majority continue to tell us they don't need a union," commented Jerry Benefield, president of manufacturing at Nissan's Tennessee plant. "Why would somebody want to pay $26 in union dues a month to get what they already have?" For the unions, it was the old problem of nonunion workers "free-riding." "At Nissan, they get the benefits without paying any dues," commented Lynn Agee, the attorney who represented the UAW.

Just before the election, Nissan management also mounted a concentrated campaign against the union, calling employees into group meetings where they were told that the UAW would call them out on strike. Company clips showing UAW leaders promoting their strike defense fund disheartened many Nissan workers, whose $15-an-hour jobs were the best they had ever had. The company also circulated a great deal of antiunion material through the in-plant television network. The UAW's effort to make an issue out of Nissan's foreign ownership also backfired, as many staff insisted on seeing the Detroit-based union, rather than the Japanese company, as the outsider. Managers encouraged these feelings by asserting that if the plant were unionized, the UAW would ensure that its laid-off northern members were given the first preference for jobs. This argument was given credence by the fact that the new Saturn plant in nearby Spring Hill was being staffed with laid-off UAW members from the North. Like southern workers before them, many Nissan staff felt that the union only wanted to organize them in order to protect its members in the North.

Nissan was also strongly supported by the press and public opinion in Rutherford County, where the plant had raised the standard of living considerably. There was no strong history of unionization in the predominantly rural county, and some observers believed that Nissan had deliberately chosen a rural location in order to keep organized labor at arm's length. Many of the Nissan workers had never held industrial jobs before and believed that they could discuss any problems they had with managers. "I just don't think we need people coming in here telling us what to do," commented Claudia Askins on the eve of the vote. "Don't get me wrong. It's not that I don't believe in change. But I'm pretty happy now. I can talk to my managers if I want to, and I just don't see how the UAW coming in here is going to make any change for the better."

These sentiments prevailed, as the union lost the election by a two-to-one margin. The defeat was widely publicized and did little to help the beleaguered labor movement, especially as pictures of procompany workers proudly sporting "Union Free and Proud" T-shirts were broadcast around the nation. "Humiliating" was the *New York Times'* verdict. The loss was significant, because until it occurred most observers had assumed that Japanese auto plants in the United States would be unionized, just as those of the "Big Three" domestic manufacturers were. Previous factories set up by Japanese car makers in the United States had been organized, although these had always been joint ventures with domestic companies and had been located in the heavily unionized Midwestern states. The Nissan defeat established that Japanese facilities in the United States could remain nonunion. In succeeding years, the UAW has been consistently unable to advance any further in Smyrna; in 1997, a lack of support forced it to abort a campaign, and in 2001 it lost a second election by a wide margin.

In the meantime, the southern car industry has continued to expand. In addition to Japanese car companies, German auto makers Mercedes and BMW both opened plants in the South in the 1990s, while in 2000 Nissan announced that it was building a second U.S. facility, this time near Jackson, Mississippi. Two years later, the Korean manufacturer Hyundai selected a site close to Montgomery, Alabama, as the location for its first U.S. plant. Following Nissan's lead, every new plant built in the South has remained nonunion. The growth of the unorganized southern car industry has contributed to the steady decline of the UAW, which hemorrhaged members throughout the 1980s and 1990s. Between 1978 and 1991, for example, the autoworkers' union, once a symbol of union power, lost 659,000 members.

While union members across the South were suffering defeats, a few were able to fight back successfully against management offensives. In the mid 1980s, workers at BASF's large chemical plant in Geismar, Louisiana, retaliated when the German company locked them out of their jobs. Representatives from the Oil, Chemical, and Atomic Workers' Union initiated a wide-ranging corporate campaign that raised many questions about BASF's environmental record, successfully utilizing workers' knowledge of past malpractice at the plant. After more than five years, the company ultimately settled with the union, abandoning most of the concessions it had originally sought. In 1990, members of the United Steelworkers in Ravenswood, West Virginia, also effectively resisted efforts by Ravenswood Aluminum Corporation (RAC) to gut their contract.

Both the Ravenswood and BASF workers succeeded through a combination of grassroots militancy and broad-based corporate campaigns that were effective at creating negative publicity for multinational companies. Both also effectively reached out to international allies, taking their disputes well beyond the plant gates. BASF workers forged bonds with environmentalists in West Germany, while Ravenswood activists worked closely with European unions. Finding that RAC was actually owned by a company controlled by corporate rogue Marc Rich, who had fled to Switzerland for tax evasion and was America's most-wanted white-collar criminal, the United Steelworkers sent delegations to Switzerland, where they protested outside Rich's corporate headquarters, and to London, where they picketed at industry conventions. BASF workers, meanwhile, disrupted the chemical giant's stockholders' meetings in Germany and brought members of the German Green Party to protest in Louisiana. Along the chemical corridor between Baton Rouge and New Orleans, where around a quarter of all U.S. petrochemicals were produced, the union and local environmentalists raised residents' concerns about industrial pollution. Highlighting that the BASF plant handled similar chemicals to the Union-Carbide facility in Bhopal, India, where a 1984 leak had killed over 3,500 people, they claimed that there was a danger of a "Bhopal on the Bayou." Activists also raised questions about the area's high cancer rate, even putting up billboards along the local interstate that claimed that the chemical corridor was in fact a "Cancer Alley." Both disputes highlighted that organized labor was still a fighting force in the region, yet they also showed that unions needed to be innovative, determined, and persistent in order to fight back effectively.

Another key element in the success of both the Ravenswood and BASF groups was the support of women for their male partners. In both locations, women organized support groups for the predominantly male workers that were particularly active in presenting the unions' case to a broader audience and securing community support. The support groups expressed the fighting determination of both sets of workers, who refused to give up despite the heavy odds stacked against them. "No matter what they did," commented a wife of a Ravenswood employee, "we always came back with another program." In an epic struggle against the Pittston Corporation in Virginia, miners' wives and other female relations also organized themselves into a ladies' auxiliary that fed strikers, walked the picket lines, and traveled across the country raising money.

Women also showed that they were willing to fight for their rights within the workforce. In 1990, female staff at the Delta Pride Company, a Mississippi-based catfish producer, successfully organized a union to deal with complaints of unhealthy working conditions and sexual harassment. In the 1980s, white farmers in Mississippi's Delta increasingly turned to raising catfish rather than cotton and other traditional crops. The industry grew rapidly, and by the early 1990s the Magnolia State produced over 600 million factory-farmed fish a year. The fish were processed in huge facilities where workers faced many of the same problems as their counterparts in the burgeoning poultry plants, particularly fast-paced, repetitive labor and overbearing managers.

Workers at the Delta Pride plant, who were predominantly African American, stood in ankle-deep water and skinned twenty fish a minute. "I was only supposed to skin 12 fish a minute," recalled Sarah White, "but they would whoop and holler at you to do as many as you could. I would do 20 a minute—that's the speed they wanted us at. If you only did 16 or 17 a minute, they would call you in and write you up." When workers developed repetitive strain injuries, the company fired them. Tied to the relentless production line, staff also found it difficult to even make trips to the restroom. "We would ask to go to the bathroom, and they would make us wait for an hour," explained White. "Then they would come inside the bathroom and holler at us that our time was up."

White took a leading role in organizing a union, and when managers resolutely refused to sign a contract, she helped lead her colleagues out on strike. Like other food processing companies, Delta Pride vigorously fought the union, firing leading activists and recruiting a black leader to preach against organized labor. On one occasion, executives even escorted $180,000 of cash into the plant in an armored truck and told workers that this was what the union would cost them in dues. Resisting these threats, more than 900 Delta women walked out, initiating the largest-ever strike by black female workers in Mississippi. As managers still refused to buckle, they followed this up by launching a boycott of the company's products that hurt profits. As was the case in other contemporary union victories, a corporate campaign coordinated by the United Food and Commercial Workers' Union (UFCW) was crucial in securing a settlement, as it attracted negative publicity for Delta Pride and hurt its sales. Workers were overjoyed when management finally recognized their union. "You talking about proud," noted White, "you talking about filled with joy—to see for once that we could stand together and fight this company." The Delta Pride victory proved difficult for the UFCW to replicate, however. Few workers were able to resist company pressure as well as the Delta Pride group, many of whom had gained experience of activism in the civil rights movement, and the union itself could not afford to run such expensive corporate campaigns very often.

In the 1980s, unions across the country were hit particularly hard by the decline of manufacturing industries, which resulted in their members being laid off. Although media images of industrial decline focused heavily on the northern "Rustbelt," the South was not spared plant closures. In fact, many of the so-called Sunbelt industries that had located in the region because of its low wages and "positive business climate" now moved onto developing countries for the same reasons. They were encouraged by policy shifts, particularly the creation of export processing zones within countries such as Taiwan, Mexico, Singapore, Hong King, and the Philippines. These zones offered multinational companies tax, labor, and environmental concessions to enable them to assemble goods for export. Initially, low-skill industries such as garments and electronics began to assemble their goods in these zones, but manufacturers of auto parts and electrical goods soon followed them. A study by sociologists John Gaventa and Barbara Ellen Smith highlights the representative case of a seat belt manufacturer that moved from Michigan to Tennessee in 1965 in search of cheaper wages. In the early 1980s, the company invested heavily in a rural, nonunion plant in a cheaper part of the South (rural Alabama), before relocating to Mexico, where assembly line staff were paid around one-sixteenth of the amount awarded to southern workers for the same job.

Decline was particularly evident in the industry that had for so long been the bulwark of the southern economy. Between 1970 and 1985, 155,000 jobs were eliminated in the U.S. textile industry, the bulk of which was located in the South. In the major textile state of North Carolina, employment in the industry dropped by 28 percent between 1973 and 1986. While many industries were hit by rising foreign competition in these years, the textile industry was particularly affected because it was labor intensive. Small capital outlays were required to start mills, and they could employ cheap labor. These features appealed to industrializing countries just as they had to New South developers after the Civil War. Developing countries also viewed their textile industry as the cornerstone of their industrialization effort and vigorously protected it through tariffs, quotas, and even import bans. Between 1973 and 1985, textile imports more than doubled, and by the end of the 1980s they claimed around a third of the market.

Some U.S. textile-makers responded to competition by investing heavily in new machinery in a brave effort to compete. By the end of the 1980s, productivity growth in textiles exceeded that in all other manufacturing industries. In the early 1980s, Burlington Industries spent around $200 million a year on capital improvements, with $70 million being used on overhauling its plant in the small town of Erwin, North Carolina, located about forty miles south of Raleigh. The investment was specifically designed to fend off foreign competition. "The only way the textile industry can survive," commented a Burlington manager, "is to be the best and most productive. Modernization is to stay ahead of both our statewide competition, but even more to stay ahead of competition worldwide." The company installed robots to carry out lifting jobs and high-speed shuttleless looms to improve productivity. The changes meant that older staff entered a workplace radically different from the old cotton mills they had first toiled in. At Erwin, workers now monitored control panels, and even the plant's dated first aid kit had been replaced by four registered nurses. "It's right much different than what we had way back," commented Bennett Blackmon, who had been an Erwin employee since 1947.

Despite the industry's optimism, these efforts to increase productivity often only delayed plant closings, as eventually the cheaper labor costs available to overseas producers gave them a compelling advantage in a highly competitive industry. In 1985, an American textile worker earning $6.71 an hour made more than thirty-three times the amount paid to their Chinese counterpart, who earned just 20 cents an hour. In addition, an increasingly automated production process could de-skill textile jobs, allowing developing producers to buy advanced machinery and operate it efficiently with newly hired staff. "They can go from zero to our quality without training—by buying equipment," related one U.S. textile machinery producer. "That's the key. They can hire a girl off the street and she'll do as well at a tenth the cost as someone who's been doing it for 20 years." Despite its extensive modernization program, employment at Burlington's plants, like that at the other leading textile companies, gradually fell over the course of the 1980s and 1990s.

Rather than trying to beat foreign competition, other companies responded by moving production to cheaper sites overseas. In the South, this trend began before the 1980s and was pioneered by apparel producers, although staple textile manufacturers soon followed suit. Item 807 of the 1963 United States Tariff Code was particularly important in driving this change, because it allowed U.S. apparel companies to cut the cloth for their garments in the United States but then export it to a factory abroad where it would be assembled. The American clothing manufacturer would then import the finished items, paying duty only on the value added, or the cost of the labor required to assemble the garment. Beginning in the late 1960s, Item 807 encouraged a gradual relocation of apparel plants to developing countries where labor costs were much lower. When the code was introduced, only 2.5 percent of clothing sold in the United States was imported, but twenty years later this figure had catapulted to 57 percent and it continued to rise in subsequent years. By the end of the twentieth century, such was the movement of U.S. apparel manufacturers abroad that it was becoming increasingly difficult to find American-made clothing in major retail stores.

Workers and union leaders did make efforts to stop the hemorrhaging of jobs. In the mid-1980s, ACTWU activists coordinated protests at several retail stores where they filled up their trolleys with imported clothing and then "forgot" their credit cards at the cash register. Union attempts to encourage the buying of American-made textiles were supported by sections of the industry, who launched a promotional campaign with the logos "Crafted with Pride in the USA" and "Made in the USA: It Matters!" Such efforts failed to halt the apparel industry's decline, as most consumers opted for the lower prices offered by foreign-made goods. Between 1972 and 1990, the number of apparel workers in the United States declined by 30 percent.

Plant closings created new obstacles for union organizers, as they gave a new legitimacy to companies' oft-repeated threats to close organized facilities. In many towns, rumors spread, encouraged by manufacturers, that organized labor was causing the mills to shut down by forcing up wage costs. Commented one resident of Dalton, Georgia, where the Crown Cotton Mills had earlier shut its doors, "Well, a lot of people give the union credit for the mill closing down." In 1985, the insecure status of the industry also hindered ongoing efforts to organize Cannon Mills in Kannapolis. David Murdock, a California financier, had recently bought the company, and the union hoped that the ending of the Cannon family's involvement would encourage workers to place their future with organized labor. ACTWU brought in twelve organizers and spent over $150,000 on the campaign, yet Murdock responded by claiming that the cost of a union contract would force him to sell. Relying on an antiunion law firm, the company displayed posters with a picture of a padlocked gate, but assured workers that if they rejected the union, their economic future would be secure. Employees reacted by heeding Murdock's advice, but only a few weeks later, the financier still sold 80 percent of Cannon to Fieldcrest Mills. At the same time, many other textile companies changed hands or merged with one another, adding to workers' fears of job loss. Between 1983 and 1988, the number of major, publicly held textile companies in the United States fell from fifteen to three, the result of mergers or selective plant closures and sales.

Over the course of the 1990s, southern textile mills shut down at a steady pace. In the major textile state of North Carolina, employment in the textile and apparel industries fell from around 300,000 in 1989 to little more than 200,000 a decade later. Inexpensive imports took their toll, claiming many mills that had survived earlier crises such as the Great Depression. In 1996, for example, the South's oldest textile mill became a victim of the textile industry's decline. Rocky Mount Mills in Rocky Mount, North Carolina, which was built in 1818 and operated through the Civil War, finally closed its doors, blaming fierce competition and poor retail sales. "It was a business decision but a very agonizing one," reflected John M. Mebane Jr., the firm's fifth-generation president.

The textile industry's decline was particularly rapid in the late 1990s and in the early years of the twenty-first century. Between 1997 and 2002, 236 textile plants shut down in the Carolinas alone, at the cost of 75,000 jobs. By the start of the new millennium, many textile communities had become ghost towns full of abandoned factories and crumbling houses, images of decline more typically associated with the northern Rustbelt. "Padlocked gates and knee-high grass surround many of the textile mills that were the lifeblood of this region for much of this last century," noted the *Charlotte Observer*. Many of the leading textile companies—Burlington Industries, Cone Mills, Fieldcrest-Cannon—were hit just as hard as smaller firms. The business pages of the nation's press reported a steady stream of layoffs and plant closings by even the largest firms. In January 1999, for example, Burlington closed seven southern plants, laying off 2,900 workers, or 17 percent of its workforce. The company blamed the surge of low-price imports from Asia for the move, yet this was not the whole story. As labor leaders bemoaned, some companies were also clearly using the North American Free Trade Agreement (NAFTA) to take advantage of Mexico's cheap labor supply and lax labor laws. In December 2000, for example, Cone Mills shut down a fabric plant in South Carolina and at the same time expanded its Mexican operations, where its famous Wrangler products were now made. Around the same time, fabric maker Guilford Mills also closed its North Carolina mill and expanded its operations in Tampico, Mexico.

Workers left behind by plant closings struggled to find comparable jobs. Many textile and apparel plants were located in small towns where they had been the main employer. For years, these companies had tried to keep higher-wage firms from locating in the area, as this would have pushed up wages and made it more difficult to recruit employees. Now, however, the economic dominance of textile companies only exacerbated the impact of plant closures, as laid-off staff often faced unemployment and underemployment that led to increased levels of home foreclosures and stress. As one 1991 study of mill closures by a trio of North Carolina–based sociologists concluded: "A reduced standard of living, forced migration, and the breakdown of rural communities are now the legacy of a capitalist industrialization process that once promised to create a New South." Due to a loophole in the law, redundant textile workers also did not receive special federal benefits such as extended unemployment compensation and help in relocating and retraining. To qualify for special trade adjustment assistance, the U.S. Labor Department had to certify that the affected jobs had been lost because of imports. Because most former textile employees had made yarn rather than finished products, they lost out, while thousands of laid-off steel, auto, shoe, and coal workers received the benefits.

Mill closures created pockets of high unemployment in parts of the South that had been heavily reliant on the textile industry. In textile-dependent areas such as Cleveland County, North Carolina, located about an hour west of Charlotte, laid-off staff vainly searched for work. Unable to break the habits of a lifetime, some continued to rise at five in the morning, ready to start the first shift in the mill. As laid-off mill worker Bessie Littlejohn explained, "You walk to the door, you stand in the door with a cup of coffee and a cigarette, and you ask yourself, 'Where do I go from here?' But no answer comes." As opportunities in textiles contracted, many found themselves working in low-paid service sector jobs with few benefits. By the end of the 1990s, some had concluded that retraining in another industry was their best option of securing better-paid work. "I'll find something else," commented laid-off worker Buddy Williams. "But I'll never take another job in textiles. There's no future in it—not when you can get someone to work for under a buck an hour." Watching other plants close their doors, those left in the vulnerable industry were understandably nervous. "I'm still getting a forty-hour week," explained one, "but it's very scary to see everything closing down around us." Even plants that did not shut often gave their staff reduced hours; yet some workers, unwilling to leave towns where they had lived all their lives, refused to quit their unstable jobs but coped by growing more of their own food and saving carefully.

Across the region, textile plant closings had a particularly harsh impact on those in their late fifties and early sixties. This older generation had planned on staying in the mills until they retired and found it very difficult to contemplate a career change. "I don't have any idea what I'll do," commented Doris Cockrell, a sixty-one-year-old Burlington employee who was laid off in 1999. "I thought I would stay here until I retired." Most older staff had only ever worked in the textile mills and struggled to come to terms with the industry's rapid decline. "It's just been textiles," commented sixty-two-year-old JoAnn Bowen, who was laid off from a Shelby, North Carolina, mill. "It's all (I've) ever (known)." Older workers found it most difficult to convince new employers to take them on, but they still lacked a sufficient income to enable them to retire completely. "The bad part about it," explained one, "was when the mill closed down, so many people were caught too old to get a job and not old enough to get social security." Many also worried about losing their health insurance, as private health plans were very expensive for those relying on unemployment benefits. "All the money you saved for retirement, you see it going away pretty fast," added another.

The textile slump changed the South's industrial landscape, as mills that had been landmarks were either demolished or stood empty and neglected. A few were converted into residential or retail units, a move that was most viable in prosperous areas with a growing population. In central

Atlanta, the large Fulton Bag mill became quality apartments, while in the booming research triangle area of North Carolina, Erwin Mill in Durham was converted into both housing and offices, while the Alberta Mill in Carrboro became a shopping mall. Many mills, however, were located in small, isolated towns where such conversion was unlikely to work, especially as there were few customers willing to rent pricey mill apartments or office lofts. In towns such as Great Falls, South Carolina, located well away from any major centers, run-down mills stood largely forgotten.

Even when they were located closer to growing centers, many mills were simply too big, too old, and too costly to renovate. In 2002, the *Charlotte Observer* reported that empty textile factories were causing headaches for city planners across the Carolinas. "There is not a big market now for four-storey, turn-of-the-century textile plants," commented Sam Bennett, city manager of Clinton, South Carolina, located in the heart of the state's old textile belt. Rather than being the economic lifeblood of communities, the textile mills were now viewed as a burden by local leaders. In a range of Piedmont towns, the vacant industrial buildings were decreasing property values and hindering efforts to redevelop downtown areas. "These abandoned plants are a huge liability to our community," concluded the mayor of Anderson, South Carolina.

In many areas, plant closures had a particularly cruel impact on African Americans who had struggled to secure good-paying jobs in manufacturing industries only to find these plants closing down just a few years later. "Once they got most of this stuff [segregation] straightened out," commented one, "they shut the factory down." Urban blacks were often the worst affected, as in cities such as Memphis and Birmingham African American communities had frequently grown up around industrial plants and were heavily reliant on them for employment. In the 1980s, a string of large plants in Memphis shut their doors, including the Firestone plant, one of the city's largest employers until its closure in 1983. As was the case elsewhere, new industry in the Memphis area increasingly located in suburban locations, bypassing inner-city neighborhoods. "There's nothing coming into Memphis at all," explained Hillie Pride, a former Firestone worker. "People are desperate since they cut out all of the plants like Firestone. No women's work, nothing for them to do. They cut out bingo and the horse track, too. There's nothing here anymore. We're just sitting here. You can't make a dime, no kind of way."

In the 1980s and 1990s, the economic progress of the southern black community as a whole was mixed. As the headlines often captured, some

African Americans did secure access to white-collar jobs. In cities such as Atlanta and Charlotte, a growing black middle-class developed, taking advantage of the removal of legal discriminatory barriers to build successful careers in business, law, and government services. At the same time, however, a parallel black underclass also grew, and despite the successes of a high-profile minority, blacks as a whole remained underrepresented in the best-paying white-collar jobs. Data collected by the Southern Regional Council highlighted that racial discrimination in employment continued to be worse in the South than in other regions, with southern blacks still the most likely to be excluded from traditionally white jobs. In 1988, 31.9 percent of all blacks in the American workforce were now employed in what the SRC classed as high-skill or high-status occupations, but in South Carolina this figure was only 17.6 percent, the lowest in the nation. Other southern states clustered at the bottom of the rankings.

Anecdotal evidence collected by the SRC confirmed that well-qualified African Americans, especially women, were still finding it difficult to secure jobs commensurate with their training. In the late 1980s, Deborah Abdullah, for example, was in the final stages of a degree in gerontology and tried to get a job as a nurse's aide in Atlanta. Employers repeatedly rebuffed her efforts. "They just said, 'We'll call you when something opens up in the laundry,'" she noted. Following continual setbacks, Abdullah eventually moved back to her home state of Arkansas, where she secured a job paying just $4.50 an hour.

Despite lingering black poverty, conservative politicians increasingly argued that there was no longer any need for affirmative action. During the Republican presidencies of the 1980s, the federal government weakened its commitment to equal employment opportunity, with both Ronald Reagan and George Bush frequently criticizing "racial quotas." Reagan also forced the resignation of liberal members of the U.S. Civil Rights Commission, appointing a conservative black opposed to affirmative action as chair. Nationally, black poverty actually increased in the 1980s, a consequence of deindustrialization, economic downturns, government policies, and the rise in the number of one-parent black families headed by women. Many of these black poor lived in the South, either in inner cities or in the countryside. In 1990, one-third of all African Americans were estimated to be living below the poverty line.

Many blacks who lived in southern cities were only able to find employment through labor pools where they were assigned casual work on a daily basis. Prospective staff showed up at the labor halls around 5 a.m.

and usually ended up with around $20 for a day's work, after deductions. Many of these workers cleaned the new office blocks and shopping malls that were springing up in the increasingly prosperous southern cities such as Atlanta and Houston. Despite the poor pay and conditions, the labor pool staff felt powerless to protest. "He (the pool owner) makes more money than you do to go out and do all the work," noted one. "They just pull all they can get out of you in a day." "To be honest, temporary service ain't nothing but a tossover from slavery," observed John Zachery, one of the few black owners of a labor pool. "It's flesh peddling. They modify it and dress it up some. But it's slavery. The difference is you pay today. Back in slavery time you told them what to do and gave them some grits and hog jowl. I'm just telling like it is."

The labor pool employees, like many working southerners, found that although they had jobs, they struggled to meet their bills and survive. They were part of the "working poor," a group that was disproportionately concentrated in Dixie. Throughout the 1980s and 1990s, southern workers in both the manufacturing and service sectors continued to be among the worst paid in the nation, a reflection of the region's history of low wages and weak labor unions. In 1988, for example, no southern state paid its manufacturing workers above the U.S. average, and Mississippi, Arkansas, North Carolina, South Carolina, and Alabama were all placed in the bottom ten. Earning around half the amount of their counterparts in the highest-paying northeastern states, workers in Mississippi consistently received the lowest wages in the nation. While the Magnolia State was a striking example, it was not unique, as many southerners labored in jobs that paid little more than the minimum wage and failed to provide health care coverage. "Today's poor aren't just the ones out on the street; it's the people working hard trying to make a decent living," noted Jennifer Morris, a single mother from Arkansas who endured low wages and irregular work. "I wish there was something that could be done to make it just a little bit easier. It seems like sometimes it's not worth it to work." Countless southern workers faced a constant struggle to survive, often living on credit and becoming, in the words of one, "Olympic champions in bill juggling." Many were only able to make ends meet by working long hours, often in more than one job.

Many of the jobs that were available were poorly paid positions in the burgeoning service sector. Jobs in retail stores and fast-food restaurants were plentiful, but they were also low-paying and offered few fringe benefits. Many laid-off manufacturing workers found jobs at Wal-Mart, the retail giant that expanded rapidly across the South in the 1980s and 1990s. In North Carolina, for example, the number of Wal-Mart stores grew from just two in 1986 to seventy-nine in 1993. In 1994, workers at Wal-Mart started on around $5.50 an hour, only $1.25 above the minimum wage, meaning that after taxes they received little more than they would get from unemployment benefits. The majority of the company's workers were part time, but only full-time employees received health insurance. Many took jobs at the firm, however, because they hoped for promotion through the ranks or because they recognized that they had few alternatives available. By 1994, Wal-Mart employed over half a million workers. Managers were keen for their "associates" to identify with the company, and prospective staff members were screened carefully to ensure their "loyalty." Like most retail companies, Wal-Mart was fiercely antiunion and fought organizing efforts, especially in the South. Until his death in April 1992, the company's expansion was overseen by founder Sam Walton, a native of Arkansas who laid down the firm's philosophy of strict cost containment. By 1991, Wal-Mart was already America's largest retailer, and the company's rapid growth showed no signs of slowing as the twenty-first century began. As the *New York Times* commented in February 2000, "the juggernaut is only gaining speed."

In the 1980s and 1990s, many workers also found that the content of their jobs changed a great deal, especially as machines carried out many tasks previously performed by hand. Many white-collar employees faced particularly big changes as computers were introduced on a widespread basis. Most acknowledged that the new machines allowed them to complete more work in less time. According to Atlanta secretary Jackie Marshall, "You get a whole lot done in half the time we used to do it, much more faster." The increased capability of computers also worried workers, however, who often viewed the new machines as a way of increasing workloads and cutting the number of staff. Many also griped that they were not rewarded for learning how to master the technology. "It doesn't add anything to our pay," complained one North Carolina secretary who had "had it out with the manager" about not being paid for learning the computer.

In addition, many workers complained that they were often not provided with sufficient training when computers were introduced. Overtime, staff also blamed the machines for a variety of health complaints, including repetitive strain injuries and eye problems. Peggy Davenport, an official with the emerging office workers' Nine-to-Five organization, summed up the mixed feelings that many office staff had toward computers: "They're great for storing material and getting your information out. But the health problems that people suffer from is what employers tend to just sweep under the rug and say, 'Well, that's just her. She's a grouch anyway,' because a lot of the problems that people have with them are like with the leg pains, back pains, headaches, blurred vision. There was this one lady who told this horror story who worked in a large insurance company here said she had to wait for thirty minutes every day after she got off work before she could go home because it took that long for her eyes to adjust. She couldn't see. And she had no provisions for eye exams on her job. Her boss would just say, 'Oh, well, you'll get over it.'"

Across the country, the introduction of computers also allowed an increasing proportion of Americans to work from home. Eliminating commuting time at a stroke, working from home also made it much easier for many employees to balance their career and family commitments. By 1993, there were an estimated 6.6 million telecommuters in the United States as a whole. Many, like contract workers for Washington-based companies who worked out of homes in Virginia, credited the practice with allowing them to spend more time with their family, yet telecommuting could also be isolating and could cause resentment from coworkers who suspected their colleagues of having an easier time. Telecommuting also sometimes produced complaints from spouses who wanted a clearer delineation between employment and recreation.

In the 1980s and 1990s, a growing proportion of southern workers were Latino immigrants. The Hispanic population began to increase in the 1980s, but it was in the 1990s that the bulk of migrants followed the paths established by the earlier pioneers. From 1980 to 1995, the Latino population in Georgia rose by 130 percent, while in the Atlanta area alone the number of Latinos increased by 260 percent between 1982 and 1992. In North Carolina, the U.S. Census Bureau estimated that the Latino community had grown at the third fastest rate in the nation over the course of the 1990s. Although the number of undocumented immigrants made it difficult to give exact statistics, well over 400,000 Hispanics were thought to be living in the Tarheel State by the end of the decade.

Several southern industries led the way in hiring increasing numbers of Latinos. Starting in the 1980s, the expanding carpet factories in Dalton, Georgia, relied on Latino immigrants to overcome the effects of a tight labor market. By 1997, almost 40,000 Hispanics were living in the Dalton area. In the space of a decade, Hispanics became a significant presence in

Dalton; in the textile city's schools, for instance, the proportion of Latino pupils shot up from 4 percent in 1989 to 42 percent in 1998. Latinos similarly played an increasingly important role in the construction industry, particularly in larger cities such as Atlanta, Houston, and Nashville. Across the South, Latino immigrants also found work in food processing plants, particularly in the poultry industry. In the late 1980s, Latinos began to be hired in large numbers by the giant Tyson Foods Company, based in northwest Arkansas. By the turn of the century, about three-quarters of Tyson's employees were Hispanic. Across the region, other Latino immigrants toiled as migrant agricultural laborers, their movements dictated by the cycles of the crops. By the mid 1980s, more than 30,000 migrants cultivated Georgia's peanuts, soybeans, grains, and cotton, replacing whites and African Americans who had often left the land in search of jobs in urban areas.

Wherever they worked, the new immigrants emphasized that they were drawn to the South in search of economic improvement. "Many people, well, we all come here to this country to progress and to make more money, or to earn more money," commented one Latino in North Carolina. Immigrants left behind countries where wages were a fraction of those in the United States. Spotlighting this, some migrants were college graduates who nonetheless took assembly line jobs because they could earn more in these positions than they could as professionals in their homeland.

By the late 1990s, Latino immigrants were a vital part of the southern economy. Increasingly dependent on the recent arrivals, employers and their allies often turned a blind eye to immigration requirements. In Georgia, so many Latino immigrants worked harvesting the state's Vidalia onions that when officials from the Immigration and Naturalization Service (INS) raided the fields, Georgia's senior senator flew down from Washington to work out a truce allowing the harvest to be completed. Referring to the Latino laborers, one elderly Georgia farmer commented, "it looks like the big farmers can't hardly get along without 'em." In the growing poultry industry, Hispanic immigrants quickly became vital because they were willing to do jobs that most native southerners refused. As one plant supervisor in Gainesville, Georgia quipped, "If there weren't Latino workers, nobody in America would be eating chicken." In a wide range of industries, in fact, Latinos took low-paying jobs that companies were finding it increasingly difficult to fill. According to Melvin Wilson, the vice president of furniture maker Hickory Chair, "It's saving some of these guys (manufacturers) around here. There is no pool of people to fill these jobs. The Latino folks have provided the bodies to do that." By the 1990s, textile manufacturers who had previously praised the qualities of native-born southern workers were now describing Mexicans in similar terms as a "godsend" and as the "lifeblood" of the industry, as these recent arrivals had allowed manufacturers to cut wages and improve productivity.

Although Latinos often carried out undesirable jobs that employers were finding it hard to fill, local residents did not always accept them as easily as employers had. In Dalton, some local people complained that Mexican immigrants were taking jobs from them in the local carpet mills. In letters to the press, disgruntled residents claimed that Latino immigrants were not assimilating enough and were not sufficiently "American," while in the schools the entry of large numbers of Latino students led some white parents to complain that the education of their own children was being neglected. Across the South, some landlords refused to accept Latino tenants, pushing them to live in run-down mobile home parks that themselves attracted complaint. Raquel Cervantes, a Mexican immigrant to North Carolina, claimed in a 1996 interview that local people viewed Latinos with suspicion. "We are always seen with mistrust," she asserted.

This mistrust was especially evident in Morganton, North Carolina, a small community in the western part of the state. In the mid 1990s, residents complained when a Latino immigrant tried to open a bodega, claiming that it would cause traffic and crime problems. A member of the Morganton Board of Adjustments, which rejected the variance request for the store, admitted that, "Some people in Morganton are frightened by the Latinos that have moved in. They talk differently, act differently and eat differently." In Siler City, a small town in central North Carolina where the number of Latino immigrants rose from just 200 in 1990 to an estimated 2,000 to 3,000 five years later, some locals also resented the influx. "We got a bunch of people who hate them," commented one man to a visiting journalist. A 1996 poll conducted by the University of North Carolina at Chapel Hill revealed that these views were quite typical, as 41 percent of respondents felt that the influx of Latinos was bad for the state, compared to 24 percent who viewed it as a positive development. The rest gave mixed responses.

African American communities had a particularly ambiguous reaction toward the new arrivals. The two groups sometimes competed for low-wage jobs and low-rent housing, causing tension. Some African Americans indeed complained that Latinos were moving ahead too fast and leaving the black community behind. "Send them back to where they came from," commented one anonymous North Carolina woman to a roving reporter. Other African Americans, however, were more sympathetic. "They're doing them just like they did us," commented a resident of Siler City. "They treated us like dogs. They can't get by with that now, but they'll get by with as much as they can."

Latino workers themselves often found it very difficult to adjust to life in the South. The language barrier was their main obstacle, as many expressed frustration with not being able to communicate effectively. In the workplace, immigrants with poor English complained that they were "outsiders" who were given inferior treatment to their English-speaking counterparts. Many were forced to rely on hand signals, demonstrations, or translators in order to communicate at work. Immigrant workers frequently had a strong desire to learn English, but they often found it hard to get to classes because they were too exhausted after finishing their long shifts. Others faced additional barriers to attending classes, such as being unable to drive or finding it hard to understand where the lessons were being held. Many immigrants complained that they were pushed into the worst jobs regardless of their qualifications, and they felt that their legal status made it difficult for them to improve their working conditions. Maria Garcia, who worked at a hog farm and processing plant in Garland, North Carolina, complained that, "'Hispano' is stereotyped as unknowledgeable and relegated to the worst jobs, though they may have knowledge to do other responsibilities." Like Garcia, many Latinos disliked the term "Hispanic," feeling that it encouraged this negative stereotyping and overlooked important cultural differences between the immigrants, who came from a wide variety of different countries.

Latino workers also faced acute difficulties in securing good housing and health care. Housing conditions were particularly poor among migrant agricultural laborers, 90 percent of whom were Latino by the end of the 1990s. An official for the Wage and Hour Division in the southeast explained that most agricultural migrants endured improvised housing that was basic at best. "Not many new facilities are being built," he explained. "Migrants are being housed in barns and abandoned restaurants or old tenant farmhouses where there are no waste facilities or water." In North Carolina, for example, migrant farm workers were usually housed in work camps consisting of trailers, old farmhouses, and renovated tobacco sheds. In Long County, Georgia, meanwhile, investigators found fifty migrant laborers living in a run-down barbecue restaurant. Federal policy often bolstered the growers' position, however, especially as workers, and not employers, were the ones most likely to be punished for violating immigration law. As had been the case throughout the post–World War II era, the threat of deportation prevented many migrant agricultural workers from organizing to improve their conditions.

By the mid 1990s, it was clear that the settlement of Latino workers was changing life in the South. In Dalton, Hispanic immigrants had established three Spanish-language newspapers, a radio station, and a soccer complex. Towns near Gainesville, Georgia, which billed itself as the "Poultry Capital of the World," had bilingual churches, restaurants, lawyers, and grocery stores, as well as a regular bus service to Mexico. Some immigrants had bought homes, encouraged by company policies that aimed to reduce turnover in the poultry plants. In many areas, retail stores and car dealers also began to make efforts to attract the growing Latino consumer market. Across North Carolina, Food Lion grocery stores began carrying traditional Latino products labeled in Spanish, while in the town of Hickory the local Chevrolet dealer turned the advertising slogan "Call Ted today!" into "Call Ted hoy!" The church was also very important to many Latino immigrants, who raised the profile of Catholicism in the predominantly Protestant Bible Belt. In 1996, for example, hundreds of Latino Catholics paraded through the town of Clinton in eastern North Carolina to celebrate the feast day of Our Lady of Guadalupe, an important religious holiday. The parade highlighted how the new immigrants were changing the culture in many small southern towns. "The Confederate soldier whose statue stands outside the county courthouse would have been amazed," wrote the Raleigh *News and Observer*. "About 700 people marched past him, dancing and singing in Spanish to the Virgin of Guadalupe."

While many Latinos had limited contact with white southerners, their presence did begin to affect white behavior. "The first Mexicans came to my park in Farmtown about 1984," reflected one owner of a mobile home–rental park in Georgia, "a few years before my husband died. They paid their rent better than the blacks and poor whites I'd been renting to. I liked them and started carrying one or two Mexican children with me to the Baptist church. Now sometimes I take ten or twelve kids with me on Sunday. . . . And some of their customs are even rubbing off on us now— refried beans, for example. The corn tortillas make good dumplings."

Latinos were similarly affected by living in the South. One Mexican interviewed by an anthropologist in the late 1990s had lived in Georgia for twelve years and had picked up the southern dialect, yet he still hoped to return to his homeland one day. "I'm fixin' to go back," he explained, "but I have three kids and I want them to go to school and go to college. But I'd like to die in Mexico."

By the mid 1990s, many Hispanic workers had in fact established roots in the South and realized that they were likely to stay. In 1995, many of those interviewed for a special feature in the *Charlotte Observer* expressed their hopes of staying permanently in the Tarheel State. Mexican immigrant Pedro Barrientos Juarez, who worked at a textile plant in Mount Airy, explained: "My dream is to buy a home. What I like about it here, I came to work. I want to work, and there's work here. There's enough work to work day and night." Across the South, Latino migrants found compelling economic reasons for staying put; they could secure jobs at wages that were higher than they could earn in their own countries, and many of the jobs could be performed without speaking English. According to Jorge Del Pinal, chief of the U.S. Census Bureau's Hispanic Statistics section, "Compared to what they are used to, it's a lot. . . . The language barrier keeps them out of the better jobs, but you don't need English skills to defeather a chicken."

While recognizing the economic advantages of staying in the South, other immigrants still felt a strong emotional pull to their homelands. Many recognized that while they could have a better material standard of living in the United States, they still missed the slower pace of life and strong community bonds that existed at home. "It's a better life there [in Mexico]," claimed one. "Not in an economic way, but the people live more happily there. They live more slowly. You're not in a rush. People have time to go to the street and talk. Somebody in the U.S., you don't even have time to know who your neighbor is."

Latino workers were crucial in fuelling the growth of the poultry industry, which became an increasingly important part of the southern economy in the 1980s and 1990s. By 1994, 84 percent of the broiler chickens produced in the United States came from the southern states. While the industry was important right across the region, Arkansas, Georgia, and Alabama led the way, together producing over 700 million birds each per year. Starting in the 1970s, large producers took over the industry from small scale farmers, setting up highly efficient, vertically integrated operations that hatched the chicks, raised them quickly into birds using scientifically formulated feed, processed them, and marketed the finished product. By this time, poultry complexes could house as many as 100,000 birds, and their efficiencies helped the price of chicken to fall, encouraging the food to become an increasing staple of the American diet. By 1993, over 200,000 people toiled in chicken processing plants, and the industry was one of the fastest growing in the country.

Jobs at poultry plants were hard, as assembly line operators performed monotonous tasks on production lines that processed 40,000 pounds of chicken a day. In 1996, a study by the U.S. Department of Labor found that the incidence of repetitive motion injuries among poultry-processing employees was five times higher than the rate in manufacturing as a whole. Most injured staff soldiered on, deterred from visiting doctors by company insurance policies with deductibles of several hundred dollars. Workers also complained that those who got hurt were fired, making them reluctant to publicize any injuries. In 1997, the Department of Labor also found that 60 percent of surveyed poultry companies were in violation of the federal Fair Labor Standards Act, with over half failing to pay staff for time spent on job-related tasks such as cleaning up. Workers also complained that they were denied breaks during the day and that they had to pay for work clothing, including protective gear. David Segars, an official with the Food and Commercial Workers' Union in Georgia, described working in southern poultry plants as "one of the dirtiest jobs there is." "The days of legal slavery are over," he added, "but I'm not sure it's over in regard to the poultry industry."

Companies themselves defended their record by stressing the difficulties of securing and training a reliable workforce in a highly competitive industry. As one academic who took a job in a Tyson poultry plant discovered, new workers were constantly being hired and received only the most basic training. From the very beginning, the nonunion poultry companies made it clear that they wanted obedient employees who would not challenge their authority; new Tyson staff received their initiation in a classroom that displayed a sign, in English and Spanish, declaring, "Democracies depend on the political participation of its citizens, but not in the workplace."

In September 1991, the poor working conditions in the southern poultry industry were vividly highlighted by a fire at the Imperial Foods plant in Hamlet, North Carolina, that killed twenty-five workers and injured another fifty. On the morning of September 3, a hydraulic line on a deep-fat fryer ruptured, igniting a blaze that swept quickly through the plant.

Like the Triangle Shirtwaist Fire of 1911, which had helped to publicize sweatshop conditions in the Progressive Era, the Hamlet fire had such devastating consequences because the factory owners had locked the doors to guard against theft, just as their counterparts had done eighty years earlier. Many trapped victims died after they were unable to kick down the locked doors. Like the earlier blaze, the Hamlet fire also helped raise public awareness of the poor conditions endured by many low-paid workers.

Emmett Roe, the plant's owner, had originally run poultry plants in the North but had been attracted to the South because he wanted to avoid unions and government regulators. In the 1980s he had opened three southern plants, and unlike his operations in the North, these factories were nonunion. In Roe's main Pennsylvania plant, which he eventually closed in 1989, workers were paid 17 percent more than their counterparts in North Carolina. Roe had also tangled with OSHA inspectors before, with one official claiming that he had "utter contempt" for the federal health and safety agency. Shortly before the Pennsylvania plant was shut, OSHA had fined the poultry operator for safety violations that included blocked exits and electrical cords lying in water.

In Hamlet, Roe also operated with little regard for safety regulations. The fire revealed failings on the part of both state and federal officials, who had allowed locked doors to stay that way despite two earlier fires. In the decade before the 1991 blaze, the number of workplaces in North Carolina increased dramatically but the number of safety inspections fell. Tarheel leaders, like their counterparts in other southern states, were primarily interested in attracting new industry and worried that a restrictive regulatory climate would deter outside investment. Following the disaster, many blamed state Labor Commissioner John C. Brooks for not bringing Roe to task sooner. Brooks, however, claimed that the legislature had not provided enough inspectors, while the legislature responded that the commissioner had not filled many of the jobs that they had funded. In the aftermath of the fire, federal and state officials also tossed allegations back and forth. "Twenty-five people lost their lives here," commented U.S. Representative Pat Roberts, a Kansas Republican. "Everyone is saying 'Not on my watch' to protect thine posterior."

Prior to the fire, some workers had worried about safety, but they were afraid to speak out. "Talking out there is like asking for a bullet in your head," commented one. Work was hard to come by in Richmond County, located an hour east of Charlotte, and the company had never had any problems recruiting staff, even though the jobs only paid around $4.75 an hour and involved monotonous tasks processing pieces of chicken. Much of the work was extremely demanding and accidents were common. In the packing room, for example, workers handled thousands of pieces of frozen chicken on each shift, causing their hands to freeze up. "After your hands had been on that cold product for so long," recalled packing room employee Doris Blue, "they would get numb. It was hard to tell if you got cut. You wouldn't know it sometimes until your hands thawed out." The pace of the line was relentless, and Imperial only allowed its employees to use the bathroom four times a shift, with each visit requiring prior permission. Under the company's "occurrence" policy, which was deeply resented, line operators were punished half an occurrence if they went to the bathroom more often, if they stayed more than five minutes, or if they went without permission. If a worker accumulated five occurrences, they would be fired. Fear of dismissal weighed heavily on Imperial staff and led many to restrict their fluid intake in an effort to avoid bathroom visits.

Following the fire, state investigators called the Imperial Foods plant a "death trap." In all, they found eighty-three safety law violations, including no sprinklers, no fire alarm, and no fire safety plan. Imperial workers had never even had a fire drill and neither federal, nor state, nor local officials had ever looked for fire and safety violations. As a consequence of these findings, Emmett Roe spent four years in prison and was fined $800,000, while the state of North Carolina was prompted to improve its health and safety inspection program. The fire, noted the *Raleigh News and Observer*, "revealed the ugly underside of the state's economy, where poor, unskilled workers afraid of losing their jobs often endure miserable, unsafe working conditions without pushing for change."

Nine years after the fire, its most famous symbol, a steel door stamped with footprints from trapped workers, hung in the Smithsonian Institute in Washington D.C. The disaster had a lasting impact on the small town of Hamlet, where few residents did not have a friend or relation who had worked at the plant. Survivors struggled to deal with what the *News and Observer* called "the disaster's legacy of nightmares and sadness, of bitterness and pain." "I remember this stuff constantly," recalled Gail Pouncy, "every day, every night. I feel like I can't breathe. I go to coughin'. And I get real hot. I feel like I'm burning." "I've never been like this before," explained another former worker, "It's like I'm a nervous wreck." Nearly a decade after the disaster, the plant still stood just outside Hamlet's downtown, but it was now abandoned and neglected. Its adjoining office had been extensively vandalized, with the words "Killers Die, 25 Lives" sprayed on the walls. "You want to know how people feel in the neighborhood?" asked one resident. "You look at that building. They've torn that place apart. Hell, they've made it look worse than the plant itself. . . . That's a pain you can't put into words. You just have to destroy something. Break the windows, tear the paper, write things on the walls." "We have to deal with this each day of our lives," added survivor Conester Williams. "Tear it down. The building should have been down long ago."

The poor working conditions highlighted by the Hamlet fire attracted the attention of unions, who saw the giant poultry plants as another opportunity to try and make ground into the South's nonunion economy. In the mid 1990s, the rapidly expanding poultry industry became the target of a major organizing campaign by the AFL-CIO. "There is a quiet resurgence in organizing," commented Richard Bensinger, executive director of the AFL-CIO's Organizing Institute, "and it is in the South and it is in the poultry industry."

As had been the case before, however, companies successfully resisted these efforts. Unions did secure some successes, such as breakthroughs at two Sanderson Farm plants in Mississippi, but the industry remained overwhelmingly unorganized. High turnover and the vulnerable status of most workers were major obstacles, especially as many recent immigrants were afraid of losing their jobs. Although conditions were poor, the $8-an-hour poultry jobs offered upward mobility for migrants from poor Latin American countries, particularly Mexicans who had left home because of the economic recession of the 1990s. Companies such as Carolina Foods Processing, located about an hour east of Hamlet, also proved successful at intimidating their employees on the eve of labor board elections, telling them that unions brought strikes and discord. As was commonplace in the region, food processing companies made effective use of captive audience meetings to highlight the disadvantages of organized labor, capitalizing on workers' fear of losing their jobs by making it clear that they would simply switch production to unorganized plants if the union was voted in. Like Tyson Foods, the nation's largest poultry company, some firms also responded to organizing efforts by granting wage increases, thus undercutting support for outside representation.

Even when poultry workers did vote for union representation, employers were reluctant to sign contracts. In 1995, a predominantly Guatemalan workforce at Case Farms in Morganton, North Carolina, stuck together and voted a union in, but their managers repeatedly refused to sign a labor agreement. In December 2001, an exhausted international union eventually withdrew from the Case Farms campaign. As was so often the case in the South, a group of workers had fought hard but had been defeated by the many obstacles arrayed against them.

The influx of Latino workers also posed new challenges for unions, who initially struggled to adjust to a different organizing climate. As AFL-CIO southern director Kirk Adams commented in 1997: "Organizing is more diverse now in the South—it's no longer just black and white." In order to reach out effectively to the new arrivals, labor leaders had to overcome the language barrier, as well as their own entrenched fears that immigrants would hurt wage rates. At the same time, union activists also hoped that these new groups might provide them with a breakthrough in the historically nonunion South. "If we reach out to the strong Latino and Asian communities," noted Adams, "who now make up a significant portion of many industries in many parts of the South, we have the opportunity to build coalitions and critical masses."

As the 1990s progressed, labor leaders did have some grounds for optimism. The continued growth of public employee unionism steadily increased the proportion of female and nonwhite union members, and the labor movement as a whole became more responsive to them. By 1996, women made up 37 percent of the AFL-CIO's membership and two out of every three new recruits. In the same year, the newly formed Union of Needletrades, Industrial, and Textile Employees (UNITE) successfully established a beachhead in the retail sector by organizing a Kmart store in Greensboro, North Carolina, after a three-year campaign that was strongly supported by the predominantly African American workforce. There were other positive signs, especially as even employees who were widely viewed as being very difficult to organize occasionally showed an interest in unions. In the summer of 1999, IBM staff in North Carolina's Research Triangle Park posted messages on the Internet supporting organizing efforts and met with union officials. The computer firm's staff was upset over the company's decision to force older employees to shift their pension plan, resulting in a big cut in benefits. "We're just beginning to make some kind of headway into high-tech," declared Communications Workers of America organizer Marilyn Baird.

As veteran labor activists knew only too well, however, in the South it was very difficult to translate union sentiment into lasting institutional gains. Organizing southern plants frequently involved lengthy battles against determined, antiunion executives, meaning that it often took many years and thousands of dollars to win bargaining rights at just one plant. In one telling case, the UFCW took over sixteen years to win bargaining rights at North Carolina's Lundy Packaging Company, and the breakthrough only came after the union was able to exert unusual outside pressure on the company. In 1978 and 1993, the UFCW had lost votes at Lundy, but in 1994 it attracted more support by spotlighting that more than 140 workers had contracted brucellosis, a rare disease, from handling infected hogs slaughtered at the plant. After the case made headlines, North Carolina Senators Jesse Helms and Lauch Faircloth helped to secure the introduction of legislation asking the federal government to buy and kill infected hog herds. The victory at the plant, which employed around 900 workers, was described as "a great day for the South, for the labor movement in the South" by UFCW official Brian Murphy.

In another high-profile case, dogged persistence produced a significant but short-lived victory for organized labor. At the large Cannon Mills in Kannapolis, North Carolina, the union did finally win an election in 1999. Between the mid 1970s and the mid 1990s, textile unions had brought four elections at the Kannapolis plants, losing each one. Given this history of defeat, the 1999 election victory at Cannon was therefore highly symbolic, as well as representing organized labor's largest-ever victory in the textile South. The *New York Times* called it a "Labor Milestone," while UNITE's organizing director proclaimed "it feels like we just organized GM." The breakthrough came after the mills had been purchased by Pillowtex, who abandoned Fieldcrest-Cannon's policy of strident opposition to organized labor. Other causes of UNITE's success were the increasing number of immigrants in the mills and the fact that more workers also supported the union as a protection against increasing workloads. Veteran labor supporters were elated to have finally won. "That was the happiest day of my life," commented Vonnie Hines, who had been trying to organize southern textile workers since the 1970s. "That one victory made up for every year, and every campaign that I went in and we lost," added a rank-and-file activist. "That one night, that one night, made up for all of that." In February 2000, the union did secure a contract with the mills' new owners, but economic insecurity continued to hang over the textile town. In the summer of 2003, workers' worst fears were realized when Pillowtex liquidated the entire site, throwing 3,400 people out of work. It was the largest layoff in North Carolina history, and it left workers economically and psychologically devastated.

In perhaps the best example of union persistence, in 2001 the United

Steelworkers finally organized the Pilkington glass plant in Laurinburg, North Carolina, at the twelfth attempt. USW activists claimed that they had managed to sign up a majority of workers in some of these earlier drives, but the company had scared off these supporters with preelection propaganda. As was the case in the Stevens and Cannon campaigns, the breakthrough came after Pilkington executives finally relented in their opposition and signed a truce agreement. The victory was widely celebrated, but as was the case at Cannon, Stevens, and Lundy, labor leaders had been pushed to expend vast resources in order to organize just one plant. As such, these gains did not offer a blueprint for successful organizing because unions could not afford to spend so much on every campaign. At Pilkington, the economic future of the plant was also uncertain, and local business leaders complained that the presence of organized labor made it less competitive. "We still don't like unions," commented Jim Frank Henderson, the executive vice president of the local Chamber of Commerce.

Henderson's remark highlights that unions in the South continue to face determined resistance, and the victories that have occurred have not changed these broader patterns. Organized labor in the South remains disproportionately weak, the percentage of unionized private-sector workers in the region consistently lagging behind U.S. averages. Outside of the well-organized public sector, southern unions have declined to a point of near extinction; between 1985 and 1998, for instance, the Bureau of National Affairs estimated that the proportion of unionized private sector southern workers fell from 7.1 percent to just 4.1 percent. In the 1980s and 1990s, there was also evidence of a worrying generation gap between union members, who were often in their forties and fifties, and younger workers who frequently acted as strikebreakers. Union workers valued the seniority protection that they had won in earlier battles, and turnover in many organized plants was low. Working in unorganized industries, the younger generation viewed their older union counterparts as pampered and out-of-touch. During the Ravenswood dispute, young replacement workers expressed open contempt for the locked out union members, whose average age was fifty-two; as they crossed the picket line, many even waved their checks and shouted "Thanks for the job, Grandpa."

The 1992 election of a Democratic president failed to significantly help the labor movement, as Bill Clinton moved the party to the center and proved increasingly unresponsive to union demands. In 1993, the new president ignored opposition to the North American Free Trade Agreement, which labor leaders viewed as a threat to their members' living standards. Even when strikers were permanently replaced in his home state, the Arkansas Democrat gave only lukewarm support to the AFL-CIO's efforts to strengthen the right to strike, underscoring that Democratic presidents were no longer as responsive to a declining labor movement. "All signs are that the White House would be happy to see the issue fade away," noted *Newsweek*. In 1992 and 1994, legislation to restrict the hiring of permanent replacements was passed by the House but was defeated by filibusters in the Senate that were led by southern representatives. Clinton, complained labor leaders, should have done more to quell this opposition, especially by leaning more on politicians from his native region.

Throughout the 1980s and 1990s, labor leaders argued that the threat of permanent replacement undermined unions by making workers fearful of strikes. Even without the threat of permanent replacement, however, the reality was that unions still faced an uphill struggle. The right to organize itself was, as the AFL-CIO's Organizing Director noted in 2000, a "legal fiction." In the 1970s, the J. P. Stevens case highlighted to a national audience that federal labor laws offered little protection to unions if companies were determined to flout them, because it took years for those who were dismissed to be reinstated with back pay. Even if a fired worker was awarded back pay, they could not recover their attorney's fees, whereas companies could deduct the award from their taxes as a legitimate business expense. By the 1990s, many corporate executives referred to NLRB back pay awards as their "hunting license," allowing them to employ an illegal but effective tactic against organizing campaigns. Companies across the United States were now copying the harsh tactics that had been pioneered in the South, ensuring that many workers would have to continue to fight hard to halt organized labor's terminal decline.

Conclusion

At the start of the twenty-first century, southern workers faced many of the same problems as their counterparts in the rest of the United States. Many had recently been laid off from jobs in manufacturing industries, just as their colleagues in the northern Rustbelt had been. From coast to coast, an increasing percentage held jobs in service industries. Work was easy to come by in this growing sector, yet jobs were often low-paying and lacked good benefits. Across the country, only a small minority of workers belonged to unions, and they had watched as the labor movement had steadily lost influence and power. Corporate opposition to organized labor was often fierce outside the South, where many strikers were also permanently replaced in the 1980s and 1990s. Throughout the postwar period, in fact, most American business executives have also been fiercely opposed to organized labor. As H. V. Reid, executive vice president of the Wilmington, North Carolina, Chamber of Commerce declared in 1975, "It's the attitude of the business community all across the country that good management doesn't need a third party (unions)."

In many ways, the behavior of southern white workers was also not very different from their counterparts elsewhere. Across the country, whites often sought to exclude blacks from their unions. Bringing the two groups together, as organizers could testify, was invariably a difficult task. In northern cities, the AFL craft unions had a long history of excluding African Americans, producing frequent complaints from civil rights organizations such as the NAACP. Throughout the twentieth century, southern workers have also consistently shown that they were capable of fighting fiercely for their rights, despite the formidable odds stacked against them.

Despite these similarities, however, a case can still be made for the South's continuing distinctiveness. Throughout the postwar period, the South has been consistently more antiunion than other parts of the United States. Like racism and poverty, both often linked to the region, antiunionism was hardly unique to the South. At the same time, however, southern antiunionism did not abate over the postwar period, and if anything, it actually became more intense. While the region certainly made progress in eliminating racism and poverty, throwing off the Jim Crow system of legal racial segregation and experiencing a faster rate of economic growth than other parts of the country, its resistance to the labor movement remained as unchanging as its fierce summers. "By the end of the 1970s," declares economic historian Bruce Schulman, "anti-unionism had practically replaced racism as the South's signature prejudice."

The South was certainly home to the most antiunion states in the country. Throughout the postwar years, North Carolina was consistently the least unionized of all. In 1984, for example, the state ranked tenth in the nation in the number of nonagricultural workers, but was fiftieth in the percentage of organized workers. Between 1970 and 1984, the Tarheel State maintained its bottom ranking for every year except one, when it was ranked forty-ninth. Antiunionism was written into North Carolina's laws, from its right-to-work act, passed shortly after Taft-Hartley, to a statute specifically forbidding collective bargaining with public employees. At the local level, too, antiunionism often had an official stamp; the Chamber of Commerce in Raleigh, for example, consistently maintained a written policy discouraging unionized industries from locating in one of the fastest-growing parts of the region. "It would be an understatement," noted a state journalist in 1984, "to say North Carolina has been antiunion over the years."

North Carolina is representative of a region that has consistently had the lowest rates of unionization in the country. In 1970, for example, only 15 percent of nonagricultural workers in the South belonged to unions, compared to 28 percent in the rest of the country. A decade and a half later, 17 percent of U.S. manufacturing employees belonged to unions, but in South Carolina this figure was just 3.6 percent. The most unionized states, in contrast, were in the Midwest and northeast, with Michigan and New York leading the way. Textiles, the South's leading employer until the late 1980s, was the only major manufacturing industry that was not heavily organized. Graphically highlighting organized labor's failure in the region, no more than 10 percent of southern textile workers ever held union cards.

Unions also remain a particularly contentious topic in the South. Few subjects provoke such strong reactions from southerners. In 1993, close friends Lori Rushmeyer and Sharon Sturgis related that they simply avoided the topic. "We can talk about a lot of things," declared Rushmeyer. "We can talk about our kids or just about anything else. But one thing we don't talk about is unions. We just don't agree about that." The topic remained particularly controversial in North Carolina. "In some places," noted the Tarheel State's *Greensboro Daily Record*, "if you want to start an argument, you talk about politics or religion. North Carolina has another perennial topic of contention—unions. . . . Scorned as pariahs by employers and many politicians, but seen as a hope for a better life by some workers, unions often seem to strike a raw nerve in this state." Across the region, in fact, even the word "union" is contentious. As one Atlanta worker commented in 1992, "Union in the South is a dirty word."

Throughout the twentieth century, southern management resisted unions with particular ferocity. In many ways, the region's employers led the way in being willing to openly violate the National Labor Relations Act. They used these tactics well before the 1980s, when open attacks on unions became commonplace across the country. In the 1960s, large construction firms such as Daniel and the Texas-based Brown and Root Company showed an increased willingness to violate the NLRA in order to maintain their nonunion status in a largely organized industry. Throughout the 1960s and 1970s, J. P. Stevens took these tactics to a new level, firing and harassing large numbers of union supporters across the region. By the late 1970s, labor leaders alleged that manufacturers were engaged in a "southern conspiracy," a "vast Dixie plot" to keep the region nonunion. Many companies were fighting unionization more than ever, utilizing the services of the growing number of labor consultants and lawyers based in the region. Throughout the postwar era, southern employers, often acting in combination with community allies, also showed a particular willingness to use violence in order to secure their goals.

Some of southern employers' opposition to unionism was clearly ideological. They genuinely disliked organized labor, and the fact that union strength was concentrated in the northern states encouraged them to see labor leaders as outsiders who did not truly understand the South. At the same time, a major part of southern antiunionism was economic. The growth of southern industry, particularly in textiles, had been inextricably linked to lower wages. As studies have shown, a wage differential of between 30 and 50 percent gave southern employers a decisive advantage over their northern counterparts. In the textile industry, for example, the decline of agriculture provided southern mill owners with a large pool of available labor, while the lack of alternative employers further strengthened their hand. In New England, by contrast, mill owners had to compete with other higher-paying industries, and this inevitably put pressure on wage levels. Southern employers clearly had a powerful economic incentive to avoid unionization, and they consistently fought to keep wages down.

The failure of organized labor to establish itself in the region was certainly not a reflection of a lack of effort. Since World War II, unions have made repeated forays into the South, recognizing the region's importance to their overall fate. "Unionization of the South is the most important organizational problem facing the CIO today," noted the CIO Organizing Committee in 1949, "and it is imperative that CIO continue and intensify its Southern drive." Although it achieved very little success, the CIO did carry on with its postwar southern drive until 1953, and even after this labor leaders continued to give a high priority to southern organizing. The failure of their efforts was important because it provided companies a growing region that they could locate in, undercutting the wages of unionized workers in the north. Even in the Sunbelt era, southern legislators and business leaders encouraged this shift by selling the region's low wages as an attraction to outside businesses, helping to ensure that the industrialization of the South has not resulted in the equalization of wage rates. Unionization has indeed been so fiercely resisted in the South partly because many southerners have feared that unions would drive up wages and make the region less attractive to outside investment. In 1963, workers in the apparel industry, which came South after World War II in order to avoid unions and reduce wage costs, earned $1.39 an hour in North Carolina compared to $2.01 an hour in New York. Even in the 1980s southern wages still held steady at around 80–85 percent of those of other regions. A "[c]entury after the New South Crusade began in earnest," notes historian Jim Cobb, "southern wage earners remained the poorest paid, most under-benefited workers in the United States."

In many respects, then, the South still provided a distinctive working environment in the last two decades of the twentieth century. In 1987, for example, seven of the bottom ten states for hourly manufacturing wages were southeastern states. In 1988, only nine U.S. states had not enacted minimum wage laws, and six of them were in the southeast. Southern workers also consistently received the lowest levels of compensation for disability and unemployment and had the highest rates of occupational disease. In addition, southern states consistently made up the largest single area in the United States with right-to-work laws. The SRC, which continued to document working conditions in its native region with impressive detail, claimed in 1988 that the southeastern states had a "dismal record" when it came to providing their employees with good conditions. Many southerners, however, continued to fight to change this, frequently turning to unions despite the vast array of obstacles facing them. Even in recent years, many veterans of the region's bitter labor battles have remained optimistic, insisting that as companies increasingly cut wages and benefits, they would eventually create the need for unions once more. "I think when people are badly enough oppressed, they'll find a way to do it," reflected veteran Memphis activist Clarence Coe, who had fought to establish a union at the city's Firestone tire plant in the 1940s. "And organizing labor is the only way."

Bibliographical Essay

The following bibliographical essay lists the secondary works I most often consulted in preparing this study. I additionally utilized primary archival collections, as well as newspaper clippings and oral history interviews. Details of such sources are provided here, especially for topics where there are few secondary sources available.

Introduction

Since the early 1980s, the field of southern labor history has grown enormously. *Like a Family: The Making of a Southern Cotton Mill World* by Jacquelyn D. Hall, James Leloudis, Robert Korstad, Mary Murphy, Lu Ann Jones, and Christopher B. Daly (Chapel Hill: University of North Carolina Press, 1987) has been particularly influential in challenging the stereotype of the docile southern worker, showing instead how mill workers developed a distinctive culture of their own in the early mill communities. Although not matching the impact of *Like a Family*, other important works published during the 1980s include David L. Carlton, *Mill and Town in South Carolina, 1880–1920* (Baton Rouge: Louisiana State University Press, 1982); Dolores E. Janiewski, *Sisterhood Denied: Race, Gender, and Class in a New South Community* (Philadelphia: Temple University Press, 1985); James A. Hodges, *New Deal Labor Policy and the Southern Cotton Textile Industry, 1933–1941* (Knoxville: University of Tennessee Press, 1986); and Barbara S. Griffith, *The Crisis of American Labor: Operation Dixie and the Defeat of the CIO* (Philadelphia: Temple University Press, 1988).

Since 1990, several scholars have built on these works, producing vivid and informative case studies of textile communities. Examples include Douglas Flamming, *Creating the Modern South: Millhands and Managers in Dalton, Georgia, 1884–1984* (Chapel Hill: University of North Carolina Press, 1992); Daniel J. Clark, *Like Night and Day: Unionization in a Southern Mill Town* (Chapel Hill: University of North Carolina Press, 1997); G. C. Waldrep III, *Southern Workers and the Search for Community: Spartanburg County, South Carolina* (Urbana: University of Illinois Press, 2000); and Michelle Brattain, *The Politics of Whiteness: Race, Workers, and Culture in the Modern South* (Princeton, N.J.: Princeton University Press, 2001). All of these works focus particular attention on the struggle to establish stable unions within small textile communities. In contrast, Michael K. Honey, *Southern Labor and Black Civil Rights: Organizing Memphis Workers* (Urbana: University of Illinois Press, 1993), explores the rise of industrial unionism in the city of Memphis. John A. Salmond, *Gastonia 1929: The Story of the Loray Mill Strike* (Chapel Hill: University of North Carolina Press, 1995), provides a narrative account of a famous southern textile strike. Studies with a state or regional focus include Robin D. G. Kelley, *Hammer and Hoe: Alabama Communists During the Great Depression* (Chapel Hill: University of North Carolina Press, 1990); Bryant Simon, *A Fabric of Defeat: The Politics of South Carolina Millhands in State and Nation* (Chapel Hill: University of North Carolina Press, 1998); and Timothy J. Minchin, *Hiring the Black Worker: The Racial Integration of the Southern Textile Industry, 1960–1980* (Chapel Hill: University of North Carolina Press, 1999).

Among the prizes awarded to works in southern labor history in recent years, Hall et al., *Like a Family*, won the Taft Prize in 1988, while Flamming, *Creating the Modern South*, won the same award in 1993. Kelley, *Hammer and Hoe*, won the Sydnor prize in 1991, and in 1994, Honey, *Southern Labor and Black Civil Rights*, won both the Sydnor Prize and the Rawlins Prize. Despite this extensive scholarship, however, the only synthetic work remains F. Ray Marshall's *Labor in the South* (Cambridge, Mass.: Harvard University Press, 1967), which concentrates largely on the 1930s and 1940s.

Several oral history collections have also explored the experiences of southern workers. Mimi Conway, *Rise Gonna Rise: A Portrait of Southern Textile Workers* (Garden City, N.Y.: Anchor Press/Doubleday, 1979), concentrates on the town of Roanoke Rapids, North Carolina, which is dominated by the J. P. Stevens plants. Utilizing a range of interviews, it focuses a great deal of attention on workers' struggle to organize in the 1960s and 1970s, part of a broader labor campaign to unionize Stevens' plants across the South. Nell Irvin Painter, *The Narrative of Hosea Hudson: His Life as a Negro Communist in the South* (Cambridge, Mass: Harvard University Press, 1979), provides an oral history of a black steelworker and former Communist Party member in Birmingham, Alabama. Oral history forms an important component of Marc S. Miller, ed., *Working Lives: The Southern Exposure History of Labor in the South* (New York: Pantheon Books, 1980). Victoria Byerly, *Hard Times Cotton Mill Girls: Personal Stories of Womanhood and Poverty in the South* (Ithaca, N.Y.: ILR Press, 1986), focuses largely on women's experiences of textile employment and contains some fine material from both black and white women. Michael K. Honey, *Black Workers Remember: An Oral History of Segregation, Unionism, and the Freedom Struggle* (Berkeley: University of California Press, 1999), focuses on African American workers in Memphis, particularly those who worked at the city's Firestone Tire plant.

For collections of essays on southern workers, see Gary M. Fink and Merl E. Reed, eds., *Essays in Southern Labor History: Selected Papers, Southern Labor History Conference, 1976* (Westport, Conn.: Greenwood Press, 1977); Robert H. Zieger, ed., *Organized Labor in the Twentieth-Century South* (Knoxville: University of Tennessee Press, 1991); Gary M. Fink and Merl E. Reed, eds., *Race, Class, and Community in Southern Labor History* (Tuscaloosa: University of Alabama Press, 1994); Robert H. Zieger, ed., *Southern Labor in Transition, 1940–1995* (Knoxville: University of Tennessee Press, 1997); and Glenn T. Eskew, ed., *Labor in the Modern South* (Athens: University of Georgia Press, 2001). All of these works include contributions from leading southern historians and cover a wide range of industries, with particular emphasis on textiles. Philip Scranton, ed., *The Second Wave: Southern Industrialization from the 1940s to the 1970s* (Athens: University of Georgia Press, 2001) is an interdisciplinary work that includes some fine case studies exploring southern industrialization. An excellent summary of the development of southern labor history as a field is provided by Michelle Brattain, "The Pursuits of Post-Exceptionalism: Race, Gender, Class, and Politics in the New Southern Labor History," in Eskew, ed., *Labor in the Modern South*, pp. 1–46.

The emergence of southern labor history as a field is also shown by the publication of articles on southern workers in leading journals. Particularly important are Jacquelyn Dowd Hall, "Disorderly Women: Gender and Labor Militancy in the Appalachian South," *Journal of American History* 73:2 (September 1986), pp. 354–82, which concentrates largely on a 1929 strike in Elizabethton, Tennessee; Bruce Nelson, "Organized Labor and the Struggle for Black Equality in Mobile during World War II," *Journal of American History* 80:3 (December 1993), pp. 952–88, which explores the ship building industry in Mobile, Alabama during World War II, concentrating especially on the racial tensions generated by the rapid expansion of the workforce; and Mary Lethert Wingerd, "Rethinking Paternalism: Power and Parochialism in a Southern Mill Village," *Journal of American History* 83:3 (December 1996), pp. 872–902, a close-grained study of mill workers in Cooleemee, North Carolina. In 1997, the summer issue of the *Georgia Historical Quarterly* was also devoted to southern labor history.

Ph.D. dissertations on southern workers offer compelling insights into southern workers in a range of other industries. They include Robert Rodgers Korstad, "Daybreak of Freedom: Tobacco Workers and the CIO, Winston-Salem, North Carolina, 1943–1950" (Ph.D. dissertation, University of North Carolina at Chapel Hill, 1987); William Powell Jones, "Cutting Through Jim Crow: African American Lumber Workers in the Jim Crow South, 1919–1960," (Ph.D. dissertation, University of North Carolina at Chapel Hill, 2000); Michelle Haberland, "Women's Work: The Apparel Industry in the United States South, 1937–1980" (Ph.D. dissertation, Tulane University, 2001). All of these dissertations include some fine oral history. As this book was being completed, Korstad's dissertation was published as *Civil Rights Unionism: Tobacco Workers and the Struggle for Democracy in the Mid-Twentieth-Century South* (Chapel Hill: University of North Carolina Press, 2003).

For early views of southern textile workers that generally stressed workers' passivity, see Lois MacDonald, *Southern Mill Hills: A Study of Social and Economic Forces in Certain Textile Mill Villages* (New York: Alex L. Hillman, 1928); Sinclair

Lewis, *Cheap and Contented Labor: The Picture of a Southern Mill Town in 1929* (New York: United Textile Workers of America and Women's Trade Union League, 1929); Harriet L. Herring, *Welfare Work in Mill Villages: The Story of Extra-Mill Activities in North Carolina* (Chapel Hill: University of North Carolina Press, 1929); Liston Pope, *Millhands and Preachers: A Study of Gastonia* (New Haven: Yale University Press, 1942); John R. Earle, Dean D. Knudson, and Donald W. Shriver Jr., *Spindles and Spires: A Re-Study of Religion and Social Change in Gastonia* (Atlanta: John Knox, 1976). Wilbur J. Cash's *The Mind of the South* (New York: Vintage Books, 1941) has also proven influential. For a fine review of much of this early literature, see Robert H. Zieger, "From Primordial Folk to Redundant Workers: Southern Textile Workers and Social Observers," in Zieger, ed., *Southern Labor in Transition*, pp. 273–94.

The upsurge of more recent historical interest in southern textile workers is capably explored by the same author in "Textile Workers and Historians," in Zieger, ed., *Organized Labor in the Twentieth-Century South*, pp. 35–59. For a range of sociological essays on the southern textile industry, see Jeffrey Leiter, Michael D. Schulman, and Rhonda Zingraff, eds., *Hanging by a Thread: Social Change in Southern Textiles* (Ithaca, N.Y.: ILR Press, 1991). Two recent works explore the 1934 General Textile Strike, the largest labor protest in southern history. Janet Irons' *Testing the New Deal: The General Textile Strike of 1934 in the American South* (Urbana: University of Illinois Press, 2000), concentrates on the South, while John A. Salmond's, *The General Textile Strike of 1934: From Maine to Alabama* (Columbia: University of Missouri Press, 2002) has a national focus.

Several historians examine broad reasons for the weakness of unions in the South including Bryant Simon, "Rethinking Why There Are So Few Unions in the South," *Georgia Historical Quarterly* 81:2 (Summer 1997), pp. 465–84, and Stephen H. Norwood, *Strike-breaking and Intimidation: Mercenaries and Masculinity in Twentieth-Century America* (Chapel Hill: University of North Carolina Press, 2002). The comparative weakness of public sector unions in the South is covered in Mark Wilkens, "Gender, Race, Work Culture, and the Building of the Fire Fighters Union in Tampa, Florida, 1943–1985," in Zieger, ed., *Southern Labor in Transition*, pp. 176–204. Bruce J. Schulman, *From Cotton Belt to Sunbelt: Federal Policy, Economic Development, and the Transformation of the South, 1938–1980* (New York: Oxford University Press, 1991) and James C. Cobb, *The Selling of the South: The Southern Crusade for Industrial Development, 1936–1980* (Baton Rouge: Louisiana State University Press, 1982) both explore southern antiunionism, especially in relation to efforts to attract outside industry to the region.

The southern press also regularly explored the reasons for the lack of unions in the region. See, for example, Kevin P. McKenna, "North Carolina Workers Shun Union Membership," *Fayetteville Observer*, September 6, 1977 (filed under "Unions" in the clipping file of the North Carolina Collection, Wilson Library, University of North Carolina at Chapel Hill, hereafter cited as NCC); Ted Reed, "Town Diversifies, Union Comes In," *Charlotte Observer*, September 3, 2001 (filed under "Labor Unions," NCC). For broader historical debate about continuing southern distinctiveness, see John Egerton, *The Americanization of Dixie: The Southernization of America* (New York: Harper's Magazine Press, 1974) and John Shelton Reed, *Southerners: The Social Psychology of Sectionalism* (Chapel Hill: University of North Carolina Press, 1983).

Chapter 1. A Double-Edged Sword: World War II and Southern Workers

For general accounts of the American experience in World War II, see John M. Blum, *V Was for Victory: Politics and Culture in American Society During World War II* (New York: Harcourt Brace Jovanovich, 1976); Richard Polenberg, *War and Society: The United States, 1941–1945* (Philadelphia: J. B. Lippincott, 1972); and Michael C. C. Adams, *The Best War Ever: America and World War II* (Baltimore: Johns Hopkins University Press, 1994).

The southern experience in World War II is covered well in southern history surveys such as Pete Daniel, *Standing at the Crossroads: Southern Life Since 1900* (New York: Hill and Wang, 1986); Numan V. Bartley, *The New South, 1945–1980: The Story of the South's Modernization* (Baton Rouge: Louisiana State University Press, 1995); and John B. Boles, *The South Through Time: A History of an American Region* (Englewood Cliffs, NJ: Prentice Hall, 1995). The war's impact on the region and its people is summarized well by Pete Daniel in "Going Among Strangers: Southern Reactions to World War II," *Journal of American History* 77:3 (December 1990), pp. 886–911. John Egerton, *Speak Now Against the Day: The Generation Before the Civil Rights Movement in the South* (New York: Alfred A. Knopf, 1994), contains some lively material on the wartime racial climate in the South.

Studs Terkel's Pulitzer Prize–winning *The Good War: An Oral History of World War II* (New York: New Press, 1984) has a broad focus, but it does include some fine interviews with both black and white southerners. Jerry Purvis Sanson, *Louisiana During World War II: Politics and Society, 1939–1945* (Baton Rouge: Louisiana State University Press, 1999) is a useful state-wide study with some material on labor and unionization.

The impact of the war on the southern textile industry is covered well in Brattain, *The Politics of Whiteness;* Flamming, *Creating The Modern South;* Waldrep, *Southern Workers and the Search for Community.* A heavy company history, Robert Sidney Smith's, *Mill on the Dan: A History of the Dan River Mills, 1882–1950* (Durham: Duke University Press, 1960), has some material on labor relations. All of these case studies also explore, in varying degrees of detail, union efforts to organize the South during World War II. For an overview that gives the perspective of the national leaders of the textile workers' union, Clete Daniel, *Culture of Misfortune: An Interpretative History of Textile Unionism in the United States* (Ithaca, N.Y.: ILR Press, 2001), is particularly informative.

For the debate about the significance of wartime work for women, see William H. Chafe *The American Woman: Her Changing Social, Economic, and Political Roles,*

1920–1970 (New York: Oxford University Press, 1972); Alice Kessler-Harris, *Out To Work: A History of Wage-Earning Women in the United States* (New York: Oxford University Press, 1982); Sara Evans, *Born for Liberty: A History of Women in America* (New York; Simon and Schuster, 1989); and particularly, Chafe's *The Paradox of Change: American Women in the 20th Century* (New York: Oxford University Press, 1991).

The mobilization of women workers in the major defense center of Mobile, Alabama is covered well in *The Mobile Press* and *The Mobile Register* between 1942 and 1945. See especially "Women Take Jobs of Men to Help Construct Ships," *Mobile Register*, September 13, 1942, p. B1 and "To the Women of Mobile," *Mobile Press Register*, February 21, 1943, p. B3.

A detailed national overview of the war's impact on black Americans is provided by Neil A. Wynn, *The Afro-American and the Second World War* (New York: Holmes and Meier, 1976). Adam Fairclough's fine summary, *Better Day Coming: Blacks and Equality, 1890–2000* (New York: Penguin Books, 2001), also examines this period's social and economic consequences for American blacks. Charles D. Chamberlain's *Victory at Home: Manpower and Race in the American South during World War II* (Athens: University of Georgia Press, 2003), is a recent work that explores the impact of World War II specifically on southern black workers.

The FEPC's efforts are detailed fully in Herbert Hill, *Black Labor and the American Legal System: Race, Work, and the Law* (Madison: University of Wisconsin Press, 1985) and Merl E. Reed, *Seedtime for the Modern Civil Rights Movement: The President's Committee on Fair Employment Practice, 1941–1946* (Baton Rouge: Louisiana State University Press, 1991). For southern white opposition to the FEPC, see Patricia Sullivan, *Days of Hope: Race and Democracy in the New Deal Era* (Chapel Hill: University of North Carolina Press, 1996) and Kari Frederickson, *The Dixiecrat Revolt and the End of the Solid South, 1932–1968* (Chapel Hill: University of North Carolina Press, 2001). The FEPC's efforts to tackle discrimination in the railroad industry are covered well in Eric Arnesen's *Brotherhoods of Color: Black Railroad Workers and the Struggle for Equality* (Cambridge, Mass.: Harvard University Press, 2001).

Case studies of black employment in the wartime South include Honey, *Southern Labor and Black Civil Rights*; Alex Lichtenstein, "Exclusion, Fair Employment, or Interracial Unionism: Race Relations in Florida's Shipyards During World War II," in Eskew, ed., *Labor in the Modern South*, pp. 135–57; Merl E. Reed, "Bell Aircraft Comes South: The Struggle by Atlanta Blacks for Jobs during World War II," also in Eskew, ed., pp. 102–34; and Jacob Vander Meulen, "Warplanes, Labor, and the International Association of Machinists, 1939–1945," in Zieger, ed., *Southern Labor*, pp. 37–57. See also Thomas A. Scott, "Winning World War II in an Atlanta Suburb: Local Boosters and the Recruitment of Bell Bomber" and Karen Ferguson, "The Politics of Exclusion: Wartime Industrialization, Civil Rights Mobilization, and Black Politics in Atlanta," both in Scranton, ed., *The Second Wave*, pp. 1–23 and 43–80 respectively.

The records of racial discrimination lawsuits brought under Title VII of the 1964 Civil Rights Act also frequently cover wartime conditions, especially in testimony given by black workers who recalled being reassigned to lower-paying jobs at the end of the conflict. In particular, this account draws on the Deposition of John Bonner, January 24, 1975, *Boles et al. v. Union-Camp* (United States District Court for the Southern District of Georgia, 1969); Trial Testimony of Horace Crenshaw, January 29, 1973, *Watkins et al. v. Scott Paper Company* (United States District Court for the Southern District of Alabama, 1971). The records of both these cases are held at the Federal Records Center in East Point, Georgia. Both cases, together with the broader context of Title VII litigation, are discussed in Timothy J. Minchin, *The Color of Work: The Struggle for Civil Rights in the Southern Paper Industry, 1945–1980* (Chapel Hill: University of North Carolina Press, 2001).

This chapter also draws on the author's interviews with black and white workers who worked in the South's wartime factories, as well as with union leaders and managers. Particularly relevant interviews include: John VanDillon, conducted on August 4, 1997 in Mobile, Alabama; Emmanuel Johnson, conducted on October 1, 1997 in Georgetown, South Carolina; Sidney Gibson, conducted on October 13, 1997 in Natchez, Mississippi; George Sawyer, conducted on October 4, 1997 in Savannah, Georgia; Alphonse Williams, conducted on July 21, 1997 in Mobile, Alabama; Russell Hall, conducted on August 4, 1997 in Pensacola, Florida; Amos Favorite, conducted on August 10, 2000 in Geismar, Louisiana. All interviews were tape-recorded and transcribed. Copies of the tapes and transcripts are currently in the author's possession.

The Mobile race riot is covered in *The Mobile Press-Register*, May 26–29, 1943, and in Nelson, "Organized Labor and the Struggle for Black Equality." For white anxieties about "Eleanor Clubs," see Bryant Simon, "Fearing Eleanor: Racial Anxieties and Wartime Rumors in the American South, 1940–1945," in Eskew, ed., pp. 83–101.

The exclusion of black women from industrial jobs in textile communities is explored well through oral interviews in Byerly, *Hard Times Cotton Mill Girls*, and Conway, *Rise Gonna Rise*. For the history of black female employment in the southern tobacco plants, see Dolores Janiewski, "Southern Honor, Southern Dishonor: Managerial Ideology and the Construction of Gender, Race, and Class Relations in Southern Industry," in Ava Baron, ed., *Work Engendered: Toward a New History of American Labor* (Ithaca, N.Y.: Cornell University Press, 1991), pp. 70–91. Also consult Tera W. Hunter, "'The Women Are Asking for BREAD, Why Give Them STONE?': Women, Work, and Protests in Atlanta and Norfolk during World War I," in Eskew, ed., pp. 62–82.

A great deal of literature explores southern workers' efforts to organize prior to World War II. These works document both the activism of southern workers and the equally fierce resistance of southern executives and their community allies. Important studies include Marshall, *Labor in the South*; Hodges, *New Deal Labor*

Policy; Melton McLaurin, *Paternalism and Protest: Southern Cotton Mill Workers and Organized Labor, 1875–1905* (Westport, Conn.: Greenwood Press, 1971) and *The Knights of Labor in the South* (Westport, Conn.: Greenwood Press, 1978); Salmond, *Gastonia 1929*; and John G. Selby, "'Better to Starve in the Shade than in the Factory': Labor Protest in High Point, North Carolina, in the Early 1930s," *North Carolina Historical Review* 64:1 (January 1987), pp. 43–64.

For the failure of the TWOC drive, as well as broader insights into the difficulties of organizing the southern textile industry, see Paul David Richards, "The History of the Textile Workers of America, CIO, in the South, 1937 to 1945" (Ph.D. dissertation, University of Wisconsin, Madison, 1978); John A. Salmond, *Miss Lucy of the CIO: The Life and Times of Lucy Randolph Mason, 1882–1959* (Athens: University of Georgia Press, 1988); Steven Fraser, *Labor Will Rule: Sidney Hillman and the Rise of American Labor* (New York: Free Press, 1991); Robert P. Ingalls, "The Wagner Act on Trial: Vigilante Violence and the Struggle to Organize Textile Workers in Fitzgerald, Georgia, 1937–1940," *Georgia Historical Quarterly* 81:2 (Summer 1997), pp. 370–94; and Leon Fink, ed., "Pages from an Organizer's Life: Don McKee Confronts Southern Millworkers—and Himself. An Excerpt from Don McKee's unpublished autobiography," *Labor History* 41:4 (November 2000), pp. 453–64.

The wartime growth of unions is explored fully in Robert H. Zieger's, *The CIO, 1935–1955* (Chapel Hill: University of North Carolina Press, 1995). There are briefer treatments in Eileen Boris and Nelson Lichtenstein, eds., *Major Problems in the History of American Workers* (Lexington, Mass.: D.C. Heath, 1991), pp. 462–95 and Robert H. Zieger and Gilbert J. Gall, *American Workers, American Unions: The Twentieth Century*, 3rd ed. (Baltimore: Johns Hopkins University Press, 2002). Nelson Lichtenstein, *Labor's War at Home: The CIO in World War II* (Cambridge: Cambridge University Press, 1982), is a national study that focuses specifically on the wartime era. Marshall, *Labor in the South* covers union history in the South during the war in full.

The wartime racial record of the union movement is summarized in Zieger and Gall, *American Workers, American Unions*. Robert J. Norrell, "Caste in Steel: Jim Crow Careers in Birmingham, Alabama," *Journal of American History* 73:3 (December 1986), pp. 669–94 is particularly critical of unions' racial record in Birmingham's steel mills. In contrast, Rick Halpern, "Interracial Unionism in the Southwest: Fort Worth's Packinghouse Workers, 1937–1954," in Zieger, ed., *Organized Labor*, pp. 158–82, examines a left-wing union that was more supportive of civil rights. For the R. J. Reynolds organizing campaign, see Korstad, "Daybreak of Freedom." Korstad's work contains vivid interview material, including the interviews with Geneva McLendon and Robert Black, who are quoted in the text. The interview with Fannie O'Neal in Brigid O'Farrell and Joyce L. Kornbluh, *Rocking the Boat: Union Women's Voices, 1915–1975* (New Brunswick: Rutgers University Press, 1996) covers the wartime organization of Reliance Manufacturing Company and the union's subsequent involvement in civil rights activities. The organization of segregated unions in the paper industry is discussed in Robert H. Zieger, *Rebuilding the Pulp and Paper Workers' Union, 1933–1941* (Knoxville: University of Tennessee Press, 1984) and Minchin, *The Color of Work*.

For information on agricultural workers during World War II, see Pete Daniel, *Breaking the Land: The Transformation of Cotton, Tobacco, and Rice Cultures since 1880* (Urbana: University of Illinois Press, 1985) and Cindy Hahamovitch, *The Fruits of Their Labor: Atlantic Coast Farmworkers and the Making of Migrant Poverty, 1870–1945* (New Brunswick: Rutgers University Press, 1997). Hahamovitch also provides a useful case study in "Standing Idly By: 'Organized' Farmworkers in South Florida during the Depression and World War II," in Zieger, ed., *Southern Labor in Transition,* pp. 15–36. For a fine recent study of the Arkansas and Mississippi Delta, see Nan Elizabeth Woodruff, *American Congo: The African-American Freedom Struggle in the Delta* (Cambridge, Mass.: Harvard University Press, 2003).

Chapter 2. The Number One Task: Operation Dixie and the Failure of Postwar Organizing

To date, Griffith's *The Crisis of American Labor* remains the only book-length study of Operation Dixie. Based on the author's pioneering access to the Operation Dixie papers in the 1980s, *The Crisis of American Labor* argues that the drive failed because of southern opposition to unionism. The Operation Dixie papers are held at the Special Collections Department of Perkins Library at Duke University, and this chapter utilizes the collection. The papers have also been microfilmed, and several libraries hold them; researchers can also purchase copies. The lack of writing on the AFL's postwar drive is largely a reflection of the fact that no comparable documentary collection exists.

Organized labor's need to unionize the postwar South, and the outcome of their efforts is covered well in Zieger, *The CIO*. Zieger and Gall, *American Workers, American Unions* summarizes national developments. The overview of the campaign provided by Marshall, *Labor in the South*, is still valuable. Salmond's *Miss Lucy of the CIO* details the work of the CIO's chief publicist in the South during Operation Dixie. In *To Win These Rights: A Personal Story of the CIO in the South* (1952 Reprint; Westport, Conn.: Greenwood Press, 1970), Mason also provides her own account of the campaign. The drive was also covered by the contemporary press, who often emphasized the "invasion" metaphor. For one of the most detailed articles, see Milton MacKaye, "The CIO Invades Dixie," *Saturday Evening Post*, July 20, 1946, pp. 12, 94–99.

Several historians have capably covered Operation Dixie at an industry level. In the key industry of textiles, Brattain, *The Politics of Whiteness*, details the campaign in Floyd County, Georgia. Brattain also provides a valuable case study in "'A Town as Small as That': Tallapoosa, Georgia, and Operation Dixie, 1945–1950," *Georgia Historical Quarterly* 81:2 (Summer 1997), pp. 395–425. The Cannon Mills' campaign is explored in Griffith, *The Crisis of American Labor* and in *Where Do You Stand? Stories from an American Mill* (2003, produced and directed by Alexandra

Lescaze, Mighty Fine Films, videocassette; 2001 prototype in author's possession). For Operation Dixie in textiles, see Minchin, *What Do We Need a Union For?*
and Flamming, *Creating the Modern South*. For the lumber industry, see Jones,
"Cutting Through Jim Crow" and "Black Workers and the CIO's Turn Toward
Racial Liberalism: Operation Dixie and the North Carolina Lumber Industry,
1946–1953," *Labor History* 41:3 (May 2000), pp. 279–306. Postwar organizing efforts in the apparel industry are covered in Dorothy DeMoss, *The History of Apparel Manufacturing in Texas, 1897–1981* (New York: Garland, 1989) and Michelle
Haberland, "Women's Work: The Apparel Industry in the United States South,
1937–1980."

The CIO's anticommunist purge has been written about in detail. For a sum-
mary, see Zieger and Gall, *American Workers, American Unions*, and Zieger, *The
CIO*. More detailed studies include Bert Cochran, *Labor and Communism: The
Conflict That Shaped American Unions* (Princeton: Princeton University Press,
1977) and Harvey A. Levenstein, *Communism, Anticommunism, and the CIO*
(Westport, Conn.: Greenwood Press, 1981). A personal account is provided by
Junius Irving Scales and Richard Nickson, *Cause at Heart: A Former Communist
Remembers* (Athens: University of Georgia Press, 1987).

Particularly influential in its criticism of the CIO's racial caution and anticommunism is Robert Korstad and Nelson Lichtenstein, "Opportunities Lost and
Found: Labor Radicals and the Early Civil Rights Movement," *Journal of Ameri-
can History* 75 (Winter 1988), pp. 786–811. Other critical accounts include Kim
Moody, *An Injury To All: The Decline of American Unionism* (New York: Verso,
1988) and two studies by Michael Goldfield: "Race and the CIO: The Possibilities
for Racial Egalitarianism During the 1930s and 1940s," *International Labor and
Working-Class History* 44 (Fall 1993), pp. 1–32 and "The Failure of Operation
Dixie: A Critical Turning Point in American Political Development?" in Fink and
Reed, eds., *Race, Class, and Community*, pp. 166–89. Goldfield's argument is also
summarized in his *The Color of Politics: Race and the Mainsprings of American Politics*
(New York: New Press, 1997). For an alternative perspective, see Alan Draper,
*Conflict of Interests: Organized Labor and the Civil Rights Movement in the South,
1954–1968* (Ithaca, N.Y.: ILR Press, 1994) and Zieger, *The CIO*.

On the difficulties of building interracial unions in the 1940s, see Halpern,
"Interracial Unionism in the Southwest"; Korstad, "Daybreak of Freedom"; and
Jones, "Cutting Through Jim Crow." For broader insights into the limits of inter-
racial unionism in an earlier period, see Eric Arnesen, "'Like Banquo's Ghost, It
Will Not Down': The Race Question and the American Railroad Brotherhoods,
1880–1920," *American Historical Review* 99 (1984), pp. 1601–33 and Daniel
Letwin, *The Challenge of Interracial Unionism: Alabama Coal Miners, 1878–1921*
(Chapel Hill: University of North Carolina Press, 1998).

While little detailed study of the AFL drive has been carried out, the effort is
summarized in Marshall, *Labor in the South* and in contemporary press clippings.
Filed under "Labor Unions," the clipping file at the North Carolina Collection

(Wilson Library, University of North Carolina at Chapel Hill) contains several articles on the AFL drive. See, for example, "AFL Launches Dixie Drive at Asheville Meet Today," *Raleigh News and Observer*, May 11, 1946; C. W. Gilmore, "Labor Unions Claim Victory in Hard-Fought Drive South," *Raleigh News and Observer*, June 29, 1947; and "AFL Meeting in Asheville to Plan Strategy Against CIO," *West Asheville News*, May 3, 1946. For an insight into the problems that AFL organizers faced, see the interview with AFL southern organizer Carmen Lucia in O'Farrell and Kornbluh, *Rocking the Boat*.

For Taft-Hartley and the right-to-work movement, as well as the broader desire of southern executives and politicians to reduce union influence after the war, see Bartley, *The New South* and Schulman, *From Cotton Belt to Sunbelt*. Southern opposition to unions is also explored in Norwood, *Strikebreaking and Intimidation*. For the broader regional context, see Boles, *The South Through Time*. The AVCO-Vultee strike is detailed in Vander Meulen, "Warplanes, Labor, and the International Association of Machinists." Waldrep's *Southern Workers and the Search for Community* details the 1949–50 strike at Clifton Manufacturing Company in Clifton, South Carolina. Minchin, *What Do We Need a Union For?*, provides an overview of the postwar textile strikes. For the postwar mobilization against unions in Memphis, see Honey, *Southern Labor and Black Civil Rights* and "Industrial Unionism and Racial Justice in Memphis," in Zieger, ed., *Organized Labor in the Twentieth-Century South*, pp. 135–57. The 1951 General Textile Strike is covered in Daniel, *Culture of Misfortune* and Minchin, *What Do We Need a Union For?*

For labor's efforts to reshape the postwar political landscape in the South, see Simon, *A Fabric of Defeat*; Robert H. Zieger, "A Venture into Unplowed Fields: Daniel Powell and CIO Political Action in the Postwar South," in Eskew, ed., pp. 158–81; Michelle Brattain, "Making Friends and Enemies: Textile Workers and Politics in Post–World War II Georgia," *Journal of Southern History* 63 (February 1997), pp. 91–138; and Flamming, *Creating the Modern South*.

Chapter 3. Split Wide Open: Black and White Workers in the 1950s

Following Operation Dixie, organizing remained a major priority for unions in the South, and several works explore the labor movement's continuing problems in this area. For overviews, see Marshall, *Labor in the South*, and Norwood, *Strikebreaking and Intimidation*. William F. Hartford, *Where Is Our Responsibility?: Unions and Economic Change in the New England Textile Industry, 1870–1960* (Amherst: University of Massachusetts Press, 1996), covers the economic decline of the northern textile industry and the way that this persistently necessitated southern organizing efforts. The importance of organizing the South to union leaders is stressed in documents held in the pamphlet collection of the AFL-CIO's Southern Regional Office Civil Rights Division Papers at the Southern Labor Archives (hereafter cited as AFL-CIO Pamphlet Collection). The archives are based at the Pullen Library, Georgia State University, Atlanta. See for example, Benjamin D. Segal, "Industrialization: Accent on the South," nd, "South," folder, box 56;

"Number One Objective: A report of the First AFL-CIO National Organizing Conference," January 6–7, 1959, "AFL-CIO Organizing Department," folder, box 8.

Daniel, *Culture of Misfortune* covers the TWUA's history in the 1950s, including the Henderson strike, the Darlington Mills case, and the continuing shift of the industry South. The Henderson strike itself is carefully detailed in both Clark, *Like Night and Day* and Linda Frankel, "'Jesus Leads Us, Cooper Needs Us, the Union Feeds Us': The 1958 Harriet-Henderson Textile Strike," in Leiter et al., eds., *Hanging by a Thread*, pp. 101–20. The Darlington mill closure is also explored in Marshall, *Labor in the South*, and Bill Arthur, "The Darlington Mills Case: Or 17 Years Before the Courts," *New South* 28 (Summer 1973), pp. 40–47. Flamming, *Creating the Modern South*, covers the 1955 Chenille organizing campaign in Dalton, Georgia.

Cobb, *The Selling of the South* and Schulman, *From Cotton Belt to Sunbelt*, both stress the South's efforts to attract outside industry. On southern economic development, see also Gavin Wright, *Old South, New South: Revolutions in the Southern Economy Since the Civil War* (New York: Basic Books, 1986). For the movement of the apparel industry South and the vain efforts of unions to stop it, see Haberland, "Women's Work."

There are several documentary collections that contain fine material on black employment in the Jim Crow South. Interviews with black and white workers conducted by the Southern Oral History Program at the University of North Carolina frequently cover civil rights questions. The interviews are all housed at the Wilson Library in Chapel Hill. See, for example, Maude Brown interview, August 3, 1979 (H-192); Carlee Drye interview, April 2, 1980 (H-5); Clyde Cook interview, July 10, 1977 (H-3). Press clippings, especially in the North Carolina Collection's file, also contain some fine material on black working conditions under segregation. Filed under "tobacco," see Betty Hodges, "History of Tobacco Workers: Part of the Female Black Experience Revealed," *Durham Morning Herald*, February 21, 1986. Under "steel," see Kevin Spear, "'It's Not Badin Anymore; It's Humdrum,'" *Winston-Salem Journal*, November 30, 1986.

The records of the Southern Regional Council (SRC), an Atlanta-based civil rights group founded in 1944, also contain much material on racial employment patterns. Throughout its history, the SRC has concentrated a great deal of attention on exploring and documenting segregation in the workplace. See especially a series of reports entitled "The Negro and Employment Opportunities in the South," which were produced in 1961–62 and include detailed studies of employment patterns in Houston, Atlanta, Chattanooga, and Miami. Copies of the reports arc on Reel 219 of the SRC Papers. The SRC Papers are held at Atlanta University but they have been microfilmed and deposited in many other libraries. Researchers can also purchase copies of the microfilm. Published in 1960, an SRC study by the renowned economist Vivian W. Henderson, "The Economic Status of Negroes in the Nation and in the South," is also detailed and informative. A copy is held in "Black Workers," folder, box 13, AFL-CIO Pamphlet Collection.

In the 1960s, a series of studies carried out by the Wharton School's Industrial Research Unit at the University of Pennsylvania explored racial employment patterns in American industries. These studies were conducted from an industrial relations perspective, drawing on the Wharton School's contacts with employers. They contain little material from workers themselves, but are still valuable, especially because they contain a large volume of useful data. See Herbert R. Northrup, Richard L. Rowan, Carl B. King, William H. Quay Jr., and Howard W. Risher Jr., *Negro Employment in Basic Industry: A Study of Racial Policies in Six Industries* (Philadelphia: Industrial Research Unit, Wharton School of Finance and Commerce, University of Pennsylvania, 1970), which contains studies on the automobile, aerospace, steel, rubber tire, petroleum, and chemical industries. Herbert R. Northrup, Richard L. Rowan, Darold T. Barnum, and John C. Howard, *Negro Employment in Southern Industry: A Study of Racial Policies in Five Industries* (Philadelphia: Industrial Research Unit, Wharton School of Finance and Commerce, University of Pennsylvania, 1970) focuses specifically on the South. The data collected by Northrup and his team in producing these studies is also available to scholars at the University of Pennsylvania's Archives and Records Center in Philadelphia. The collection is entitled the "Wharton's School's Industrial Research Unit Papers" and consists largely of data and research reports that often include quotations from company executives.

Several published oral history collections contain valuable insights into black working conditions in the Jim Crow era. For black domestic workers, including the interview with Katie Geneva Cannon, see Byerly, *Hard Times Cotton Mill Girls*. The interviews with Winnie Hefley, Sallie Hutton, Aletha Vaughn, Essie Favrot, Eugenia Bowden, Corinne Cooke, and Louise Webster are all in Susan Tucker, *Telling Memories Among Southern Women: Domestic Workers and Their Employers in the Segregated South* (Baton Rouge: Louisiana State University Press, 1988). Honey, *Black Workers Remember* includes some fine material, especially on conditions in the rubber industry. Painter's *The Narrative of Hosea Hudson* contains Hudson's insights on black working conditions in Birmingham's steel industry in the Jim Crow era. Robert Armstead, *Black Days, Black Dust: The Memories of an African American Coal Miner* (Knoxville: University of Tennessee Press, 2002), is an oral history of a black coal miner in West Virginia as told to scholar S. L. Gardner.

For insights into workers' experience of the segregated workplace, this chapter also utilizes the author's interviews. The following interviews were particularly relevant: Otis Walker conducted on July 24, 1997 in Apalachicola, Florida; Cleveland Bailey, conducted on July 24, 1997 in Port St. Joe, Florida; State Stallworth, conducted on July 8, 1998 in Moss Point, Mississippi; Sammie J. Hatcher, conducted on October 10, 1997 in Mobile, Alabama; Leroy Hamilton, conducted on

July 25, 1997 in Woodbine, Georgia; Sidney Gibson, conducted on October 13, 1997 in Natchez, Mississippi; James Tyson, conducted on October 3, 1997 in Savannah, Georgia; Joe McCullough, conducted on October 3, 1997 in Savannah, Georgia. All interviews were tape-recorded and transcribed, and copies of the tapes and transcripts are currently in the author's possession.

In recent years, historians have also produced many valuable published studies of black employment in the South. The steel industry has been particularly well documented. See, for example: Norrell, "Caste in Steel"; Judith Stein, *Running Steel, Running America: Race, Economic Policy, and the Decline of Liberalism* (Chapel Hill: University of North Carolina Press, 1998); Bruce Nelson, "'CIO Meant One Thing for the Whites and Another Thing for Us': Steelworkers and Civil Rights, 1936–1974," in Zieger, ed., *Southern Labor in Transition*, pp. 113–45; and Judith Stein, "Southern Workers in National Unions: Birmingham Steelworkers, 1936–1951," in Zieger, ed., *Organized Labor in the Twentieth-Century South*, pp. 183–222.

Scholars have also carried out important work on other industries. Jones, "Cutting Through Jim Crow," explores the history of segregation in the southern lumber industry and includes the interviews with lumber workers Orrie Tyson and John Oatis. Korstad, "Daybreak of Freedom," utilizes some fine interview material with black tobacco workers. Sally McMillen, "No Easy Time: Rural Southern Women, 1940–1990," in R. Douglas Hurt, ed., *The Rural South Since World War II* (Baton Rouge: Louisiana State University Press, 1998), pp. 59–94, estimably covers domestic employment. For the paper industry, see Minchin, *The Color of Work*. Rick Halpern, "The CIO and the Limits of Labor-Based Civil Rights Activism: The Case of Louisiana's Sugar Workers, 1947–1966," in Zieger, ed., *Southern Labor in Transition*, pp. 86–112, examines race relations in the sugar industry. On black workers' strategies of coping with discrimination in the workplace, Robin D. G. Kelley, "'We Are Not What We Seem': Rethinking Black Working-Class Opposition in the Jim Crow South," *The Journal of American History* 80:1 (June 1993), pp. 75–112, has been particularly influential. Jack E. Davis, *Race Against Time: Culture and Separation in Natchez Since 1930* (Baton Rouge: Louisiana State University Press, 2001) contains some lively material on black employment in Natchez, Mississippi.

Many of these studies concentrate particular attention on the racial record of unions. For insight into the debate about organized labor and race, see Bruce Nelson, "Class, Race and Democracy in the CIO: The 'New' Labor History Meets the 'Wages of Whiteness,'" *International Review of Social History* 41 (1996), pp. 351–74; Goldfield, "Race and the CIO"; and Brattain, "The Pursuits of Post-Exceptionalism." Studies of specific unions include Halpern, "Interracial Unionism in the Southwest"; Nelson, "'CIO Meant One Thing'"; and Brattain, *The Politics of Whiteness*. For broad discussions of the literature on black workers and organized labor, see also Eric Arnesen, "Following the Color Line of Labor: Black Workers and the Labor Movement before 1930," *Radical History Review* 55 (1993), pp. 53–87 and Rick Halpern, "Organized Labor, Black Workers, and the Twentieth Century South: The Emerging Revision," in Melyvn Stokes and Rick Halpern, eds., *Race and Class in the American South Since 1890* (Providence: Berg, 1994), pp. 43–76.

Draper, *Conflict of Interests*, summarizes the Front Royal case and the broader impact of "Massive Resistance" on organized labor in the South. For Front Royal, see also Julius Duscha, "Segregationist Local Embarrassing to Labor," *Washington Post*, May 23, 1960, p. A15 and "Proceedings of the Eleventh Biennial Convention of the Textile Workers Union of America," May 30–June 3, 1960. Patrick J. Maney, "Hale Boggs, Organized Labor, and the Politics of Race in South Louisiana," in Zieger, ed., *Southern Labor in Transition*, pp. 230–50, examines the changing racial climate of the 1950s and its implications for liberal Democrats who tried to court labor support. Frederickson, *The Dixiecrat Revolt* explores southern employers' fears of a permanent FEPC.

The development of the company-owned textile mill village is explored by, among others, Cathy L. McHugh, *Mill Family: The Labor System in the Southern Cotton Textile Industry, 1880–1915* (New York: Oxford University Press, 1988); Hodges, *New Deal Labor Policy*; Hall et al., *Like a Family*; and Flamming, *Creating the Modern South*. The best account of the causes and consequences of the sale of company-owned housing by textile firms is Toby Moore, "Dismantling the South's Cotton Mill Village System," in Scranton, ed., *The Second Wave*, pp. 114–45. Richard Thorpe, *Cotton Mill Cowboys And Other Characters I've Known: A Humorous Look at Life in a Mill Village* (Greenville, SC: Richwood Press, 1984) provides a personal, lighthearted account of life in a mill village. For a contemporary perspective of social change in mill villages, see Harriet L. Herring, *Passing of the Mill Village: Revolution in a Southern Institution* (Chapel Hill: University of North Carolina Press, 1949). For the sale of lumber company housing, see Jones, "Cutting Through Jim Crow."

In the 1950s, automation and industrial decline was already beginning to eliminate manufacturing jobs. For the postwar decline of the southern coal industry, see Bartley, *The New South* and Melvyn Dubofsky and Warren Van Tine, *John L. Lewis: A Biography* (New York: Quadrangle, 1977). There are relevant interviews in Studs Terkel, *American Dreams: Lost and Found* (London: Hodder and Stoughton, 1980). See especially Terkel's interviews with Gaynell Begley and Pat and Tom Gish. Traditional labor-based "black" positions were disproportionately affected by automation and deindustrialization. Armstead's *Black Days, Black Dust* and Painter's *The Narrative of Hosea Hudson* detail the black experience of deindustrialization in the coal and steel industries respectively.

Chapter 4. Civil Rights Struggles

The upsurge of black protest in the 1960s has been treated extensively by historians. On the sit-in movement, see especially William H. Chafe, *Civilities and Civil Rights: Greensboro, North Carolina and the Black Struggle for Freedom* (New York: Oxford University Press, 1980). Among the many useful histories of the civil rights movement, see Robert Weisbrot, *Freedom Bound: A History of America's Civil Rights Movement* (New York: Norton, 1990) and Robert Cook, *Sweet Land of Liberty?: The African-American Struggle for Civil Rights in the Twentieth Century* (London: Longman, 1998), a recent synthesis with a full bibliography. For useful overviews of civil rights protest, see William H. Chafe, *The Unfinished Journey: America Since World War II* (New York: Oxford University Press, 1986)and Fairclough, *Better Day Coming*.

For general overviews of black economic progress in the 1960s, see James C. Cobb, *Industrialization and Southern Society, 1877–1984* (Lexington: University Press of Kentucky, 1984) and David R. Goldfield, *Black, White, and Southern: Race Relations and Southern Culture, 1940 to the Present* (Baton Rouge: Louisiana State University Press, 1990). Black economic conditions in the rural South are covered well in Hurt, ed., *The Rural South Since World War II*. Adam Fairclough, *Race and Democracy: The Civil Rights Struggle in Louisiana, 1915–1972* (Athens: University of Georgia Press, 1995) provides a statewide study that includes material on employment. An NAACP Legal Defense Fund pamphlet, "Jobs for Blacks: Building the Economic Base for Full Equality," (in "Black Workers," folder, box 13, AFL-CIO Pamphlet Collection), contains useful data on black employment in the 1960s.

For more detailed insights into black economic conditions in the 1960s, Ray Marshall and Virgil L. Christian Jr., eds., *Employment of Blacks in the South: A Perspective on the 1960s* (Austin: University of Texas Press, 1978) contains a wealth of data. The studies contained in Northrup et al., eds., *The Negro in Southern Industry* and Northrup et al., eds., *Negro Employment in Basic Industry* explore the integration of facilities, jobs, and unions well and contain lots of data and contemporary interview material with southern executives. For detailed studies of the racial integration of the textile and paper industries in the 1960s, see Minchin, *Hiring the Black Worker* and *The Color of Work*. Brattain, *The Politics of Whiteness*, covers the integration of the mills in the important textile area of Floyd County, Georgia. Several of the interviews extracted in Byerly, *Hard Times Cotton Mill Girls* stress the benefits of African American women's entry into textile jobs, while Haberland, "Women's Work," covers the integration of southern apparel plants. For race relations in the steel industry, see Stein, *Running Steel, Running America* and Nelson, "'CIO Meant One Thing for the Whites and Another Thing for Us.'" For black efforts to integrate the railroads, see Arnesen, *Brotherhoods of Color*.

This chapter also utilizes the author's interviews with Leroy Hamilton, conducted on July 25, 1997 in Woodbine, Georgia; Allen Coley, conducted on October 13, 1997 in Natchez, Mississippi; Mervin Taylor, conducted on July 20, 1999 in Bogalusa, Louisiana; Julius Chambers, conducted on June 28, 1996 in Durham, North Carolina; Alphonse Williams, conducted on July 21, 1997 in Mobile, Alabama; Horace Gill, conducted on July 22, 1997 in Mobile, Alabama; Joe McCullough, conducted on October 3, 1997 in Savannah, Georgia; Wayne Glenn, conducted on July 18, 1997 in Nashville, Tennessee; Elboyd Deal, conducted on

March 11, 1996 in Kannapolis, North Carolina; Robert B. Lincks, conducted on July 17, 1995 in Greensboro, North Carolina; Chuck Spence, conducted on July 17, 1997 in Nashville, Tennessee. All interviews were tape-recorded and transcribed, and copies of the tapes and transcripts are currently in the author's possession.

For the decline of industries that traditionally employed blacks, see Ronald L. Lewis, *Black Coal Miners in America: Race, Class, and Community Conflict, 1780–1980* (Lexington: University Press of Kentucky, 1987); Stein, *Running Steel, Running America*; Haberland, "Women's Work"; Armstead, *Black Days, Black Dust*; and Arnesen, *Brotherhoods of Color*.

The rise of the Republican Party in the South is summarized well in Bartley, *The New South*; Boles, *The South Through Time*; and Goldfield, *Black, White, and Southern*. The definitive biography of George Wallace is Dan T. Carter's *The Politics of Rage: George Wallace, the Origins of the New Conservatism, and the Transformation of American Politics* (New York: Simon and Schuster, 1995). For southern workers' support of Wallace, see Robert J. Norrell, "Labor Trouble: George Wallace and Union Politics," in Zieger, ed., *Organized Labor in the Twentieth-Century South*, pp. 250–72.

The rise of public employee unionism is covered in Thomas R. Brooks, *Toil and Trouble: A History of American Labor* (New York: Delacorte Press, 1964) and in Zieger and Gall, *American Workers, American Unions*. For a southern focus, see Wilkens, "Gender, Race, Work Culture" and Darryl Paulson and Janet Stiff, "An Empty Victory: The St. Petersburg Sanitation Strike, 1968," *Florida Historical Quarterly* 57:4 (April 1979), pp. 421–33. The Florida teachers' strike is explored in James Sullivan, "The Florida Teacher Walkout in the Political Transition of 1968," in Zieger, ed., *Southern Labor in Transition*, pp. 205–29. The *New York Times* also covered the dispute. See especially "Florida Teachers Reject Pay Offer," *New York Times*, February 16, 1968, p. A16; Martin Waldron, "Florida Teachers Called Insecure," *New York Times*, March 17, 1968, p. 37; and Martin Waldron, "Some School Boards in Florida Bar Striking Teachers' Return," *New York Times*, March 10, 1968, p. 10.

For an excellent account of the 1969 Charleston Hospital workers' strike, see Leon Fink and Brian Greenberg, *Upheaval in the Quiet Zone: A History of Hospital Workers' Union, Local 1199* (Urbana: University of Illinois Press, 1989). The local press in Charleston also covered the 1969 hospital workers' strike in detail. See, for example, Stewart R. King, "Abernathy Pledges Support to Strikers," *Charleston News and Courier*, April 1, 1969, pp. 1A, 7A and Stewart R. King, "Negotiations Deadlocked in County Hospital Dispute," *Charleston News and Courier*, July 1, 1969, pp. 1A, 2A. For the settlement of the Charleston strike, see also, "Charleston Finale," *New York Times*, July 22, 1969, p. 38.

The 1968 strike by sanitation workers in Memphis has been covered well by scholars. Joan Turner Beifuss, *At The River I Stand* (Memphis: St. Luke's Press, 1990) is based on a large body of oral history interviews with strike participants. A broader work on black labor in Memphis, Honey's *Black Workers Remember* includes lively interviews with some of those involved in the strike. Honey's "Martin Luther King, Jr., the Crisis of the Black Working Class, and the Memphis Sanitation Strike," in Zieger, ed., *Southern Labor in Transition*, explores the role of the civil rights leader in the walkout. *Southern Labor and Black Civil Rights*, by the same author, concentrates on the period before the strike but provides important context for understanding it. Steve Estes, "'I AM A MAN!': Race, Masculinity, and the 1968 Memphis Sanitation Strike," *Labor History* 41:2 (May 2000), pp. 153–70, explores the role of gender in the walkout.

Chapter 5. Southern Workers in the Sunbelt Years

The term "Sunbelt" largely derived from a series of front-page articles in the *New York Times* published between February 8 and 13, 1976. Other papers copied the term, and even the London *Times* produced a special Sunbelt supplement (see *The Times*, September 29, 1977.) For an important contemporary account, see Kirkpatrick Sale, *Power Shift: The Rise of the Southern Rim and Its Challenge to the Eastern Establishment* (New York: Random House, 1975). For historical discussions of the Sunbelt term and what it represented, see Schulman, *From Cotton Belt to Sun Belt*; Bartley, *The New South*; and Boles, *The South Through Time*.

Much of the Sunbelt economic growth was a reflection of southern leaders' intensive efforts to attract outside industry to their region. James C. Cobb, *The Selling of the South: The Southern Crusade for Industrial Development, 1936–1980.* (Baton Rouge: Louisiana State University Press, 1982) remains the standard work on these efforts. Despite the headlines about southern economic growth, Cobb emphasizes that southern industry remained overwhelmingly low wage and nonunion. For the opposition of low-wage industries to the influx of higher-wage employers, see also Kevin P. McKenna, "Native N.C. Industry View Outside Threats," *Fayetteville Observer*, September 7, 1977, filed under "Unions," NCC.

Much of the Sunbelt growth bypassed the South's African American population. For overviews of black economic progress in the 1970s, see Goldfield, *Black, White, and Southern*; Schulman, *From Cotton Belt to Sun Belt*; Minchin, *The Color of Work*; and Minchin, *Hiring the Black Worker.* For women's economic progress, see Chafe, *The Paradox of Change*; Sara M. Evans, *Born for Liberty: A History of Women in America* (New York: Simon and Schuster, 1989); and Wilkens, "Gender, Race, Work Culture."

Legal decisions from the 1970s highlight the barriers that continued to block black access to higher-paying jobs in many southern industries. See especially *Baxter v. Savannah Sugar Refining Corporation*, U.S. Court of Appeals, 5th Circuit, 1974, (495 F.2d 437); *Cathey et al. v. Johnson Motor Lines*, United States District Court for the Western District of North Carolina, 1974, (398 F. Supp. 1107); *Franks v. Bowman Transportation Company*, U.S. Court of Appeals, 5th Circuit, 1974 (495 F.2d, 398); *Bing et al. v. Roadway Express*, U.S. Court of Appeals, 5th Circuit, 1971, (444 F.2d 687).

This chapter also draws on the author's interviews with Laura Ann Pope, conducted on April 1, 1996 in Andrews, South Carolina; Willie Ford, conducted on October 10, 1997 in Mobile, Alabama; Julius Chambers, conducted on June 28, 1996 in Durham, North Carolina; Plez Watson, conducted on July 19, 1997, in Mobile, Alabama; and Gladys Harvey, conducted on August 21, 2000 in Gonzales, Louisiana.

DeMoss, *The History of Apparel Manufacturing* and Haberland, "Women's Work," cover the Farah strike. The struggle is also well detailed in Homer Bigart, "Classic Labor-Organizing Drive Splits El Paso," *New York Times*, September 11, 1972, pp. 57, 58 and in Philip Shabecoff, "Meany Cites Gain in Farah Strike," *New York Times*, February 26, 1974, p. 21. The papers of the Amalgamated Clothing Workers' of America, held at the Southern Labor Archives at Georgia State University, also contain a limited amount of material on the strike. See especially Folder 18, Box 789.

The strike at Oneita Knitting Mills is covered in Carolyn Ashbaugh and Dan McCurry, "On the Line at Oneita," in Miller, ed., *Working Lives*, pp. 205–14 and in "A Talk with the Oneita Strikers," *The Call*, June 1973, pp. 12–13. See also Haberland, *Women's Work* and Minchin, *Hiring the Black Worker*.

For the Stevens campaign, see Conway, *Rise Gonna Rise*; Daniel, *Culture of Misfortune*; and Brent D. Glass, *The Textile Industry in North Carolina* (Raleigh: North Carolina Division of Archives and History, 1992). James A. Hodges, "J. P. Stevens and the Union: Struggle for the South," in Fink and Reed, eds., *Race, Class, and Community*, pp. 53–64, is a fine summary. Hodges has also written an interesting piece on the links between the film *Norma Rae*, which is loosely based on the story of real-life Stevens' worker Crystal Lee Sutton, and the campaign. See James A. Hodges, "The Real Norma Rae," in Zieger, ed., *Southern Labor in Transition*, pp. 251–72. Barry E. Truchil, *Capital Labor Relations in the U.S. Textile Industry* (New York: Praeger Press, 1988), puts the dispute in a broader industrial relations context. The ACTWU papers, held at the Catherwood Library at Cornell University, also contain a great deal of material on the Stevens campaign. The records of the early part of the campaign are held in the TWUA Papers at the State Historical Society of Wisconsin in Madison, Wisconsin.

The fight to organize J. P. Stevens was also covered extensively in the contemporary press. See, for example, Ed McConville, "Dirty Tricks Down South," *The Nation*, Feb. 9, 1980, pp. 142–45; Merle Kellerhals, "Unions Making Inroads in Battle of the Sunbelt," *Raleigh News and Observer*, November 22, 1979; A. H. Raskin, "J. P. Stevens: Labor's Big Domino," *New York Times*, August 15, 1976, pp. C3, 11; George Tucker, "The Struggle to Organize J. P. Stevens," *Political Affairs* 57 (May 1978), pp. 2–9; and Walter Guzzardi Jr., "How the Union Got the Upper Hand on J. P. Stevens," *Fortune*, June 19, 1978, pp. 86–98.

Information about efforts to organize the southern furniture industry is drawn chiefly from newspaper clippings in the North Carolina Collection, as the industry has not received the same amount of attention from scholars as many others.

Relevant clippings are filed under "Furniture Industry" and "Furniture Industry—Unionization." "Furniture Industry Started in High Point Back in 1888," *Greensboro Daily News*, June 15, 1930, summarizes the industry's early history. See also Jane Hall, "N.C. Furniture Industry Grows Bigger," *Raleigh News and Observer*, July 10, 1966. For labor relations, see "Unionization Efforts Have Fallen Flat in Carolina," *Durham Sun*, March 22, 1978; Mary Bishop, "Campaign to Unionize Furniture Workers Planned," *Charlotte Observer*, November 4, 1977; and "Union Loses 1st Election in Caldwell," *Charlotte Observer*, March 10, 1977. Filed under "Unions," see also John Byrd, "Unions Are Losing Ground in N.C.," *Winston-Salem Journal*, April 3, 1978. The earlier failure of organizing efforts in the southern furniture industry is detailed in Selby, "'Better to Starve in the Shade than in the Factory.'"

On brown lung disease, see Hall et al., *Like a Family*; Conway, *Rise Gonna Rise*; and Bennett M. Judkins and Bart Dredge, "The Brown Lung Association and Grass-Roots Organizing," in Leiter et al., eds., *Hanging by a Thread*, pp. 121–36. Between February 3 and 6, 1980, the *Charlotte Observer* ran a detailed series of articles on the disease, which later won the Pulitzer Prize. These articles are particularly valuable to scholars and are included in the North Carolina Collection's clipping file under the heading "Brown Lung Disease."

On southern tolerance of environmental pollution, see Cobb, *The Selling of the South* and *Industrialization and Southern Society*; Craig. E. Colten, "Texas v. the Petrochemical Industry: Contesting Pollution in an Era of Industrial Growth," in Scranton, ed., *The Second Wave*, pp. 146–67; Albert E. Cowdrey, *This Land, This South: An Environmental History* (Lexington: University Press of Kentucky, 1983); and Timothy J. Minchin, *Forging a Common Bond: Labor and Environmental Activism in the BASF Lockout* (Gainesville: University Press of Florida, 2003). For the national context, see Carolyn Merchant, ed., *Major Problems in American Environmental History* (Lexington, Mass.: D.C. Heath, 1993) and Samuel P. Hays, *A History of Environmental Politics since 1945* (Pittsburgh: University of Pittsburgh Press, 2000).

For general studies of the growth of public employee unionism, see Richard N. Billings and John Grenya, *Power to the Public Worker* (Washington: Robert B. Luce, Inc., 1974); and Zieger and Gall, *American Workers, American Unions*. Filed under "Unions," the press clippings in the North Carolina Collection also document the growth in public unionism in North Carolina and the South as a whole. See especially Susan Jetton, "Carolinas Public Employees 'Organizing Like Mad,'" *Charlotte Observer*, March 8, 1976; Rick Nichols, "Union Activity Mushrooms Among Public Workers," *Raleigh News and Observer*, January 18, 1976; "North Carolina Gets Taste of City Unions," *Durham Morning Herald*, January 4, 1976; and "Unions Still Hoe a Tough Row in N.C.," *Charlotte Observer*, February 5, 1979.

The organization of the Domestic Workers' Union is outlined in "Helpers' Helper," *Atlanta Journal-Constitution* magazine, January 13, 1982. This account also utilizes the papers of the Domestic Workers' Union, held by the Southern Labor Archives at Georgia State University. For the Duke Hospital Workers' struggle, see Karen Brodkin Sacks, *Caring by the Hour: Women, Work, and Organizing at Duke Medical Center* (Urbana: University of Illinois Press, 1988).

The growth of teachers' unions is explored in Sullivan, "The Florida Teacher Walkout." See also Eugene J. Didier, "AFT-AFL-CIO: Growth in the South," "American Federation of Teachers" folder, box 59, AFL-CIO Pamphlet Collection. See also the clippings filed under "Teachers-Unions" in the North Carolina Collection, especially "N.C. Teachers Reportedly Want Aid in Starting Union," *Asheville Citizen*, September 2, 1971; "N.C. Teacher Unions Growing," *Raleigh News and Observer*, November 16, 1972; and Rick Edmonds, "Organizing: N.C. Laws Hinder Teachers' Efforts," *Winston-Salem Journal*, August 1, 1976.

For the continuing importance of textiles to the southern economy in the 1970s, see Conway, *Rise Gonna Rise*, and Henry P. Leiferman, "Trouble in the South's First Industry: The Unions are Coming," *New York Times Magazine*, August 5, 1973, p. 10. For workers' continuing complaints about workloads, see Flamming, *Creating the Modern South*. Filed under "Textile Industry," the North Carolina Collection's clipping file also contains many articles on the industry that explore a diverse range of topics, including working conditions, social change in textile communities, and the rising threat posed by imports. See, for example, Don Bedwell, "Frightened Industry Clamors for Protection from Cheap Imports," *Charlotte Observer*, April 24, 1977; Conrad Paysour, "Textiles at Crossroads," *Greensboro Daily News*, September 11, 1977; "Mimi Conway, "Working Hard for Little in a Southern Textile Mill," *Fayetteville Observer-Times*, September 9, 1979; and Rick Gray, "N.C. Textile Industry Is in 'Period of Transition,'" *Winston-Salem Journal*, December 30, 1979.

Chapter 6. Toward a New Century

A substantial literature explores the causes of organized labor's decline in the 1980s and 1990s. For detailed secondary studies, see Michael Goldfield, *The Decline of Organized Labor in the United States* (Chicago: University of Chicago Press, 1987); David Brody, "Labor's Crisis in Historical Perspective," in George Strauss, Daniel G. Gallagher, and Jack Fiorito, eds., *The State of the Unions* (Madison: Industrial Relations Research Association, 1991), pp. 277–311; Moody, *An Injury to All*; and Bruce Nissen, ed., *U.S. Labor Relations, 1945–1989: Accommodation and Conflict* (New York: Garland, 1990). Thomas Geoghegan provides a more journalistic account in *Which Side Are You On?: Trying to Be for Labor When It's Flat on its Back* (New York: Farrar, Straus, and Giroux, 1991).

The press also covered union decline well. See, for example, "As Rolls Drop and Ways Change, Unions Retreat," *Boston Globe*, September 7, 1992, pp. 1, 10. The particular difficulties faced by unions in the South, especially North Carolina, are explored in clippings held at the NCC. Filed under "Unions" or "Labor Unions," see especially Dave Baity et al., "Workers Reject Unions in 3 Carolinas

Elections," *The Charlotte Observer,* August 29, 1981; Michael Flagg, "Hard Times for Unions," *Raleigh News and Observer,* April 18, 1983; John Byrd, "N.C. Unions Lose Gains in Recession," *Winston-Salem Journal,* November 21, 1982; and Jack Betts, "A New Day in Dixie," *Charlotte Observer,* August 28, 1994.

For the upsurge in the hiring of permanent replacements, C. Perry, A. M. Kramer, and T. J. Schneider, *Operating During Strikes: Company Experience, NLRB Policies, and Government Regulations* (Labor Relations and Public Policy Series, No. 23, Industrial Research Unit, Wharton School, University of Pennsylvania, 1982), has been widely viewed as an influential strikebreaking guide for employers. Much of the literature on permanent replacement is found in industrial relations and legal journals. See, for example, Roger D. Staton, "Hiring of Replacement Workers: An Insidious Weapon Against Labor or Management's Last Bargaining Chip?" *Labor Law Journal* (January 1994), pp. 25–32 and John F. Schnell and Cynthia L. Gramm, "The Empirical Relations Between Employers' Striker Replacement Strategies and Strike Duration," *Industrial and Labor Relations Review* 47:2 (January 1994), pp. 189–206. These studies include a great deal of data documenting the increasing prevalence of the tactic, but they are short of material from replaced workers themselves. In contrast, Julius Getman, *The Betrayal of Local 14: Paperworkers, Politics, and Permanent Replacements* (Ithaca, N.Y.: ILR Press, 1998), covers the human impact of the tactic eloquently.

In exploring the rise of concessionary bargaining and the increasing prevalence of permanent replacements, this chapter also draws on the author's interviews with Don Low, conducted on July 10, 1998 in De Ridder, Louisiana; Johnny Sharp, conducted on July 10, 1998 in De Ridder, Louisiana; Bruce Carpenter, conducted on July 6, 1998 in Crossett, Arkansas; Wayne Fisher, conducted on July 1, 1998 in Creola, Alabama; Frank Bragg, conducted on June 18, 1998 in Nashville, Tennessee; Pat Clancy, conducted on July 2, 1998 in Creola, Alabama; Lynn Agee, conducted on June 26, 1998 in Nashville, Tennessee.

Union efforts to ban the hiring of permanent replacements are detailed well through congressional hearings, which contain revealing testimony from labor, management, and government officials. See, for example, U.S. Congress, House, Committee on Education and Labor, *Legislative Hearing on H.R. 5,* Hearings, 103rd Cong., 1st Sess. (Washington D.C., 1993); U.S. Congress, House, Committee on Education and Commerce, *Striker Replacement Legislation,* Hearings, 102nd Cong., 1st Sess. (Washington D.C., 1991).

For Nissan's decision to locate in the South and the opposition the Japanese company provoked from unions, see Lamar Alexander, *Steps Along the Way: A Governor's Scrapbook,* (Nashville: Thomas Nelson Publishers, 1986). While he was governor of the Volunteer State, Alexander played an important role in wooing Nissan to locate there, and his papers contain a great deal of correspondence with Nissan executives. The papers are held at the Tennessee Department of Archives and History in Nashville. See especially Lamar Alexander to Takashi Ishihara, December 24, 1985; Lamar Alexander to Marvin T. Runyon, December 24, 1980;

Takashi Ishihara to Lamar Alexander, September 12, 1983; Lamar Alexander to friends, October 20, 1983—all in reel 196, box 657, folder 3.

For the Nissan campaign, one of the most informative accounts is David Gelsanliter, *Jump Start: Japan Comes to the Heartland* (Farrar, Straus, Giroux: New York, 1990). The campaign, together with Nissan's decision to locate in Tennessee, is also covered in a study conducted by a group of Swedish social scientists. See Christian Berggren, Torsten Bjorkman, and Ernst Hollander, *Are they unbeatable?: Report from a field trip to study transplants, the Japanese owned auto plants in North America* (Stockholm: Royal Institute of Technology, 1991). Karsten Hulsemann, "Greenfields in the Heart of Dixie: How the American Auto Industry Discovered the South," in Scranton, ed., *The Second Wave*, pp. 219–54, summarizes the growth of the southern auto industry. John Junkerman, "Nissan, Tennessee: It ain't what it's cracked up to be," *The Progressive*, June 1987, pp. 16–20, details workers' complaints about the relentless pace of the assembly line. The UAW's defeat at Nissan is also explored in Warren Brown, "Behind the UAW's Defeat in Tennessee," *The Washington Post*, July 30, 1989, p. H3 and in Tas Papathanasis, "Smyrna: The Crucible of America," *The Christian Science Monitor*, August 11, 1989, p. 19.

Tom Juravich and Kate Bronfenbrenner, *Ravenswood: The Steelworkers' Victory and the Revival of American Labor* (Ithaca, N.Y.: ILR Press, 1999) offers a fine account of the RAC lockout. For the BASF lockout, see Minchin, *Forging a Common Bond*. The Delta Pride strike and the growth of the Mississippi catfish industry is covered in a special issue of *Southern Exposure*, 19:3 (Fall 1991).

For the movement of "Sunbelt" industries to the developing world, see John Gaventa and Barbara Ellen Smith, "The Deindustrialization of the Textile South: A Case Study," in Leiter et al., eds., *Hanging by a Thread*, pp. 181–96 and Jefferson Cowie, *Capital Moves: RCA's Seventy-Year Quest for Cheap Labor* (Ithaca, N.Y.: Cornell University Press, 1999). Haberland, "Women's Work," covers the decline of the southern apparel industry. For the national decline of manufacturing industries, see Barry Bluestone and Bennett Harrison, *The Deindustrialization of America: Plant Closings, Community Abandonment, and the Dismantling of Basic Industry* (New York: Basic Books, 1982).

The decline of the textile industry in the leading textile state of North Carolina is summarized briefly in Brent D. Glass, *The Textile Industry in North Carolina* (Raleigh: North Carolina Division of Archives and History, 1992). Gaventa and Smith's "The Deindustrialization," gives an overview of the industry's broader regional decline. See also Rhonda Zingraff, "Facing Extinction?" in Leiter et al., *Hanging by a Thread*, pp. 199–216. The North Carolina Collection's clipping file also contains some insightful stories on the decline of the textile industry under the heading "Textile Industry." See especially, "High-Tech Takes Off in Textiles," *Greensboro News and Record*, May 8, 1983; Cindy Dunlevy, "Textiles Face Import Competition; 518 Plants Close from '77–'82," *Greensboro Daily News*, April 20, 1980; and Marsha Blakemore, "Imports Only Half the Textile Problem," *Winston-*

Salem Journal, September 22, 1985. For more recent stories, see Irwin Speizer, "Crisis in Asia Costs N.C. Jobs in Textile Mills," *Raleigh News and Observer*, January 31, 1999; Ken Moritsugu, "Where Looms Have Ceased," *Charlotte Observer*, September 17, 2001; and Jane Seccombe, "Textile Losses Highest in N.C.," *Winston-Salem Journal*, October 5, 2001. Filed under "Textile Mills," see Charles Lunan, "Empty Mills Burden Carolinas," *Charlotte Observer*, July 22, 2002 and "Textile Heritage Stripped Away," *Charlotte Observer*, July 21, 2002, both of which explore the difficulties in finding new uses for the disused textile mills.

The national press also documented southern textile mill closings. For closure examples, see, "Burlington to Close 2 Plants and Cut 1100 Jobs," *New York Times*, June 6, 1996, p. D4; "Cone Mills to Close U.S. Plant and Expand in Mexico," *New York Times*, December 14, 2000, p. C4; "Guilford Mills is Moving Some Operations to Mexico," *New York Times*, July 28, 2000, p. C4; and "Burlington Industries to Cut Jobs and Close Plants," *New York Times*, January 27, 1999, p. C4. John Holusha's "Squeezing the Textile Workers," *New York Times*, February 21, 1996, pp. D1, D20, is a more general piece.

At the national level, both Fairclough, *Better Day Coming*, and Cook, *Sweet Land of Liberty*, outline the persistence of black poverty in the post–civil rights era. Goldfield, *Black, White, and Southern*, focuses specifically on the South. For the impact of plant closures on African Americans in Memphis, see Honey, *Black Workers Remember*. For continued black poverty in the rural South, see David S. Cecelski, *Along Freedom Road: Hyde County, North Carolina and the Fate of Black Schools in the South* (Chapel Hill: University of North Carolina Press, 1994) and Hurt, ed., *The Rural South Since World War II*.

Southern Regional Council (SRC) reports offer a wealth of information on southern workers in the 1980s. The reports give especially valuable insights into continued black poverty in the South. Particularly informative are reports produced by the Council's Southern Labor Institute. Set up in 1985, the institute was designed to "strengthen the historical commitment of the Southern Regional Council to address the problems of low wages and non-union working conditions in the South and to unite the goals of the civil rights movement with the struggle for economic justice." Its main emphasis was on research and education, and it produced a large number of reports documenting the fact that southern workers were less well paid, had fewer benefits, and were less likely to belong to a union than their counterparts in other regions. See "The Climate for Workers in the United States" (1988) and "The Climate for Workers in the United States" (1990). On day labor pools, see "Hard Labor: A Report on Day Labor Pools and Temporary Employment," (1988). Copies of all reports are available from the SRC, located in Atlanta, Georgia, and are also in the author's possession.

On the growth of Wal-Mart, see Jacques Steinberg, "Retail Giant Becomes a Job-Seeker's Oasis," *New York Times*, January 24, 1994, pp. B1, B2; Leslie Kaufman, "Wal-Mart Has Its Ups and Downs," *New York Times*, February 16, 2000, pp. C1, C13; Thomas C. Hayes, "Behind Wal-Mart's Surge, a Web of Suppliers," *New York Times,* July 1, 1991, pp. D1, D2. In addition, see Brian D. Ubell, "The Locational Strategy of Wal-Mart Stores in North Carolina and Their Impacts on the Local Retail Environments" (undergraduate thesis, University of North Carolina, 1995).

The impact of computers on the workforce is explored well in a series of interviews with Atlanta office workers held at the Southern Labor Archives at Georgia State University under the title "Working Women in Atlanta Oral History Project." Sacks, *Caring by the Hour,* has some material on the introduction of computers in the health care sector, while Peter Rachleff and the Work Environment Project, *Moving the Mail: From a Manual Case to Outer Space* (Morgantown, W.Va.: The Work Environment Project, 1982), details worker opposition to automation in the postal service. For the rise in working at home, see Robert E. Calem, "Working at Home, for Better or Worse," *New York Times,* April 18, 1993, pp. C1, C6.

A series of essays by southern anthropologists, Arthur D. Murphy, Colleen Blanchard, and Jennifer A. Hill, eds., *Latino Workers in the Contemporary South* (Athens: University of Georgia Press, 2001), is indispensable for understanding the causes and consequences of the growth in the number of Latino workers in the southern states. Particularly valuable in this volume are Deborah A. Duchon and Arthur D. Murphy, "Introduction: From *Patrones* and *Caciques* to Good Ole Boys"; Grieg Guthey, "Mexican Places in Southern Spaces: Globalization, Work, and Daily Life in and around the North Georgia Poultry Industry"; James D. Engstrom, "Industry and Immigration in Dalton, Georgia"; and Jack G. Dale, Susan Andreatta, and Elizabeth Freeman, "Language and the Migrant Worker Experience in Rural North Carolina Communities." Another important secondary work on Latino workers in the South, Leon Fink's, *The Maya of Morganton: Work and Community in the Nuevo New South* (Chapel Hill: University of North Carolina Press, 2003) offers a fine case study of efforts by a predominantly Guatemalan workforce at Case Farms in Morganton, North Carolina, to organize a union.

The Southern Oral History Program at the University of North Carolina, Chapel Hill, also contains several interviews with Latino immigrants to the Tarheel State, grouped under the collection title "Engineering Latino Communities: Oral Life-Stories in Rural Eastern North Carolina." Filed under "Hispanics in North Carolina," the North Carolina Collection's clipping file contains a wide variety of stories exploring the rapid growth of Latino communities in North Carolina. See especially Frank Elliott, "Drawn by Desire for a Better Life, More Hispanics Settling in N.C." *Charlotte Observer,* September 24, 1995; Ben Stocking, "Hispanic Culture Comes to Downtown Clinton," *The News and Observer,* December 9, 1996; Ben Stocking, "Challenge of an American Dream: Newcomers Seek Place to Belong as Blacks, Whites Struggle to Adjust," *The News and Observer,* January 14, 1996; Ned Glascock, "How Many N.C. Hispanics?" *The News and Observer,* November 16, 2000; John Boyle, "Hispanics Vital Part of Economy,"

Asheville Citizen-Times, June 19, 1999; Jef Feeley and Gail Smith, "Hispanic Migration," *Winston-Salem Journal*, April 23, 1995; and Ben Stocking, "Hispanic Wave Has Tar Heels on Edge, Polls Show," *The News and Observer*, March 9, 1996.

A fascinating, accessible insight into working conditions in southern poultry plants is provided by the firsthand experiences of anthropologist Steve Striffler, who took a job at a Tyson plant in Arkansas. See Steve Striffler, "Inside a Poultry Processing Plant: An Ethnographic Portrait," *Labor History* 43:2 (August 2002), pp. 305–13. For another firsthand insight into conditions in the poultry factories, see "Voices and Choices: Workplace Justice and the Poultry Industry," *Southern Changes* 23:1 (Spring 2001), pp. 3–7. On union efforts to organize the poultry plants, see Ronald Smothers, "Unions Head South to Woo Poultry Workers," *New York Times*, January 30, 1996, (clipping in "Food and Commercial Workers Union, United," folder, box 26, AFL-CIO Pamphlet Collection) and Preston Quesenberry, "The Climate for Workers in the United States, 1997," *Southern Changes* 19:3–4 (Fall/Winter 1997), pp. 3–20.

The account of the Imperial Foods fire in Hamlet, North Carolina, is based largely on a series of detailed articles on the fire and its aftermath in the *Raleigh News and Observer*, December 8–11, 1991. There are also other articles in the North Carolina Collection clipping file under the heading "Hamlet, NC—Imperial Foods—Fire." See especially Irwin Speizer, "Hamlet Fire's Ultimate Scar," *Raleigh News and Observer*, February 15, 2000.

The 1999 election victory at Cannon Mills in Kannapolis, North Carolina, is covered in David Firestone's "Union Victory at Plant in South Is Labor Milestone," *New York Times*, June 25, 1999, p. A16; in Lescaze's documentary film, *Where Do You Stand? Stories from an American Mill* (2003); and in Daniel's, *Culture of Misfortune*. In the fall of 2003, the *Charlotte Observer* covered the closure of the Kannapolis mills in some detail. See, for example, Tony Mecia, "Pillowtex Judge OKs Sale," *Charlotte Observer*, October 8, 2003, p. 1D and Sara Leitch, "Unemployed Residents Can Get Free Food," *Charlotte Observer*, October 3, 2003, p. B2. For the Lundy and Pilkington victories, see Larry Bingham, "Lundy Union Victory Certified," *Fayetteville Observer-Times*, September 7, 1994 and Ted Reed, "Town Diversifies, Union Comes in," *The Charlotte Observer*, September 3, 2001, both filed under "Labor Unions," NCC. In the same clipping file, Sabrina Jones, "State of the Unions," *Raleigh News and Observer*, September 5, 1999, provides a general exploration of the state of organized labor in the South at the end of the 1990s.

Conclusion

The similarities between the South and the rest of the country are explored well in Simon, "Rethinking Why There Are So Few Unions in the South"; Zieger, "Introduction: Is Southern Labor History Exceptional?" in Zieger, ed., *Southern Labor in Transition*, pp. 1–13; and Brattain, "The Pursuits of Post-Exceptionalism." In contrast, the persistence of southern antiunionism is detailed in Schulman, *From Cotton Belt to Sunbelt*; Marshall, *Labor in the South*; and Norwood, *Strike-*

Breaking and Intimidation. For the continuing wage differential, see Cobb, *Industrialization and Southern Society* and Schulman, *From Cotton Belt to Sunbelt.*

Filed under "Unions," newspaper clippings held at the North Carolina Collection explore well the consistent weakness of unions in the South, especially North Carolina. See Tom Minehart, "N.C. Remains Near Bottom in Unionization," *Durham Sun,* July 11, 1986; "N.C. The Country's Least Unionized State," *Durham Morning Herald,* May 15, 1977; Jay Hamilton, "Union Influence," *Weekender,* November 13, 1980; Stan Swofford, "The State of Unions in North Carolina," *Greensboro News and Record,* March 18, 1984; and George P. Antone, "The 50th State: Will N.C. Workers Accept Unions?" *Charlotte Observer,* March 3, 1977. See also Jim Wrinn, "Textile Town on Edge as It Faces the Big Divide," *Charlotte Observer,* July 6, 1993, filed under "Kannapolis, N.C."

Despite the growth in southern labor history, much remains to be done. Although an increased sensitivity to gender has also informed the new scholarship, historians have not explored gender dynamics as fully or effectively as they have those of race. The unionized industries that new labor historians concentrated on were mainly male dominated, both in the South and outside it, and historians have often concentrated on particularly active or "heroic" women at the expense of women's broader struggle to secure equal rights in the workplace and in the union movement. As Michelle Brattain has noted recently, "there are still nagging gaps in southern working-class women's history." On these points, see Ava Baron, "Gender and Labor History: Learning from the Past, Looking to the Future," in Ava Baron, ed., *Work Engendered: Toward a New History of American Labor,* (Ithaca, N.Y.: Cornell University Press, 1991), pp. 1–46; Brattain, "The Pursuits of Post-Exceptionalism"; and Mary E. Frederickson, "Heroines and Girl Strikers: Gender Issues and Organized Labor in the Twentieth-Century American South," in Zieger, ed., *Organized Labor in the Twentieth-Century South,* pp. 84–112.

Scholarship has also concentrated much more on CIO unions than their AFL counterparts. AFL craft unions, which were the first unions to establish themselves in the region, have been particularly overlooked. These unions' record of racial exclusion has not endeared them to scholars, but they certainly need to be explored further. For studies that do explore AFL unions, see Zieger, *Rebuilding the Pulp and Paper Workers' Union;* Minchin, *The Color of Work;* and Marshall, *Labor in the South.*

Much more also needs to be learned about unorganized southern workers. A disproportionate amount of recent scholarship has concentrated on organized workers, partly because unions offer one of the best ways of obtaining information about working conditions. Unions create records, whereas less visible unorganized workers remain difficult for the historian to reach. As a result, the vast majority of recent community studies have focused on unionized communities or have been focused around one local union. Exploring nonunion workers remains particularly important in a region where union members were always a small minority.

In all of these areas, historians' efforts will undoubtedly be circumscribed by available sources. Oral history, which has emerged as a central feature of recent work, clearly offers a way to explore these areas more, although more written sources are also needed to support interview material. The continuing growth of archive sources, and the vitality of the field as a whole, ensures that future studies will undoubtedly continue to take southern labor history forward into new and vibrant areas.

Index

Index · 225

in, 128; failure of, 52, 60, 63; field staff in, 49; funding of, 49, 52; gains in, 55; in Georgia, 47; harassment of activists in, 43, 51; labor drives following, 197; lumber industry in, 196; NLRB in, 43, 44; in North Carolina, 42, 46–47; opposition to, 40–42, 46, 52; preelection tactics during, 151; racial issues in, 51–52; textile industry in, 49–50, 52, 196; TWUA in, 49, 52; UAW in, 49; violence during, 4. *See also* Congress of Industrial Organizations (CIO)
Operation Sunbelt, 2, 130
Ormet Aluminum plant (Baton Rouge, La.), 25

Packinghouse Workers Organizing Committee, 27–28
Palmer, E. M., 126
Paper industry: African Americans in, 75, 97, 119, 122; integration of, 99–100, 105, 122; pollution by, 139–40; segregation in, 105–6, 195, 200; union-avoidance strategies in, 150–52; unions in, 106, 195; workplace discrimination in, 98
Pascagoula (Miss.), defense industry in, 12
Pearson, Virgil, 101
Pedigo, Joe, 69
Pepper, Claude, 34
Person County (North Carolina), economic development in, 134
Peterson, Esther, 125
Petrochemical industry: African Americans in, 97; growth in, 70
Phenix Chair Company (West Jefferson, N.C.), 135
Philippines, industrial relocation to, 158
Philips, Kevin, 117
Pigeon River (N.C.), industrial pollution in, 139
Pilkington glass plant (Laurinburg, N.C.), USW campaign at, 179–80, 212
Pillowtex company, layoffs by, 179
Pitts, William, 138–39
Pittston Corporation (Virginia), 157
Plant closings: effect on older workers,

163; impact on African Americans, 164–66; in North Carolina, 161–62; southern, 126; in textile industry, 68, 160–64, 210. *See also* Deindustrialization
Plants, southern: closing of, 126; conversion of, 163–64; derelict, 163; nonunion, 132–33, 134, 174. *See also* Textile industry, southern
Police officers, unionization of, 141–42
Pollution, industrial, 139–40
Poor People's Campaign (1968), 113
Pope, Laura Ann, 128
Port Gibson (Miss.), antiunionism in, 42
Potofsky, Jacob, 41
Poultry industry: AFL-CIO campaign in, 177; Latino workers in, 169, 173–74, 177; nonunion employees in, 174; repetitive motion injuries in, 174; strikes in, 177–78; working conditions in, 212. *See also* Imperial Foods plant (Hamlet, N.C.)
Pouncy, Gail, 176
Poverty: African American, 102, 117, 120, 165–66
—southern: in postwar era, 102, 139, 182–83; prewar, 8, 9; Roosevelt administration on, 9; in Sunbelt era, 117
Powell, Daniel, 62
Press: opposition to Operation Dixie, 41
Pride, Hillie, 164
Professional Air Traffic Controllers Organization (PATCO), walkout by, 148
The Progressive (journal), 153
Progressive Party, 47
Proximity Mill (Greensboro, N.C.), 54–55
Public employees, southern: African American, 119, 142; of Florida, 141; hospital workers, 112–15; sanitation, 2, 95, 109–12, 141; strikes by, 108–16; unionization of, 4, 6, 140–44; wages of, 142; in Wilmington, 144
Public employment, worker attitudes toward, 108–9
Public space, segregation of, 94
Puckett, Charlie, 58
Pugh, Ernest B., 50
Pulp and paper industry. *See* Paper industry

Tim Minchin is senior lecturer in North American history at La Trobe University in Melbourne, Australia. He has authored four books on the topic of labor as well as several articles and pamphlets. In 1999, he was awarded the Richard A. Lester Prize for the Outstanding Book in Labor Economics and Industrial Relations for his *Hiring the Black Worker*.